THE FIRST-BOOK MARKET

THE FIRST-BOOK MARKET

Where and How to Publish
Your First Book and Make It a Success

Editor
Jason Shinder

Associate Editor
Amy Holman

Editorial Assistants
Kathleen Adams
Elizabeth Wilson

MACMILLAN • USA

MACMILLAN
A Simon & Schuster Macmillan Company
1633 Broadway
New York, NY 10019-6785

Macmillan Publishing books may be purchased for business or sales promotional use. For information please write:

Special Markets Department
Macmillan Publishing USA
1633 Broadway
New York, NY 10019

Library of Congress Cataloging-in-Publication Data

The first-book market: where and how to publish your first
    book and make it a success / editor, Jason Shinder;
    assistant editor, Amy Holman ; editorial assistants,
    Kathleen Adams, Elizabeth Wilson.
        p.   cm
    Includes bibliographical references (p.) and index.
    ISBN 0-02-862248-0
    1. Authorship. I. Shinder, Jason, 1955– . II. Holman, Amy.
    PN151.F55   1998
    808'.02—dc21   98-12215
                                                    CIP

Printed in the United States of America

10 9 8 7 6 5 4 3 2 1

Book design by Barbara Kordesh

In memory of Allen Ginsberg

1926–1997

What lovest well remains, the rest is dross
What lovest well shall not bereft from thee
What lovest well is thy true history

—Ezra Pound
Pisan Cantos

In an age defined by its modes of production, where everybody tends to be a specialist of sorts, the artist ideally is that rarity, a whole person making a whole thing.

—Stanley Kunitz

CONTENTS

Acknowledgments

THANKS to the people from the many organizations who responded to editorial questionnaires and/or phone interviews.

Although listings in this book were based on the questionnaires and phone interviews, two general resource books were also called upon, if necessary, to verify select information. These books were *Grants and Awards Available to Writers* (Editor, John Monroe; PEN, American Center) and *The Writer's Market* (Editor, Kirsten C. Holm; *Writer's Digest*).

Thanks also to the many authors who contributed comments and advice regarding their first-book experiences. Special thanks to Terry McMillan, Nancy Means Wright, Anna Monardo, and Sadi Ranson for their critical essays. And thanks to the Associated Writing Program and *Poets & Writers* for their help in securing and/or permitting the reprinting of select pieces.

Amy Holman, Associate Director of Information Services at *Poets & Writers*, was very much a part of the book's development, especially in securing comments from authors and developing portions of the various listings.

Katie Adams and Elizabeth Wilson created and researched a database of all the listings, and provided assistance on various other matters of research and technology. Without their hard work, responsibility, and quality of dedication, this book would not have been completed. Rodney Phillips, Director of the Berg Exhibition Room, Center for the Humanities at the New York Public Library, generously offered rare research and exhibition documents regarding the publishing information of the first books of our country's most distinguished authors. His many years of hard work on behalf of writers and books is of the highest quality and impact. Thanks also to editor Ruth Greenstein for her practical, important, and friendly advice introducing each part of the book.

Finally, thanks to Natalie Chapman, Publisher of Macmillan Books, for thinking a resource for unpublished first-book authors was a much-needed and important project, and to Betsy Thorpe, Editor at Macmillan Books, for her hands-on, invaluable input regarding every aspect of the book.

FROM THE EDITOR

A typical conversation I often have when people ask me how to get their first book published usually begins with the answer, "Send it out." My response always amuses and confuses them.

To whom? Where? When? It's not that simple. How can you just send it out?

You can do it, I tell them.

Oh, you mean anyone can get published?

No. But everyone can send out their first books, and there are plenty of awards and publishers favorable toward first-book authors. But to begin with, of course, you have to write a book of the highest quality and originality possible. And for most people the way to write a first book of the highest quality takes years of hard work, and, more often than not, hands-on assistance from another writer and/or teacher.

You mean anyone with a good first book can get published?

No. But if the book is one *you* are truly satisfied with, and passionate about, it has a better chance of satisfying an agent or editor, and, later, its readers.

OK. What if I already have a first book I'm happy with?

Well, you first have to identify what publishing opportunities are currently available, especially those that are favorable toward first books. You then need to decide which publishing possibilities you, and/or your agent, are willing to pursue.

Do I need an agent?

Well, yes. And no. You certainly do not need an agent to submit your manuscript to awards for unpublished first-book manuscripts, the prize of which is usually publication. (In fact, most of the publishing opportunities in this book do not require an agent to pursue.)

Yet it's clearly in your best interest to work with an agent when submitting your manuscript to a major publisher, especially as they largely ignore unagented manuscripts. But, on the other hand, there are many publishers who are favorable to first books, even those that may be sent without an agent.

Where can I find out about these contests? How do I know which publishers are favorable to first-book authors? How have other writers published their first books? How . . .

At this point in the conversation, I would usually begin listing several of the hundreds of such contests and publishing opportunities, and/or referring them to sections within dozens of various reference books. As the founder and director of the fifteen-year-old YMCA National Writer's Voice, a network of literary arts centers at YMCAs in over twenty-five states, and core faculty member of the graduate writing programs at Bennington College and The New School for Social Research, I've had the opportunity to gather a great deal of information about first books and speak to a good deal of authors about their first-book experiences. As a result, I've also had the pleasure to develop and teach a unique workshop specifically targeted to help writers with excellent first-book manuscripts secure publication.

This book, then, is a compilation of all that I've discovered as I've helped writers achieve their first-book publication goals. It is the first book to comprehensively present all the awards, contests, and publishing opportunities exclusively about first-book publication. Although self-publishing, or vanity/subsidy press publishing are viable options, and sometimes very successful ones, this book focuses its attention on standard publishing—where a for-profit or not-for-profit publisher agrees to assume all production and many promotional costs of your book, based on the book's quality and appeal to the publisher. With such publishing, authors usually receive a cash advance before publication, and a percentage of royalties on the retail (or sometimes wholesale) sales of the books once such sales pay back the cash advance.

The First-Book Market also includes first-hand accounts by several of our country's distinguished writers on their insights into first-book publication. In addition, interspersed in each part of the book and arranged chronologically are publishing and historical information about the first books of many of America's most important writers over the last two centuries.

I hope these personal and historical accounts will illuminate the various and unique routes toward publication—as well as the constants of hard work, patience, faith, the love of writing and literature and the toughly earned joy it can bring—that distinguishes the rich and exciting adventure of first-book publication.

"I greet you," as Ralph Waldo Emerson said to Walt Whitman on the publication of his first poetry book, *Leaves of Grass*, "at the beginning of a wonderful career."

User's Guide

Parts two, three, and four of this book regarding awards and publishers include listings of specific opportunities for your unpublished first book. Each listing contains basic information regarding deadlines, entry fees, etc., and whenever possible, information regarding previous winners, judges, and/or editorial comments from the publisher or award's administrators.

After you've identified an opportunity you want to pursue, send a self-addressed stamped envelope (SASE) to the address in the listing and carefully review all the submission requirements. Your chance to have your manuscript receive serious consideration, or any consideration, depends upon following any directions to the letter. In some cases, application forms need to be sent along with your manuscript. These forms will be sent to you with the information regarding submission requirements.

The listings in the chapters "Awards Exclusively for Unpublished First-Book Manuscripts" and "Awards Favorable to Unpublished First-Book Manuscripts" are also arranged by award in the prize index and by their particular genre in the genre index. Many listings also let you know how long it will typically take for the organization to respond to your submission.

Finally, each listing has a symbol indicating what genre or genres the contest or award applies to, as follows:

C	Children's	**P**	Poetry
D	Drama	**SF**	Short Fiction
F	Fiction	**SP**	Screenplays
J	Journalism	**TR**	Translation
NF	Nonfiction	**YA**	Young Adult

Please note: Listings are based on questionnaires and/or phone interviews. Listings are not advertisements. The results of contact with listed awards, contests, and publishers are not the responsibility of the editor.

PART 1

"What Lovest Well Remains": Writers on Their First Books

INTRODUCTION

Ruth Greenstein

For most writers, the road to publishing that first book is long and far and full of rocks and ruts. Others get lucky and find their way with hardly a hitch. This part of *The First-Book Market* features real-life stories from contemporary writers of various stripes on their own first-book publication experience. While each of these writers has found his or her own road to publication, many offer the same admonitions on how to stay on that road until you reach your destination. Here, in short, is a listing of those suggestions that come up again and again:

Build up to the book

A writer's first book is almost never his or her first publication. Don't rush into trying to publish a whole book. Start slow. Take workshops. Get plenty of feedback on your work from peers and professionals. Self-publish. Publish small pieces in small magazines. (See the Resources section, page 281, at the back of this book for the names of directories that list such magazines.) Keep an eye out for local magazines and journals that specialize in the subjects about which you write. Start your own small magazine.

> **What You've Heard Is True**
>
> ◆
>
> **An MFA Thesis Is Not a Book**
> In most cases, especially for writers at the beginning of their careers, a thesis for a graduate writing program is simply a collection of their work to date. A book, on the other hand, is a meticulously arranged collection of a writer's very best work. The book as a whole is no different than its individual elements, in that each should reflect a single vision. As writer Nick Carbó reminds us later in this section, do not make the mistake of assuming that your thesis is a publishable book.
>
> —J. S.

Gestate

Many writers warn that it is impossible to view their own work critically without some time and distance from it. Don't send out your work right after it's finished. "No wine before its time," says Ron Carlson, with homage to the ad writers at Gallo. Let your writing sit awhile. Then give it a fresh look and see if it still works for you.

Revise and Retry

One of the wonderful things about the publishing business is that people and projects are constantly in flux. Take advantage of this. Get feedback on why your work has been rejected and revise it accordingly. Then go out and pursue new opportunities. For example, if your manuscript has been rejected by an editor at your favorite publishing house, chances are that by the time you've revised your work, that editor will be working elsewhere and may want to reconsider your project at his or her new house. Meanwhile, there will likely be a new editor at the original publisher whom you can also approach.

What You've Heard Is True

◆

Alan Dugan waited until he was thirty-nine to submit his first book, *Poems*, for publication. When he finally did, it received the Yale Series of Younger Poets Award, the Pulitzer Prize, the National Book Award, the National Book Critics Circle Award, and the Prix de Rome.

—J. S.

Love the work

Don't lose sight of the goal, which must be the process of writing and the work itself, not the recognition that may or may not eventually come from it. Keep your focus there.

Network

Don't try to do it alone. Behind nearly every successful writer is a loyal peer support system that helped him or her get there. Talk to other writers and learn from their experiences as well as your own. Go to literary events and meet people in the business. Seek out editors who may be interested in your work.

Persevere

Learn to take rejections in stride. Consider each disappointment as one more stepping stone that leads to your goal. Don't pace yourself against other writers; remember that everyone finds his or her own road. Try out some of the suggestions from writers like Toi Derricotte for submitting and resubmitting your work. Create your own routines for keeping your writing in circulation.

Keep the faith

Be prepared for the long haul. If you're truly committed, the journey should not be a painful one. Consider the first-book experiences of writers like Anna Monardo and her twelve-year journey into publication. Remember that for most writers, the old adage paraphrased by Carolyn Forche holds true: "It takes years to become an overnight success."

Ruth Greenstein has been in the publishing business for nine years and has edited a wide range of fiction, nonfiction, and poetry. She has worked for Harcourt Brace & Company, The Ecco Press, and independently as an editor, writer, and publishing consultant.

What You've Heard Is True

◆

Every Return Brings You Closer to Your Goal
The return of your writing from an editor is not a rejection of you as a writer or as a person. It is information you can use in your pursuit of three objectives:

1) identifying how to make your writing as strong as possible
2) identifying opportunities to build relationships with editors
3) identifying opportunities to publish your work

In this way, consider every return of your work as a cause for celebration. The sooner you receive such returns, the closer you will be to finding the appropriate place for your work.

William Kennedy's Pulitzer Prize–winning novel, Ironweed, *was rejected by more than ten publishers before it found a home.*

—J. S.

Writers on Their Own First Books

"Write the Book You Want to Write, Not the One You Think Will Sell"

Cathryn Alpert

Cathryn Alpert had the ideal first-book experience. "Before I was a third of the way into *Rocket City,* Greg Michalson of *The Missouri Review* and the fiction editor for MacMurray and Beck, asked to see it. His call came out of the blue and very early in the morning. I remember he woke me and I had no idea who he was, how he found me, or what he was talking about, as I'd never heard of MacMurray and Beck and had never sent any work to *Missouri Review.* I had been published twice in *Puerto Del Sol,* which he mentioned, but I failed to see the connection," Ms. Alpert says. "I am not much of a morning person." In fact, she would not have sent her completed manuscript if he had not sent a follow-up letter. Two weeks after she did, Michalson called to offer to publish *Rocket City.* Ms. Alpert secured Felicia Eth to be her agent, "whom I'd once seen give an excellent and very savvy talk about book publishing. She negotiated the terms of the contract with MacMurray and Beck, and upon the book's publication, brought it to the attention of Marty Asher at Vintage, who purchased the paperback rights."

Vintage sent Ms. Alpert on a national book tour, garnering serious publicity for *Rocket City.* Between the hardcover and paperback editions, she'd recorded an interview and read excerpts from the novel for Kay Bonetti of the American Audio Prose Library and gave about twenty readings and book signings throughout her home state of California. The hardcover edition was chosen for Barnes & Noble's Discover Great New Writers Series, but it was the national book tour afforded by Vintage that gave her the sense that her book was actually being read.

Ms. Alpert had heard horror tales about the fate of "mid-listed" writers in the big houses and although she did not have any knowledge of working with any kind of publisher to begin with, she's glad she started small. "MacMurray and Beck put everything it had behind *Rocket City*. Both Greg Michalson and Fred Ramey, the editor in chief, spent hours on the phone with me, discussing everything from commas to semicolons to how I envisioned the cover. They were both wonderful—patient and nurturing—and two of the best editors I've ever had. I wouldn't trade that experience for anything."

Ms. Alpert's beginning as a writer can be traced back to her reading and rereading *Stuart Little*, E. B. White's first book for children. "Stuart Little was my first picaresque hero, whose story of longing and differentness [sic] simply broke my heart." *Sense and Sensibility,* by Jane Austen, is her favorite nineteenth century first novel, if only for its intelligence, which includes "Austen's wit, social acuity, sparkling language and innate sensitivity to nuance." Amy Tan's *The Joy Luck Club* is "as perfect a first book as has ever been written." Ms. Alpert lists some other firsts, including David Bowman's *Let the Dog Drive* and Laurie Hendrie's *Stygo,* among others.

The nonfiction firsts are *Girl Interrupted,* by Susanna Kaysen, "for its lyrical lack of sentimentality" and *Reeling and Writhing,* by Candida Lawrence, "for its understated humor." And Michael Harrington's *The Other America,* "a book about poverty in America that controverted twelve years of programming by my white, upper-middle-class, Nixon-adoring parents."

She says, "write the book you want to write, not the book you think will sell," because "dedicated and committed publishers, both large and small, remain. Find an agent with whom you have rapport. Can you call your agent at home on a Sunday or does the thought of such an intrusion make you break out in hives? Your agent should be your partner. Find one who makes you feel comfortable." She says not to resist changes suggested by your editor because "editors exist in the world to make you look good. Although the changes suggested for *Rocket City* were minor, they were crucial to the betterment of the novel."

"Don't be wary of small publishing houses. The downside is money. They don't pay much in the way of advances, and often don't have the budget to support such luxuries as book tours and trips to the ABA. The upside is the individual attention they can give you, especially if they're a new house and only releasing one or two titles a season." But she warns writers not to get hung up on publication, either. "Losing sight of the goal—which is writing—is the quickest way to box in your imagination. Write well, and the rest will follow."

Cathryn Alpert's first novel is Rocket City, *published by MacMurray and Beck and reprinted by them in 1996. She is a "recovering academic" with a Ph.D. in theatre and lives with her family in Aptos, California.*

"They Make You Think You Have a Book When You Graduate"

Nick Carbó

Nick Carbó, a Filipino-American poet, whose first book, *El Grupo McDonalds,* was published by Tia Chucha Press in Chicago, recommends three first books: *White Elephants,* by Reetika Vazrani, Beacon Press, 1996; *Likely,* by Lisa Coffman, Kent State University Press, 1997; and *Ismaila Eclipse* by Khaled Mattawa, Sheep Meadow Press, 1995. These poets won prizes and fellowships and Mr. Carbó suggests that if you look at how the poems in these books are ordered, that will help you put together your own poetry collections.

"It just took me so long," he says when asked about the publication of his first book. "For those who go through MFA programs, they make you think you have a book when you graduate—with your thesis—but most of the poems aren't really finished. In the two years it took me to put together a manuscript only ten poems from the thesis survived. Most I wrote after. It was four years after graduating that the book was accepted."

Mr. Carbó says to send to publishers and competitions. "Of course that's a lot of rejections in four years. The publisher that finally accepted me, Luis Rodriguez at Tia Chucha, publishes a lot of ethnic writers, including Elizabeth Alexander, so I definitely had a better chance. You can't send blindly." The anthology of Filipino and

Filipino-American poetry Mr. Carbó edited, *Returning A Borrowed Tongue,* was accepted by Coffee House Press around the same time as *El Grupo McDonalds,* so he had the good fortune of two books coming out the same year. "It's dry for a while and it suddenly rains," he says.

Nick Carbó recently edited the anthology Returning a Borrowed Tongue: Filipino/Filipina Poetry *(Coffee House Press). He teaches at The New School for Social Research in New York City.*

•◆•

"Write Only What You Love"

Ron Carlson

Ron Carlson's favorite first book is F. Scott Fitzgerald's *This Side of Paradise,* "not because the novel is so 'young' and dear and tender toward its confused protagonist Amory Blaine, but because it, more than any other first book I know, reveals so clearly how it was constructed, pasted together, stitched, and ironed," he says, revealing the editorial eye of one who teaches creative writing. "It's some kind of fresh, untutored, or barely tutored, scrapbook with just a nod at narrative. Sophomoric and self-conscious half the time, lyric and uninhibited others, the novel ultimately carries, despite Fitzgerald's efforts in the final pages to make it important. I read it when I was nineteen and I moved my bed over by the window. If I had waited a year, the answer to this question would have been different."

Mr. Carlson's advice is not limited to writers of first books, but can be applied to every process of writing. "Keep your head down; stay in the room; write only what you love; don't write it for other people; if someone else could write the book you're working on, let them."

"I wrote my first novel, *Betrayed by F. Scott Fitzgerald,* because I was young and because I wanted to; I was not in a program or school. I had too great affection for many curiosities I'd come across and I wrote a book to claim them," he says, adding, "I'm from Utah and no one had asked me to please write a book. When I had most of a draft, I looked in the *Literary Market Place* in the library for publishers and came across W. W. Norton in New York City."

He ran his finger down the list of editors, "until I was halfway past the presidents and chairman and vice presidents to the editors and then to the name, Carol Houck Smith, and it looked like a good name, a person at that place in the list who might not be too busy."

The sequence of events that followed Mr. Carlson's query, in which he admitted that much of the novel was set in Utah, has comic twists worthy of his own fiction. "She wrote back that she would read the book, to send it, and then a month later she wrote back that Norton wanted to publish the book. We spoke on the telephone and at the end of the call, I had to ask her to send back the two-page synopsis of the last section of the book, because I had neglected to keep a copy. I didn't know then that they had decided to publish the book whether I could finish it or not. We've laughed about that many times since," he says, "but there is a nice part two-thirds through where Larry is walking through town in the twilight and I guess the book could've ended there."

Still in Utah in 1977 when the novel came out, he received a call from Carol Houck Smith with the report that the daily *New York Times* had reviewed the book and that she had good news and bad news. "I asked for the good news and it was good news indeed, as she read the review and it was the perfect review. I was thrilled. 'Your picture is in the paper too by the review,' she said, and I asked her how I looked. She said I looked good.

"The bad news was simply that it was a blackout in New York, the paper never hit the streets. So my picture and that review of *Betrayed by F. Scott Fitzgerald,* my first novel, published when I was twenty-nine, is in a collector's edition of that famous paper—an irony I now appreciate."

Mr. Carlson's advance back then "was minuscule, but what it has meant since to me and to my career is immeasurable. Carol and I have worked on all five of my books," he says, stating that *Betrayed. . .* is still in print. His latest collection of stories, *The Hotel Eden,* was published in 1997. And like his favorite first book, "it is a book I see now that is a bit of a scrapbook, but it's a good story, and even though I've evolved as a writer in the years since, I'm sticking to it."

Ron Carlson's latest book is a collection of stories, The Hotel Eden *(W. W. Norton, 1997). He directs the writing program at Arizona State University.*

❧❀❧

"An Editor Is Not God"

Toi Derricotte

Toi Derricotte sent her first book, *The Empress of the Death House,* Lotus Press, 1978, out to African American publishing houses, "since several of the poems were about race" and they'd be more open to publishing her work at that time. "I got a letter from Broadside Press saying that the editor, Dudley Randall, was interested but not publishing books at this time. He recommended Naomi Long Madgett at Lotus Press and she accepted my book, *The Empress of the Death House,* shortly after I sent it.

"I had been writing seriously, often several hours a day seven days a week, for about ten years when my first book was published. I did not get much guidance. I am scrupulous and like to turn over finished manuscripts to my publishers. I didn't take any money at all on the sale. And now that I think about it, I have never been sent any money from sales of the book, though it's in third or fourth printing, I think. I don't keep up with money matters concerning poetry book sales, especially since most poets don't make that much on sales. However, I am delighted that the publisher has kept my book in print for almost twenty years!"

Ms. Derricotte named three books that most impressed her when she began writing seriously and she still thinks they are wonderful: *A Street in Bronzeville,* by Gwendolyn Brooks; *Howl,* by Allen Ginsberg; and *Colossus,* by Sylvia Plath. Her advice to writers refers to the build-up to a book, publishing the poems in magazines. She says to make a list of the magazines you want to be published by and rotate poems to all those magazines until all poems have been read by all magazines. "Remember if you like a certain editor's taste, that editor may be one likely to like your taste. Wait until you have enough poems to send out several to each of those magazines on your list at the same time.

So you won't be disappointed, count on one acceptance out of fourteen or fifteen tries." Ms. Derricotte offers a method by which to handle responses to these mailings. "Use a post office box so that you can go pick up your news of acceptances and/or rejections when you're in the right mood. When you get poems back, repackage them—have an envelope ready to go—and send them out quickly to another magazine on your list. In this way, editors get accustomed to your work and name. If you get a personal note from an editor, however brief, keep sending to that editor, even if it takes eighty tries.

"Remember," she concludes, "an editor is not God, only a person with a certain viewpoint, certain taste; therefore, don't let rejection slips stop you from writing or sending out."

Toi Derricotte's most recent book is The Black Notebooks *(W. W. Norton, 1997).*

"Learn From the Insights of Another Writer"

John Haines

In his favorite first book, poet and creative nonfiction writer, John Haines, who lives in, and writes often about, Alaska was "deeply impressed by a novel, *The Sleepwalkers*, by the German writer Hermann Broch. I have forgotten how I first came upon Broch's novel, but I read it in the standard translation by Willa and Edwin Muir early in the 1980s. I read it slowly, a chapter or two a day, absorbing page by page and episode by episode the three interconnected sections of the book, in which the various characters mingled, then separated, to meet again at a later time in greatly changed circumstances brought on by the First World War as it affected Prussian and Austrian empires, challenging and altering all traditional values in the general upheaval of the age." Mr. Haines praises the novel as a first book and also recognizes Broch's succeeding works as "distinctive and individual, each of them in its own way attempting to define some aspect of this modern period." He even reread *The Sleepwalkers*, aloud, to a close friend, with renewed insight and admiration.

"I remember quite vividly that when copies of my first book, *Winter News*, arrived in the mail in the spring of 1966, I was afraid to open it, fearful of what I might find there: mistakes, bad lines, poems I no longer liked, etc.," Mr. Haines says, a bit shy about recalling the publication of his first book. "I had similar reactions when a magazine arrived with a poem of mine featured. I read nearly everything else in the journal before I turned to my own work. I'm not sure why I reacted this way, and I don't know if it is common with other writers. I've long since put that sort of thing behind me, yet I still feel a certain hesitation when I turn to, say, a poem of mine in *The New Criterion*, [even though] I'm naturally eager to see it there, [and] pleased that the editors thought enough of the poem to publish it."

Mr. Haines also speaks on the favorable reaction to his first collection of poems, published when he was forty-two, since "it had its source in a part of the country remote from the major literary activities in cities like New York. I have to say I feel quite fortunate in having that early reception, with all the invitations to read that followed, the correspondence with other poets, the request for poems from many editors. Meanwhile, I had begun work on an entirely new collection of poems, one that would take me a long way from the setting in that first slim book."

Mr. Haines speaks about the critical aspect of being a writer, how one eagerly reads reviews and comments made of one's work, especially in the case of a first book. "We want to know what others think of the work, whether they like it, whether they understand what it is one is trying to do. And I know it can be disappointing, sometimes irritating, when we feel that the reviewer has somehow misread the work, failed to appreciate just what it was one intended in a particular poem or essay. I recall reacting with a mixture of amusement and resentment in the case of a well-known university poet condescending to a remark on what he called 'Mr. Haines's few artful but subdued triumphs,' etc. I have since had the occasion to review a book by this same poet, in which I was tempted to, as we say, 'get even'! Well that's the literary life, isn't it? But in this case I tried to be fair, while also being honest about some fairly serious flaws I found in the poems.

"I think it's important not to take this sort of thing too seriously," Mr. Haines continues in his advice to writers. "Especially in the case of a first book, and to see if there is not something to be learned from a critic's remarks. After all, he or she might be of some help in achieving a firmer grasp on verse technique, a deeper insight on whatever it is one is attempting to say. There have been examples of writers who have refused to read a review of their book, and there may be some wisdom in that—a refusal to allow the potential distraction from one's real work. Finally, this is a matter of individual disposition, ideally tempered by an honest desire to learn, if possible, from the insights of another writer."

John Haines's recent books include the collection of essays, Fables and Distances *(Graywolf) and the poetry book,* A Guide to the Fourchambered Heart *(Larkspur Press). He lives in Anchorage, Alaska.*

"A Novel Can Be Workshopped to Death"

Shelby Hearon

In 1967, Shelby Hearon sent her first novel, *Armadillo in the Grass,* over the transom without a name, without knowing writers or editors, to Knopf because they had beautiful books. In her letter she said that if they didn't love this to send it back to her and she would send it elsewhere. Judith Jones, her current editor, took it. Her first reader read it, then the second reader, and then, Judith. "That was back when they had first readers," Ms. Hearon says.

And while it's amazing to have one's first novel accepted by a big house on the first try, Ms. Hearon is quick to say that she worked on that novel for five years and didn't show it to anybody, and still never shows her novels to anybody until they are finished. Her advice to novelists is the advice she gives to people she's taught—"you have to learn to tell if it's good. A novel can be workshopped to death."

Three first novels sprung to Ms. Hearon's mind as her favorites: *Mysteries of Pittsburgh,* by Michael Chabon; *The Movie Goer,* by Walker Percy; and *Mona In The Promised Land,* by Gish Jen.

Shelby Hearon's latest novel, Footprints, *was published by Knopf. She lives in Burlington, Vermont.*

‹◆›

"Who Wrote This Way Before?"

Gail Mazur

Gail Mazur is limiting her choices to the "most astonishing first books that had an enormous impact on me." Ms. Mazur imagines the debut of Elizabeth Bishop's *North & South*. "To guess what it must've been like to have opened this book in 1946, by a new poet, with 'The Map,' 'The Man-Moth,' 'The Weed,' 'Cirque d' Hiver,' 'Roosters,' 'The Fish'—well, why guess, read it, and read Randall Jarrell's piece on Bishop. These early poems were 'echt-Bishop': lucent, lucid, luscious! And this poet, who would become known for, among more significant attributes, perhaps, the economy of her output, continued until her death in 1979 to write brilliant poems, always, it seems to me, at the top of her form."

James Tate's *The Lost Pilot* is her second choice. "At 23, Tate's poems already had the bravura, zany lyricism, courage, and poignancy that was to grow steadily in the following decades. These poems certainly triggered poems in me, for which I am still grateful."

Ms. Mazur will never forget the feeling she had when she read Frank Bidart's *Golden State* in manuscript form in the early '70s, that this would be *the* new American voice in poetry. "Who wrote this way before Bidart?" she asks. "Twenty-odd years later, a body of work, an individual, unmistakable voice, at the center of our senses of poetry at the end of the century."

Gail Mazur's first book of poetry, Nightfire, *was published by David R. Godine in 1978. Her most recent collection,* The Common, *is with the University of Chicago Press, 1995. She teaches at Emerson's Creative Writing Program and is the founder and director of the Blacksmith House Poetry Center in Cambridge, Massachusetts.*

"Wordly Matters and Matters of Art Are Different"

Robert Pinsky

The United States Poet Laureate, Robert Pinsky, is glad his first manuscript did not get published as his first book, although he tried. When the second manuscript was taken, he was thirty-four, and he "felt extremely old with a much delayed first book." He'd been publishing a lot in little magazines since he was very young and he just swept a lot of them into the manuscript, *Sadness & Happiness*, "and now I just wish they were swept out to sea."

Naturally, age influences Mr. Pinsky's interest in other poets' first books, and he separates his favorites into past and present. "Historically, *Prufrock and Other Observations*, (T. S. Eliot), because he was so young, and *A Boy's Will*, (Robert Frost), because he was so old." He also cites William Carlos Williams's first book, "because of its saucy address to the readers on the cover." Mr. Pinsky also likes Anne Winter's *The Key to the City*, which came late, and had seven poems about New York City that are the best. When he taught Mark Halliday's *Little Star* at Berkeley, the students liked it so much, "I was sure *Little Star* would become a best-seller." Carl Phillips's *In the Blood* was written and published while he was in the Boston University Creative Writing program, and it was followed by an even better book.

Mr. Pinsky's advice to writers is "to remember that everyone is different, there's no one manner in which first books come." And on the line of perseverance, to remember the importance of acceptance of a different pace for each poet. "Worldly matters touch art, but are not necessarily matters of art," Mr. Pinsky says. "With the publication and reception of the first book, one cares so much, so it's hard." It's important not to confuse the two realms. "Worldly matters and matters of art are different."

Robert Pinsky's latest books include The Figured Wheel: New and Selected Poems *(Farrar, Straus, & Giroux, 1996) and an award-winning translation of Dante's* Inferno. *He teaches at Boston University.*

"I Laugh at an Advance"

Terese Svoboda

"After graduating from Columbia, I worked on my poetry for ten years and won a first-book contest with the University of Georgia. No editorial guidance was offered but workshops contributed a lot in the shaping of individual poems. No advance. My first book of prose took fifteen years to write, ditto about the workshops, but in particular an exhilarating experience with Gordon Lish taught me that I might as well write the way I pleased since goddamn nobody would ever publish it. It won the Bobst Prize, the Great Lakes New Writers Award, and was runner up for the Paterson Prize." *Cannibal* was published in 1995 with NYU Press. "It went through three agents, a hundred rejections—thirteen alone in the form that won the prizes. No advance. I laugh at an advance.

"Whereas a first book of poetry is regarded as a poet's first mewlings, the first book of prose must soar impossible heights, as reflected in the bidding wars. The prose writer is like a film director; if he hasn't scored a sell-out by the third time, he's out. The poet is just beginning to be recognized by the third book." However, Ms. Svoboda knows that poets can also be selected by big houses after publishing with smaller presses because they work so hard promoting their own work.

Thus, her advice to writers is threefold and simple—perseverance, constant review of your own work, and belief in your own voice. "By the way, NYU's prize is the only one that offers cash, a fabulous cocktail party, lots of photographers, and a catered dinner party for intimate friends and family after the awards ceremony. They really make a big deal out of a first book. The Great Lakes New Writers Award is another stroke of genius in that the award is a reading series throughout the Great Lakes region, giving the writer a chance to tap a new audience and gain experience reading in public."

Terese Svoboda's favorite first books include Anne Caston's book, *Flying Out with the Wounded* and David Rivard's *Torque*. Her own first book of poetry, *All Aberration*, was published in 1985.

Terese Svoboda's most recent books include the novel Cannibal *(NYU Press) and the poetry book* Mere Mortals *(University of Georgia Press). She teaches at Williams College.*

"Small Presses Are the Way to Go"

Karen Tei Yamashita

Karen Tei Yamashita has no idea what her favorite first books are because she doesn't ever pay attention to whether a book is the author's first or second or fifth. She has an inch stack of rejection letters for her own first effort, *Through the Arc of the Rain Forest*, eventually published by Coffee House Press. "I took a one-day class at UCLA on how to publish it and wrote a note to Alan Lau, who wrote back one of his funny postcards suggesting three publishers interested in Asian American writers. I wasn't sure about that because the book is not necessarily about Asian Americans but I went ahead and sent queries. The University of Washington didn't want fiction, Graywolf looked at it, but Coffee House took it." It took Allen Kornblum of Coffee House to recognize what Ms. Yamashita was doing with the novel, which is slipped between the genres.

"I knew nothing about the business but I learned very quickly. Sue Ostfield, the publicist, was marvelous, and walked me through the process. Allen has a great love of the publishing business." She says that she didn't meet them in person until the ABA book fair held that year in Las Vegas. "A strange place for a book fair. I enter this huge hall and the small presses are all in one row. I have a great respect for the independent presses. I don't want any to die and it's sad that the NEA didn't come through."

Ms. Yamashita says that small presses are the best options for literature, except that they are overloaded. Every year Coffee House's submissions get more overwhelming. "I believe they are the way to go. Small presses have small staffs who know you, who've all read your book and believe in you. I think, unless you have a blockbuster and can get an agent, they are the best way. Not a lot of money, but nobody's looking to make a lot with a first book."

Ms. Yamashita mentions a detail that often comes into play with small presses, that the publishers are willing to consider the author's input when it comes to the cover design. "Allen called me and asked me if I had any idea of color for the cover. I thought that was strange, but he said that people have strong associations with color, some can be bad. I told him that my husband was an artist," she laughs. "I couldn't see his face because this was the telephone but he probably thought, 'oh no.' But he asked me to send him a sample— and that's the cover of the book. That can happen at a small press."

All of Karen Tei Yamashita's books are published with Coffee House Press. Through the Arc of the Rain Forest *was published in 1990 and* Tropic of Orange *in 1997. She teaches at UC Santa Cruz.*

PART 2

FIRST LIGHT: AWARDS FOR UNPUBLISHED FIRST-BOOK MANUSCRIPTS

INTRODUCTION

Ruth Greenstein

The many organizations that sponsor literary contests and awards are an excellent venue for writers seeking recognition and publication for a first-book manuscript. But before sending out your manuscript, there are a number of questions you can ask yourself to help ensure that your work is in suitable shape and that you are sending it to the most appropriate and promising places.

Have I received several professional opinions on the quality of my manuscript?

Family and friends are often good sounding boards, but only a professional such as a writing teacher, an editor, or a published writer can give you the kind of knowing critique that will help you produce a publishable work. If you are not sure of where to find such professionals, the Resources section of this book (page 281) will help steer you in the right direction.

Have I prepared my manuscript in a suitable format?

One of the hazards of home computing is that it enables people to do too much with the format of their work. I recommend that writers avoid using fancy typography. A clean-looking page in a plain and readable typeface such as Courier, Times Roman, or a classic book font will let your words be seen without distracting your readers. Be sure your manuscript is properly paginated and cleanly photocopied, and that it includes appropriate front and back matter, if necessary.

Have I determined which types of contests and awards are the most suitable for my work?

This is where *The First-Book Market* comes in. The listings that follow are divided into two categories: Awards Exclusively for Unpublished First-Book Manuscripts and Awards Favorable to Unpublished First-

Book Manuscripts. Awards for longer manuscripts such as novels and works of nonfiction can be found in these sections, while awards for shorter works that lend themselves to the chapbook format can be found in Part 3.

Have I done enough research?

Once you've read through the listings and noted which awards seem suitable for your work, request the guidelines for each award that interests you and review them carefully. Then have a look at the books published by past winners, and find out what you can about the writers who are judging the awards. Does the style and quality of your work seem consistent with the work written by past winners? If it differs dramatically from that of previous winners, you may want to focus your efforts (and dollars) elsewhere.

To how many places should I send my work?

The awards game is a game of odds: the more places you send your work, the greater your chances are of winning. However, there is no point in sending your work to places that are not appropriate, nor in submitting your work to several places when the guidelines require that your submission be exclusive. So after carefully researching each award that interests you and ruling out those that don't fit, I would recommend you send your work to every place that remains on your list—or as many of them as time and money allow.

In general, after heeding the advice of peers and mentors, guidelines and guidebooks, the best way to learn is by doing. So, send out your manuscript, hope for the best, remember that the decisions of judges are subjective, and don't let yourself be discouraged by rejection.

WINNING AN AWARD: DOES IT CHANGE YOUR LIFE?

Nancy Means Wright

For most writers winning a prestigious contest seems a fantasy, a panacea, a way out of anonymity. We know the odds: literary competitions like the AWP Award Series or the National Poetry Series can receive up to a thousand manuscripts, asking fees that range from ten to thirty dollars—and the fruits of our time and money will most likely be a form letter of rejection. Still, there is something in us that loves a contest, and we rush to apply. Someone, we reason, has to win—and for a time at least, rise like a fragile balloon into the public eye.

Who are these winners, and how did they do it? How has the prize altered their lives and work? Is it really the panacea it seems? What did they do after the initial euphoria paled, after the champagne and the congratulatory calls—that moment of "apotheosis," as Sondra Spatt Olsen, winner of the '91 Iowa Short Fiction prize for *Traps*, terms it? To answer these questions, I interviewed nine poets and writers, whose wins date from 1981 to 1994.

Most of these winners had been submitting for months, even years. Six months before her novel, *Cannibal*, won the '93 Bobst prize, Terese Svoboda had thought of "giving up fiction entirely, because I hadn't had any interest in a story of mine for six years." Sondra Olsen admits to dark night fantasies that "maybe I'm too New York, too old, too out of touch with what's going on." David Rivard was twice a nonwinning contest finalist before taking the '87 Starrett Poetry prize for *Torque*. "On the one hand, it was great to be getting closer to publishing a book—in another sense enormously frustrating. When you're getting close you end up feeling, well, okay, your work is as good as the ones who get published. But why were they chosen, and why not you?"

But ultimately he was chosen, and although "no planes pulled banners across the sky," the prize, he allows, "is a boost in confidence, and it guarantees a certain amount of attention. It probably gets new poems past the screeners, and read seriously."

For others, too, the win had positive results. Terese Svoboda was approached by a "prestigious agent"; for Sondra Olsen there were magazine solicitations, readings in bookstores and colleges. Annabel Thomas, who won the Iowa in '81 for *The Phototropic Woman,* and then an Ernest Hemingway Foundation Special Citation in '82, found herself a sudden celebrity: her original, mythic stories adapted for theater, her book in demand for college lit classes. Moreover, the award offered a chance to get out of a small farm community in Ohio and meet other writers—in her day there were few MFA programs.

For some winners, though, the results were bittersweet. Lamar Herrin had already published three novels with major publishers before he won the '91 AWP for a novel, *The Lies Boys Tell.* He entered the contest because W. W. Norton, a commercial firm, would publish the winning manuscript. "But I don't think they publicized it at all. They said they'd set up readings—but even after a long, rave review in the *Times,* and a film option, they didn't do it." When Alan Hewat was awarded the '86 Hemingway Foundation award for his "ragtime" novel, *Lady's Time,* submitted by Harper & Row's Ted Solataroff, there was only a brief notice in the *Times.* And when Harper sent him to New Orleans, where the novel was set, "it wasn't even in the bookstores. This was a literary novel by an unknown." Though it earned back its $10,000 advance, went into paperback, and was optioned for film, the book was ultimately remaindered.

More harrowing still, the contest brought on a "writing block" for Elizabeth Inness-Brown, whose collection, *Satin Palms*, was published by Fiction International as the result of an '81 AWP competition. Since the publisher was a "one-man operation," there was limited distribution of the thousand copies printed. Although the collection was subsequently awarded the St. Lawrence Short Fiction prize, the then twenty-seven-year-old felt she "had to produce a novel, had to top what I'd already done." For the next five years she couldn't write; she felt "tremendous guilt. Like other women in our culture I thought: Was it just luck? Am I really any good on my own or because a mentor was always there in the wings?"

For most of the nine writers, though, the win has led to new openings in their work, an opportunity to take more risks. In re-thinking *Torque,* David Rivard had come to see "an ongoing betrayal" of the voice of his Massachusetts Catholic, working-class background. "But I now [feel I've] reached a point where I could begin to explore other ways of writing, other forms, altering my sense of the subject I was dealing with." Terese Svoboda, who had concentrated on poetry and translations, is now moving deeper into prose; and Sondra Olsen is working on linked stories that for the first time will touch on her childhood, on "recovered memories" of an extended family lost in the Holocaust. And poet Allison Joseph, winner of the '92 Ampersand Press Women Poets Series prize, and then the *Ploughshares*/Zacharis Award for her coming-of-age collection, *What Keeps Us Here,* is writing poems on darker themes: "dealing more directly with racism than I'd allowed myself to do before."

And so, with the contest behind them, the winners write on and market their work—often fruitfully. Graywolf Press has just published *Wise Poison,* a second collection by David Rivard, which won the '96 James Laughlin Award from the Academy of American Poets. University of Georgia Press has issued *Mere Mortals,* a second collection by Terese Svoboda; and Allison Joseph has now had manuscripts accepted, almost simultaneously, by the University of Pittsburgh Press and by Carnegie Mellon. Elizabeth Inness-Brown placed a second book of stories on her own after an agent had given up: in '92 *Here* was accepted by Louisiana State University Press. In '94 Annabel Thomas won the Helicon Nine Willa Cather Fiction prize after entering *Knucklebones,* a book of stories, in two other contests. Finding a home for a novel, though, seemed a dead end. A self-styled recluse and "second generation hill-billy," Thomas was approached by agents after the Iowa win, but found them "turned off" by her Appalachian settings and dialect.

Because "agents want novels," Inness-Brown and Olsen have been stretching themselves to be more commercial—"to prove to myself I can do it," says Inness-Brown. But the process can be harrowing, according to Olsen, for a writer whose method of revision is to "cut it, make it tighter, smaller." Inness-Brown is just finishing that first novel for her agent in the wings, but Olsen has a completed work, "a comedy of manners" set in academe, that agents inform her is "hard to place. They want the big seller—maybe their jobs depend on it," says Olsen, who describes her work as "subtle, low-key." Alan Hewat had "a rush from agents" when a story came out in *Esquire,* "but when they saw my nonsensational-type fiction, they got sort of demure. The obvious subtext was 'This is not a blockbuster.'" Terese Svoboda, who calls her work "idiosyncratic," had found—and lost—two agents before signing up with a third. Lamar Herrin, whose earlier novels were placed by his agent (who failed to sell *The Lies Boys Tell* before the author entered the AWP), admits that these days "it would be harder to get an agent for a literary novel—much harder." "Driven to write," Herrin still has four orphan novels in his desk.

How, then, I asked, do these writers, after that moment in the sun, deal with rejections? How do they dredge up the courage to resubmit? "You get used to them," Herrin allows, but he only revises after he hears the same complaint, "rejection after rejection. Then I'll give thought to it." Terese Svoboda tends to work quickly; at first she is "terribly satisfied. I think it's the best thing anyone has ever written. And almost without exception I have got the book back ten minutes, it seems, after I've sent it out. Then I always reexamine it and make changes."

One could conceivably send the same work to a contest over and over again, Annabel Thomas observes, "but it pays to improve it." She lets a new manuscript rest for a while before she begins her process of "re-visioning." While the work "cools off," she studies the stories of other authors, learning from them techniques she had hoped to accomplish in hers. "When I finally take it up again, I can see its flaws."

For writers of collections, rejection seems a process of reorganizing: "taking out a story, adding a story, trying to package it differently, giving it a different title or spin," advises Elizabeth Inness-Brown, who continually "revamped" her work after *Here* was rejected "everywhere in the first round of submissions." "Of course the frustration of not winning the contest," says Sondra Olsen, "is that you are left clueless about what went wrong." In resubmitting her latest collection for the Heinz she reversed the order of her first and last stories "to amazingly different effect. Who knows if this is a real improvement or just wishful thinking? Without critical feedback, it's like reading entrails." Allison Joseph agrees that "rejections are frustrating—it's difficult to publish a second book," but feels that "if the writing is important enough, you'll come back to it." She would "love" to publish with a feminist or African American press, "but presses once committed to these writers are losing their funding.

They can't publish more than one book every two years. I don't know when," she says, "or if, it will happen to me again."

"You simply get the rejections and go on," says Terese Svoboda, who, as a sometime judge, finds many manuscripts "worthy of publication, but with nothing particularly driving them." Svoboda would go the contest route "at any time," and so would David Rivard, along with poet Belle Waring, a staff nurse who had published "only a few poems" before winning the '89 AWP for *Refuge*. Both poets had a positive experience with the University of Pittsburgh Press, a series publisher. But Rivard "worries" about contests that are "one-shot deals," that publish a single book but can't promote it or keep it in print. He worries that contests are an inadequate response to the trade presses "having by and large abandoned poetry." He worries about the screeners, "their lack of experience at judging the work of others." The final judging, he argues, "is only as good as the judge himself," and "judges seem to be drawn from a fairly small pool." He worries, too, that despite the large number of contests, "the dominant aesthetic simply reinforces itself, is not reinventing itself. Would a Muriel Rukeyser or George Oppen win a prize these days?"

"You realize there are so many different voices," says Allison Joseph, who has served as both final and preliminary judge for AWP contests. "It's practically impossible to choose one. I keep on reading and listening for something that appeals to me. But what appeals to me may not be what appeals to the final judge. So there's a very big chance element to contests."

With contests publishing one out of a thousand, and talented writers dropping through the holes—how, then, I asked, do these immensely talented, largely unagented writers survive?

Through connections with other writers, some suggest; through endorsements of their work, and recommendations: poets David Wojahn and Alice Fulton gave Rivard and Waring, respectively, a leg up onto the faculty at Vermont College's MFA program. "Ultimately the prize meant job offers that would otherwise have been out of reach, since to that point I had no real teaching experience," says Waring, who now combines nursing with teaching writing to patients at a Washington, D.C. children's hospital; her second collection of poems, *Dark Blonde,* is forthcoming from Sarabande Books. Sondra Olsen and Terese Svoboda belong to city writers' groups; Alan Hewat has an agent patiently awaiting a novel— although "it's a couple of years since I've had time or energy," says Hewat, who at fifty-five, with a new baby, combines work as a rural Vermont mail carrier with freelance editing. Annabel Thomas, who tried teaching but found it "pumped the creative fountains dry," helps with her husband's veterinary practice. And with her children and grandchildren, has "other people's lives to watch, and write about."

Others, though, appear to thrive in academe. Inness-Brown has a "really great teaching job" at St. Michael's College (Vermont), for which she gives the AWP prize credit. Rivard is a part-time lecturer at Tufts; Joseph teaches poetry writing at Southern Illinois University in Carbondale, where she lives with her husband, poet Jon Tribble. She finds that talking about the writing process with her students "helps when I return to my own writing." Lamar Herrin, who passed through careers in pro baseball and the movies (he appeared in *Flaming Star* with Elvis Presley) to ultimately write, has tenure at Cornell. He likes teaching, but finds "teaching energy similar to writing energy: you come away a bit drained. So you've got to figure ways to do two things."

But mostly these writers survive through the act of writing itself. "It's not attention and awards that sustain you," says Rivard, "the work itself sustains." And Terese Svoboda adds, "The world measures success by money, and most writers can't. It seems to me the point of it all is not the book party and certainly not the royalty statement, but the wonderful moment when the story or poem comes together." Inness-Brown tells her students "to focus on the writing first, and publishing after"; and then to "always keep something in the mail." The key to success, she insists, "is persistence, making a job of it, making it methodical."

For Annabel Thomas, survival means "detaching" a submission from her ego, sending it out "as unemotionally as if I were playing Ping-Pong—for fun, not to win. Otherwise it's easy to take each returned manuscript as an announcement that I'm a failure, and so I find myself hurtling into a depression that will dry up the creative juices." She would agree with Sondra Olsen, who feels that too close an attachment "can be counterproductive to one's stamina and productivity." So Thomas just keeps "rewriting and sending out." Without the contests, she allows, "my work would be mustering in some basement or periodical nobody reads any more. Out of the contests came readings, friendships with other writers and overworked editors of literary journals who took time to write a line or two on a rejected manuscript."

And so the contest survives, and the numbers of applicants proliferate. The country is "flooded with good writing," claims Lamar Herrin, who to date has only entered one contest, but sees the publishing of serious fiction "increasingly being left to regional and university presses." It's up to them, he says, and often through contests, "to take up the slack that's being created by commercial houses."

"It would be a cold world out there without them," agrees Terese Svoboda, to whom any university press with a deadline is a "contest." For Svoboda, who is "always" circulating a new collection, the contest offers above all a time frame in which "to get something organized," and get it out. She figures the period of gestation—the time it takes to get a book published—to be about five years. "So staying at it is the most important aspect. You're always learning, trying something new. You're always getting bored with what you've just finished. You're always trying to make it better."

Winning a contest then, these nine interviewees might conclude, is no panacea: there will always be disappointments, there will always be rejections—those nagging self-doubts. But there will be moments of intense gratification as well. Most would agree with Elizabeth Inness-Brown that the true reward comes when one has a book that one "can be proud of," that one can "show to people."

The contest, it would seem, in spite of the cost, in spite of the odds, is a reasonable gamble.

Nancy Means Wright is the author of six books, including the recent Mad Search *(St. Martin's Press). Her fiction, nonfiction, and writing for young adults has appeared in leading magazines nationwide. She is currently a lecturer at Marist College.*

2

AWARDS EXCLUSIVELY FOR UNPUBLISHED FIRST-BOOK MANUSCRIPTS

ACADEMY OF AMERICAN POETS

Contest/Award Name: Walt Whitman Award

*P

Award Director: India Amos

Prize: $5,000, one-month residency at the Vermont Studio Center, and publication by Louisiana State University Press

Entry Fee: $20

Deadline: 11/15

Open to: All U.S. citizens who have neither published nor committed to publish a volume of poetry 40 pages or more in length and in an edition of 500 or more copies, either in the United States or abroad.

Number of applications received last year: 1,079

Award has been in existence: since 1975

Mail to: Academy of American Poets

Address: 584 Broadway, Suite 1208, New York, NY 10012-3250

Phone: (212) 274-0343   **Fax:** (212) 274-9427

Category: Original Poetry, by a single poet, in English

Contest results announced: May

Past Winners: *Bite Every Sorrow*, Barbara Ras, 1997; *Madonna Anno Domini*, Joshua Clover, 1996; *Resurrection*, Nicole Cooley, 1995; *Because the Brain Can Be Talked into Anything*, Jan Richman, 1994; *Science and Other Poems*, Alison Hawthorne Deming, 1993; *The Fire in All Things*, Stephan Yenser, 1992; *From the Iron Chair*, Greg Glazner, 1991; *The Cult of the Right Hand*, Elaine Terranova,

1990; *The Game of Statues*, Martha Hollander, 1989; *Blackbird Bye Bye*, April Bernard, 1988; *The Weight of Numbers*, Judith Baumel, 1987; *Fragments from the Fire*, Chris Llewellyn, 1986; *Bindweed*, Christianne Balk, 1985; *For the New Year*, Eric Pankey, 1984; *Across the Mutual Landscape*, Christopher Gilbert, 1983; *Jurgis Petraskas*, Anthony Petrosky, 1982; *Whispering to Fool the Wind*, Alberto Rios, 1981; *Work, for the Night is Coming*, Jared Carter, 1980; *Shooting Rats at the Bibb County Dump*, David Bottoms, 1979; *Wonders*, Karen Snow, 1978; *Guilty Bystander*, Lauren Shakely, 1977; *The Hocus-Pocus of the Universe*, Laura Gilpin, 1976; and *Climbing into the Roots*, Reg Saner, 1975

Past Judges: C. K. Williams, 1997; Jorie Graham, 1996; Cynthia Macdonald, 1995; Robert Pinsky, 1994; Gerald Stern, 1993; Richard Howard, 1992; Charles Wright, 1991; Rita Dove, 1990; W. S. Merwin, 1989; Amy Clampitt, 1988; Mona Van Duyn, 1987; Maxine Kumin, 1986; Anthony Hecht, 1985; Mark Strand, 1984; Michael S. Harper, 1983; Philip Levine, 1982; Donald Justice, 1981; Galway Kinnell, 1980; Robert Penn Warren, 1979; Louis Simpson, 1978; Diane Wakoski, 1977; William Stafford, 1976; and William Meredith, 1975

Publication and Promotion: Press releases sent to publications around the country. Louisiana State University Press publishes award-winning books. The number of copies printed each year varies; the hardback print run for the 1996 winner was about 7,000, of which the Academy purchased 6,000. Paperback publication is at the discretion of the publisher; LSU has printed paperbacks of all its winners so far.

Advice: Do not send your manuscript without the entry form or fee. Keep a copy of your manuscript; no manuscripts will be returned. Fasten your manuscript securely with a binder clip; do not use report covers, binding, or staples. Submission period is from 9/15 to 11/15.

AMERICAN POETRY REVIEW

Contest/Award Name:
Honickman First Book Prize

---

*P

Prize: $3,000 and publication

Entry Fee: $20

Deadline: 10/31

Open to: All U.S. poets

Award has been in existence: 1997 is the first year.

Mail to: American Poetry Review

Address: Honickman First Book Prize, The American Poetry Review-1, 1721 Walnut St., Philadelphia, PA 19103

Phone: (215) 496-0439

Category: Poetry

Advice: Submission period from 8/1 through 10/31. Write and send SASE for guidelines.

AWP/St. Martin's Press

Contest/Award Name:
AWP/St. Martin's Press Young Writer's Award

---

* F

Prize: $2,000 against royalties, publication, and standard royalties

Entry Fee: $15—nonmembers; $10—members of AWP

Deadline: 2/28

Open to: Writers born after February 28, 1965 (33 years or younger) who have not yet published a manuscript

Number of applications last year: 400

Award has been in existence: 1997 is the first year.

Mail to: AWP Award Series in (genre entered), The Associated Writing Programs

Address: Tallwood House, Mail Stop 1 E3, George Mason University, Fairfax, VA 22030

Phone: (703) 993-4301

Category: Novel

Contest results announced: August

Publication and Promotion: Award announced in *Poets & Writers, AWP Chronicle,* and newsletters.

Advice: Submission period from 1/1 to 2/28. Send SASE for complete guidelines.

AWP

Contest/Award Name:
AWP Award Series in Poetry

---

*P

Prize: $2,000, publication, and standard royalties

Entry Fee: $15—nonmembers; $10—members of AWP

Deadline: 2/28

Open to: All authors writing original works in English. Book-length MSS—48 pages minimum.

Number of applications last year: 1,000

Award has been in existence: since 1991

Mail to: AWP Award Series in Poetry, The Associated Writing Programs

Address: Tallwood House, Mail Stop 1 E3, George Mason University, Fairfax, VA 22030

Phone: (703) 993-4301

Category: Poetry

Contest results announced: August

Past Winners: *It Is Hard to Look At What We Came to Think*, Michelle Glazer, 1996; *The Ocean Inside Kenji Takezo*, Rick Noguchi, 1995; *Possible Songs*, Ruth L. Schwartz, 1994; *Some Are Drowning*, Reginald Shepard, 1993; *The New World*, Suzanne Gardinier, 1992; and *The Red Line*, Betsy Sholl, 1991

Past Judges: Jorie Graham, 1996; Olga Broumas, 1995; William Matthews, 1994; Carolyn Forche, 1993; Lucille Clifton, 1992; and Ron Wallace, 1991

Publication and Promotion: Award-winning book is published by University of Pittsburgh Press. Award is announced in *Poets & Writers* and newsletters.

Advice: "Only submit really finished work. Put your best work forward—the best 60 pages." Submission period from 1/1 to 2/28. Send SASE for complete guidelines.

AWP

Contest/Award Name:
AWP Award Series in Short Fiction

*SF

Prize: $2,000, publication, and standard royalties

Entry Fee: $15—nonmembers; $10—members of AWP

Deadline: 2/28

Open to: All authors writing original works in English. Book-length MSS—150–300 pages minimum.

Number of applications last year: 400

Award has been in existence: since 1990

Mail to: AWP Award Series in Short Fiction, The Associated Writing Programs

Address: Tallwood House, Mail Stop 1 E3, George Mason University, Fairfax, VA 22030

Phone: (703) 993-4301

Category: Short Fiction

Contest results announced: August

Past Winners: *A Private State*, Charlotte Bacon, 1996; *Black Maps*, David Jauss, 1995; *Read This and Tell Me What It Says*, A. Manette Ansay, 1994; *The Price of Tea in China*, E. Bumas, 1993; *The Last Good Man*, Daniel Lyons, 1992; *Wanting Only to Be Heard*, Jack Driscoll, 1991; and *Wild Desire*, Karen Brennan, 1990

Past Judges: George Coumo, 1996; Lorrie Moore, 1995; Elizabeth Tallent, 1994; Grace Paley, 1993; Bret Lott, 1992; Antonya Nelson, 1991; and Ron Hansen, 1990

Publication and Promotion: Award-winning book published by the University of Massachusetts Press. Award announced in *Poets & Writers* and newsletters.

Advice: Send only finished work. Submission period from 1/1 to 2/28. Send SASE for complete guidelines.

AWP

Contest/Award Name:
AWP Award Series in Creative Nonfiction

*NF

Prize: $2,000, publication, and standard royalties

Entry Fee: $15—nonmembers; $10—members of AWP

Deadline: 2/28

Open to: All authors writing original works in English. Book-length MSS—150 to 300 pages minimum.

Number of applications last year: 100

Award has been in existence: since 1992

Mail to: AWP Award Series in Creative Nonfiction, The Associated Writing Programs

Address: Tallwood House, Mail Stop 1 E3, George Mason University, Fairfax, VA 22030

Phone: (703) 993-4301

Category: Creative Nonfiction

Contest results announced: August

Past Winners: *Moses Unchained*, Marilyn Moriarty, 1996; *Because I Remember Terror, Father, I Remember You*, Sue William Silverman, 1995; *Memory Links*, William F. Van Wert, 1994; *Green Dreams: Essays Under the Influence of the Irish*, Michael Stephens, 1993; and *The Roads Taken: Travels Through America's Literary Landscapes*, Fred Setterberg, 1992

Past Judges: Lucy Grealy, 1996; Adam Hochschild, 1995; Patricia Hemple, 1994; Phillip Lopate, 1993; and Stanley Lindberg, 1992

Publication and Promotion: Award-winning book published by University of Georgia Press. Award announced in *Poets & Writers* and newsletters.

Advice: Submission period from 1/1 to 2/28. Send SASE for guidelines.

BANTAM DOUBLEDAY DELL

Contest/Award Name:
Delacorte Press Prize for a First Young Novel

---

*YA

Prize: $1,500 cash prize, $6,000 advance against royalties, and book contract

Entry Fee: $0

Deadline: 12/30   **Postmarked:** 12/30

Open to: All U.S. and Canadian writers who have not previously published a young adult novel. Foreign-language manuscripts and translations are not eligible. Manuscripts submitted to a previous Delacorte Press contest are not eligible.

Number of applications last year: 300

Mail to: Delacorte Press Prize for a First Young Novel

Address: 1540 Broadway, New York, NY 10036

Phone: (212) 354-6500   **Fax:** (212) 782-9062

Category: Young Adult

Contest results announced: 4/30

Past Winners: *Breaking Boxes*, A. M. Jenkins, 1996; *Under the Mermaid Angel*, Martha Moore, 1994; *Life Belts*, Jane Hosie-Bounar, 1992; *Squashed*, Joan Bauer, 1991; *Lizard*, Dennis Covington, 1990; *Hank*, James Sauer, 1989; *Ozzy on the Outside*, R. E. Allen, 1988; *Cal Cameron by Day, Spider-Man by Night*, A. E. Cannon, 1987; *The Impact Zone*, Ray Maloney, 1985; *Walk Through Cold Fire*, Cin Forshay-Lunsford, 1984; and *Center Line*, Joyce Sweeney, 1983

Past Judges: Editors of Delacorte Press Books for Young Readers

Publication and Promotion: Publication of hardback and paperback by Bantam Doubleday Dell, Books for Young Readers

Advice: Read books for appropriate age group and follow the contest rules. Submission period from 10/10 to 12/30.

Bantam Doubleday Dell

Contest/Award Name:
Marguerite de Angeli Contest

*YA

Prize: $1,500 cash prize, $3,500 advance against royalties, and book contract

Entry Fee: $0

Deadline: 6/30   **Postmarked:** 6/30

Open to: All U.S. and Canadian writers who have not previously published a novel for middle-grade readers. Foreign-language manuscripts and translations are not eligible.

Number of applications last year: 250

Mail to: Marguerite de Angeli Contest, Bantam Doubleday Dell BFYR

Address: 1540 Broadway, New York, NY 10036

Phone: (212) 354-6500   **Fax:** (212) 782-9062

Category: Contemporary or historical fiction set in North America, for readers age 7–10.

Contest results announced: 10/31

Past Winners: *Beastle*, Vickie Winslow Wolfinger, 1995; *Seth and Samona*, Joanne Hyppolite, 1993; and *Jackson Jones and the Puddle of Thorns*, Mary Quattlebaum, 1992

Past Judges: Editors of Books for Young Readers

Publication and Promotion: Publication of hardback and paperback by Bantam Doubleday Dell, Books for Young Readers

Advice: Read books for appropriate age group and follow the contest rules. Submission period from 4/1 to 6/30.

Barnard College

Contest/Award Name:
Barnard New Women Poets Prize

*P

Award Director: Claudia Rankine

Prize: $1,000 and publication by Beacon Press

Entry Fee: $0

Deadline: 10/15

Open to: All unpublished women writers

Number of applications last year: 550 to 700

Award has been in existence: since 1985

Mail to: Barnard College

Address: 3009 Broadway, New York, NY 10027-6598

Phone: (212) 854-2116/2038

Category: Poetry

Contest results announced: 6/1

Past Winners: Reetika Vacirani, Donna Masini, Dorothy Barresi, Barbara Jordan, Patricia Storace, and Mary Campbell

Past Judges: Marie Ponsot, Molly Peacock, Colleen McElroy, Mona Van Duyn, Eavan Boland, and Marilyn Hacker

Publication and Promotion: Announcements in major literary publications that include *Poets & Writers, American Poetry Review,* and the *AWP Chronicle.* Publication by Beacon Press of over 1,500 copies.

Advice: Send SASE for guidelines. Review the 12 volumes previously published.

BREAD LOAF WRITER'S CONFERENCE

Contest/Award Name:
Bakeless Literary Publication Prizes

*F/NF/P

Award Director: Michael Collier

Prize: Publication by Middlebury College/University Press of New England and fellowship to attend Bread Loaf Writer's Conference

Entry Fee: $10 for each submission and each genre entered

Deadline: 3/1   **Postmarked:** 3/1

Open to: Writers who have not yet published a book—any writer in any country writing in English

Number of applications last year: 1,200 in all genres for 1996

Award has been in existence: since 1996

Mail to: Bread Loaf Writer's Conference

Address: Bakeless Prizes, Middlebury College, Middlebury, VT 05753

Phone: (802) 443-5000   **Fax:** (802) 443-2087

Category: Fiction, Poetry, and Creative Nonfiction

Contest results announced: August

Past Winners: Mary Jo Bang, 1996, poetry; and Katherine Hester, 1996, fiction

Past Judges: Edward Hersh, 1997, poetry; Francine Prose, 1997, fiction; and Patricia Hemple, 1997, nonfiction; Garrett Hongo, 1996, poetry; Joanna Scott, 1996, fiction; and Alec Wilkinson, 1996, nonfiction

Publication and Promotion: Publicity varies. Award announced in *Poets & Writers*. Award-winning book published in the University Press of New England.

FC2

Contest/Award Name:
National Fiction Competition

---

*F

Award Director: Curtis White

Prize: Publication and a reading

Entry Fee: $15

Deadline: 11/15   **Postmarked:** 11/15

Open to: No restrictions

Number of applications received last year: 400

Award has been in existence: since 1977

Mail to: FC2

Address: Illinois State University, Campus Box 4241, Normal, IL 61790-4241

Phone: (309) 438-2111/ext. 3025   **Fax:** (309) 438-3523

Category: Fiction

Contest results announced: Spring

Past Winners: *City in Love*, Alex Shakar; *Angry Nights*, Larry Foundation; and *The Alphabet Man*, Richard Grossman

Past Judges: Carol Maso, Kathy Acker, Paul Auster, and Tobi Olsen

Publication and Promotion: Announcements in *Poets & Writers and AWP*. Promotion also includes sending flyers out to past applicants.

FOUR WAY BOOKS

Contest/Award Name: Intro Series in Poetry

*P

Award Director: Martha Rhodes

Prize: $2,500 and publication

Entry Fee: $15

Deadline: 5/15

Open to: All U.S. Poets

Number of applications last year: 1,500

Award has been in existence: since 1993

Mail to: Four Way Books

Address: PO Box 535, Village Station, New York, NY 10014

Phone: (617) 837-4887

Category: Poetry

Contest results announced: January of each year

Past Winners: *Strike Root*, Anne Babson Carter, 1996; *Eye of the Blackbird*, Mary Ann McFadden, 1995; *Be Properly Scared*, M. Wyrebek, 1994; and *Corporal Works*, Lynn Domina, 1993

Past Judges: Grace Schulman, 1996; Chase Twichell, 1995; Gregory Orr, 1994; and Stephen Dobyns, 1993

Publication and Promotion: Contest is promoted through readings, primarily ads, direct mail, etc. Books can be ordered through any bookstore. 1,000 paperback copies printed.

Advice: Please do not send only copy or accompanying art work.

GIBBS SMITH, PUBLISHER

Contest/Award Name:
Peregrine Smith Poetry Competition

---

*P

Award Director: Gibbs Smith; Gail Yngue, Poetry Editor

Prize: $500 and publication

Entry Fee: $15

Deadline: 4/30   **Postmarked:** 4/30

Open to: Poets who have not published a book-length work

Number of applications last year: Approximately 400

Award has been in existence: since 1986

Mail to: Gibbs Smith, Publisher

Address: P.O. Box 667, Layton, UT 84041

Phone: (801) 544-9800

Category: Poetry

Contest results announced: Three to four months after deadline

Past Judges: Christopher Merrill

Past Winners: *Perfect Hell*, H. L. Hix, 1996; *The Uses of Passion*, Angie Estes, 1995; *Buying Breakfast for my Kamakazee Pilot*, Norman Stock, 1994; and *1-800-HOT-RIBS*, Catherine Bowman, 1993

Publication and Promotion: Contest is announced in *Poets & Writers*. Award-winning book is published by Gibbs Smith, Publisher. Paperback published by Peregrine Smith Books.

Advice: Send SASE for guidelines.

HELICON NINE EDITIONS

Contest/Award Name:
Willa Cather Fiction Prize

*F

Award Director: Gloria Vando Hickok

Prize: $1,000 and publication

Entry Fee: $15

Open to: All fiction writers in the United States

Number of applications last year: 300

Award has been in existence: since 1991

Mail to: Helicon Nine Editions

Address: 3607 Pennsylvania Ave., Kansas City, MO 64111

Phone: (816) 753-1095

Category: Fiction

Contest results announced: varies

Past Winners: *Eternal City*, Molly Shapiro, 1996; *Knucklebones*, Annabel Thomas, 1994; *Galaxy Girls: Wonder Women*, Anne Whitney Pierce, 1993; *Value of Kindness*, Ellyn Bache, 1992; and *Sweet Angel Band*, R. M. Kinder, 1991

Past Judges: Daniel Stern, Carolyn Doty, James B. Hall, Hilary Masters, and Leonard Michaels

Publication and Promotion: Announcements in literary magazines—main source *Poets & Writers*. Award-winning book published by Helicon Nine. Number of copies include: Fiction—1,200 to 1,500 copies first print run (Baker & Taylor, distributor).

Advice: All MSS must be professional looking.

HELICON NINE EDITIONS

Contest/Award Name:
Marianne Moore Poetry Prize

*P

Award Director: Gloria Vando Hickok

Prize: $1,000 and publication

Entry Fee: $15

Open to: All poets in the United States

Number of applications last year: 600

Award has been in existence: since 1991

Mail to: Helicon Nine Editions

Address: 3607 Pennsylvania Ave., Kansas City, MO 64111

Phone: (816) 753-1095

Category: Poetry

Contest results announced: varies

Past Winners: *Prayer to the Other Life*, Christopher Seid, 1996; *A Strange Heart*, Jane O. Wayne, 1995; *Night Drawings*, Marjorie Stelmach, 1994; *My Journey Toward You*, Judy Longley, 1993; *Women in Cars*, Martha McFerren, 1992; and *Black Method*, Biff Russ, 1991

Past Judges: James Tate, David Ignatow, Richard Howard, Colette Inez, Mona Van Duyn, and David Ray

Publication and Promotion: Announcements in literary magazines—main source *Poets & Writers*. Award-winning book published by Helicon Nine. Number of copies include 1,000 first print run (Baker & Taylor, distributor).

Advice: All MSS must be professional looking. We are looking for thematic poetry.

INTERNATIONAL READING ASSOCIATION

Contest/Award Name: Children's Book Award

*C

Award Director: Judith Meagher

Prize: $500 for each of three prizes for first and second book

Entry Fee: $0

Deadline: 12/1   **Postmarked:** 12/1

Open to: Authors whose early works show unusual promise for a career in children's literature. Book has to be published this year. Includes first or second book.

Award has been in existence: since 1975

Mail to: c/o Judith Meagher

Address: University of CT, School of Education, 249 Glenbrook Rd., Storrs, CT 06268-2064

Phone: (302) 731-1600

Category: Younger Readers (four to 10); Older Readers (16+); Informational Books (four to 16+)

Contest results announced: May 3rd through the 8th at the Int'l Reading Assoc. Annual Conference.

Past Winners: Ingrid Slyder, Elizabeth Mann and Margaret Peterson Haddix, 1997; Chris K. Soentpiet, Elizabeth Alden and Susan Quinlan, 1996; Trudy Krisher and Gary Bowen, 1995; Deborah Hopkinson and Nellie S. Toll, 1994; and Karen Hesse, 1993

Publication and Promotion: Award is announced in newspapers, *Int'l Reading Assoc. Journal,* as well as press releases.

Advice: Meet the deadline.

THE JAMES JONES LITERARY SOCIETY

Contest/Award Name:

The James Jones First Novel Fellowship

---

*F

Award Director: Kaylie Jones

Prize: $2,500

Entry Fee: $15

Deadline: 3/1

Open to: All U.S. writers who have not previously published novels

Number of applications last year: over 500

Award has been in existence: since 1992

Mail to: The James Jones First Novel Fellowship

Address: Department of English, Wilkes University, Wilkes-Barre, PA 18766

Phone: (717) 831-4200

Category: Fiction

Contest results announced: 9/1

Past Winners: *The Hindenburg Crashes Nightly*, Greg Herbeck, 1996; *Where the Sea Used to Be*, Rick Bass, 1995; *Tale of a Two-Hearted Tiger*, Tanuja Desai, 1995; *The Frequency of Souls*, Mary Kay Zuravleff, 1994; and *Eden Undone*, Nancy Flynn, 1993

Past Judges: Kaylie Jones, Kevin Heisler, J. Michael Lennon, Patricia Heaman, and Jon Shirota

Publication and Promotion: Award announcement is distributed to all writing programs across the country. Award also advertised in *Poets & Writers* and other literary publications. Presently designing a web page to post award ad on English department bulletin board on the Internet.

Advice: The award is intended to honor the spirit of unblinking honesty, determination, and insight into modern culture exemplified by the late James Jones, author of *From Here to Eternity*, and other prose narratives of distinction. Failure to comply with MS guidelines may disqualify entries. Please send SASE for complete guidelines.

KENT STATE UNIVERSITY

Contest/Award Name:
The Stan and Tom Wick Poetry Prize

*P

Award Director: Maggie Anderson, Director

Prize: $2,000 and publication by Kent State University Press

Entry Fee: $15

Deadline: 5/1   **Postmarked:** 5/1

Open to: All poets writing in English who have not yet published a full-length collection of poems (a volume of 48 or more pages published in an edition of 500 or more).

Number of applications last year: 675

Award has been in existence: since 1994

Mail to: Stan and Tom Wick Poetry Prize

Address: Kent State University, Department of English, P.O. Box 5190, Kent, OH 44242-0001

Phone: (330) 672-2676   **Fax:** (330) 672-3152

Category: Poetry

Contest results announced: Fall of each year

Past Winners: *Already the World*, Victoria Redel, 1994; *Likely*, Lisa Coffman, 1995; and *Intended Place*, Rosemary Willey, 1996

Past Judges: Marilyn Hacker, 1997; Yusef Komunyakaa, 1996; Alicia Ostriker, 1995; and Gerald Stern, 1994

Publication and Promotion: Award announced through advertisements in literary magazines, e.g., *Poets & Writers, The Boston Review of Books, Threepenny Review,* etc., and through direct mailings. Kent State University Press publishes hardback and paperback copies of award-winning book. Number of copies: 300 hardback/1,200 paperback. Books can be obtained through bookstores everywhere and through the Kent State University Press, Kent State University, P.O. Box 5190, Kent, OH 44242-0001, 1-800-247-6553.

Advice: Follow our guidelines regarding length, format, etc., to ensure that your manuscript is considered for the contest. Submission period from 2/1 to 5/1. To receive a copy of the guidelines, send a SASE to the Stan and Tom Wick Poetry Contest at Kent State University, Department of English.

MID-LIST PRESS

Contest/Award Name: First Book Awards

*F/NF/P/SF

Prize: $1,000 and publication (fiction, short fiction, and nonfiction), $500 and publication (poetry)

Entry Fee: $10

Deadline: 2/1 for novels and poetry; 7/1 for short fiction and creative nonfiction

Open to: Any writer who has not yet published: a collection of short stories, poetry (including chapbooks), a novel, or a work of nonfiction

Number of applications last year: 350 (poetry), 350 (novel), 270 (short fiction), 100 (nonfiction)

Mail to: Mid-List Press

Address: 4324 12th Avenue South, Minneapolis, MN 55407

Phone: (612) 822-3733

Category: Fiction, Nonfiction, Poetry, and Short Fiction

Contest results announced: In the summer *AWP Chronicle*

Past Winners: Fiction: *The Mensch*, David Weiss, 1996; *The Latest Epistle of Jim*, Roy Shepard, 1995; *Jump*, John Prendergast, 1994; *Felicity*, Kristen Staby Rembold, 1993; *News from Fort God*, William Sutherland, 1992; and *Same Bed, Different Dreams*, Hugh Gross, 1990. **Poetry:** *Brokern Helix*, Dina Ben-lev, 1996; *My World, My Fingerhold, My Bygod Apple*, Neva Hacker, 1995; *The Only Time There Is*, Jeff Worley, 1994; *Words on the Moon*, Douglas Gray, 1993; *Scavenging the Country for a Heartbeat*, Neil Shepard, 1992; *Instruments of the Bones*, Stephen Behrendt, 1991; *On the Other Side of the River*, J. E. Sorrell, 1991; and *Discriminating Evidence*, Mary Logue, 1990. **Short Fiction:** *The Sincere Café*, Leslee Becker, 1995. **Nonfiction:** *Thistle Journal and Other Essays on Building a House*, Daniel Minock, 1996

Past Judges: Mid-List Editorial Board

Publication: Award-winning book is published. Number of copies: 1,000 to 3,000 (novel, short fiction/nonfiction); 50 to 1,000 (poetry)

Advice: Entries must be ready for publication. Creative nonfiction may include, but is not limited to, memoirs, autobiographies, nature writing, travel writing, personal essays, literary journalism, social communication, and cross-disciplinary work. Mid-List does not discriminate against genres, but they are not interested in formula writing—only new and innovative writing. Most important aspect of writing (fiction) is character and story (not plot-driven writing).

NATIONAL WRITERS ASSOCIATION
Contest/Award Name: NWA Novel Contest

*F

Prize: $500 and Clearinghouse representation (first place); $250 (second place); $150 (third place)

Entry Fee: $35

Deadline: 4/1

Open to: Open to all U.S. writers

Mail to: NWA Novel Contest

Address: National Writers Assoc., 1450 S. Havana, Suite 424, Aurora, CO 80012

Phone: (303) 751-7844

Category: Fiction

Advice: The purpose of the National Writers Association Novel Contest is to encourage the development of creative skills, and to recognize and reward outstanding ability in the area of novel writing.

NATIVE WRITERS CIRCLE OF THE AMERICAS
Contest/Award Name:
North American Native Authors First Book Awards

*NF/P

Award Director: Joseph Bruchac

Prize: $500, publication by Greenfield Review Press, and standard royalties (usually 10% of the sale price of the book)

Entry Fee: $0

Deadline: 3/15   **Postmarked:** 3/15

Open to: Native Americans of the United States, Canada, and Mexico, including those of Aleut, Inuit, or Metis ancestry.

Number of applications last year: 60

Award has been in existence: since 1990

Mail to: Native Writers Circle of the Americas

Address: The Greenfield Review Literary Center, P.O. Box 308, 2 Middle Grove Rd., Greenfield Center, NY 12633

Phone: (518) 584-1728

Category: Nonfiction and Poetry

Contest results announced: Winners are announced 5/1 at the Native Writers Circle Awards Banquet held each year in Norman, OK. Winners invited to attend this banquet.

Past Winners: D. L. Birchfield (Choctaw-Chickasaw) and Robert J. Perry (Chickasaw), 1997, prose; Deborah Miranda (Ohlone-Costanoan) for Poetry, 1997. Charles Ballard (Quapaw), 1996, poetry. Glen Twist (Cherokee), 1995, prose; Denise Sweet (Anishinabe), 1995, poetry. Gus Palmer, Jr. (Kiowa), 1994, prose; and Tiffany Midge (Lakota), 1994, poetry

Publication and Promotion: Contest promoted through press releases and banquet. The Greenfield Review Press publishes award-winning book.

Advice: Follow the guidelines.

NEW YORK UNIVERSITY PRESS
Contest/Award Name:
Poetry and Fiction Awards (formerly the Bobst Award)

*F/P

Award Director: Niko Pfund

Prize: $1,000 and publication

Entry Fee: $0

Deadline: 1st Friday of each May

Open to: Any writer of poetry and/or fiction

Number of applications last year: 368 (poetry); 240 (fiction)

Award has been in existence: since 1990

Mail to: New York University Press

Address: 70 Washington Square South, 2nd Floor, New York, NY 10012-1091

Phone: (212) 998-2575

Category: Fiction and Poetry

Contest results announced: varies

Past Winners: *Bye Bye*, Jane Ransom, 1996, fiction; *Flying Out with the Wounded*, Anne Caston, 1996, poetry; *Bird-Self Accumulated*, Don Judson, 1995, fiction; *Rodent Angel*, Debra Weinstein, 1995, poetry; *The Lost & Found and Other Stories*, Anne Marsella, 1994, fiction; *Human Nature*, Alice Anderson, 1994, poetry; *Cannibal*, Terese Svoboda, 1993, fiction; *Men Living on a Side and Other Poems*, and Stephan Torre, 1993, poetry

Past Judges: Judges for 1997 included Barbara Eppler and Terese Svoboda.

Publication and Promotion: Announcement in *Poets & Writers* and other literary publications

Advice: Include your recommendation letter with your own letter. Try to do something different—no romance novels, fantasy, etc. Also, do not submit too lengthy a manuscript.

Owl Creek Press

Contest/Award Name: Owl Creek Poetry Prize

*P

Award Director: Rich Ives

Prize: $750 and publication

Entry Fee: $0

Deadline: 2/15

Open to: All U.S. poets

Number of applications last year: 200

Mail to: Owl Creek Press

Address: 2693 South West Kamano Drive, Kamano Island, WA 98292

Phone: (360) 387-6101

Category: Poetry

Contest results announced: Four to five months after deadline

Past Winners: Sue Ellen Thompson, 1996, and Deborah Gregerman, 1997

Past Judges: Rich Ives (final judge) and selected screeners who vary on an annual basis

Publication and Promotion: Contest announced in *AWP* and *Poets & Writers*

PEN AMERICAN CENTER
Contest/Award Name: PEN/Norma Klein Award

*C

Award Director: John Morrone

Prize: $3,000 biennially

Entry Fee: $0

Deadline: 12/15   **Postmarked:** 12/15

Open to: U.S. writers of children's literature. Open to the "adventuresome, innovative spirit that characterizes the best children's literature and Norma Klein's own work." Also, nomination necessary.

Number of applications last year: 40

Award has been in existence: since 1991

Mail to: PEN American Center

Address: 568 Broadway, 4th Floor, New York, NY 10012-3225

Phone: (212) 334-1660

Category: Children's Literature

Contest results announced: May

Past Winners: Rita Williams Garcia, 1997; Angela Johnson, 1995; Graham Salisbury, 1993; and Cynthia Grant, 1991

Past Award-Winning Books: *Blue Skin of the Sea*, Graham Salisbury, 1993; and *Humming Whispers and Toning the Sweep*, Angela Johnson, 1995

Publication and Promotion: Contest announced in *Poets & Writers, AWP*

Advice: Nominations must come from authors and editors.

PEN American Center

Contest/Award Name:
Renato Poggioli Translation Award

*TR

Award Director: John Morrone

Prize: $3,000 for first book in progress, Italian into English

Entry Fee: $0

Deadline: 12/31   Postmarked: 12/31

Open to: All U.S. writers

Number of applications last year: 15 to 20

Award has been in existence: since 1978

Mail to: PEN American Center

Address: 568 Broadway, 4th Floor, New York, NY 10012-3225

Phone: (212) 334-1660

Category: Translation

Past Winners: Ann McGarrell, *The Faith of Isis* by Vittoria Ronchey, 1997; and Luis Rozier, *Little Jesus of Sicily* by Fortunato Pasqualino, 1996

Quarterly Review of Literature

Contest/Award Name: QRL Poetry Book Series

*PL/P/TR

Award Directors: Theodore and Renee Weiss

Prize: $1,000 and 100 copies of publication. Four to five winners published in one volume.

Entry Fee: $20 (includes subscription)

Deadline: 5/30 and 10/30

Open to: Any book-length collection of poems (original or translated), book-length poem, or poetic play. English language submissions from foreign countries welcome.

Number of applications last year: 500 submissions for five awards

Award has been in existence: since 1978

Mail to: Quarterly Review of Literature Poetry Book Series

Address: 26 Haslet Ave., Princeton, NJ 08540

Phone: (609) 921-6976

Category: Poetic Plays, Poetry, and Translation

Contest results announced: Approximately three months

Past Winners: Julia Mishkin, 1984; Anne Carson, 1983; Wislawa Szymborska, 1981; Jane Hirshfield, 1981; and Reginald Gibbons, 1978

Past Judges: Theodore and Renee Weiss

Publication and Promotion: Volume is published by QRL in both hardcover and paperback. Approximately 2,500 copies printed. Promoted through mailings to a wide range of reviewers and libraries.

Advice: Familiarize yourself with the Poetry Series. Manuscripts declined one year may be revised and resubmitted. Send SASE for guidelines and application forms.

SARABANDE BOOKS
Contest/Award Name:
Kathryn A. Morton Award for Poetry

*P

Award Director: Sarah Gorham, Editor in Chief

Prize: $2,000, publication, and a standard royalty contract

Entry Fee: $15

Deadline: 2/15   **Postmarked:** 2/15

Open to: Any writer of English who is a citizen of the United States, except employees of Sarabande Books, Inc. Submitted MS must be an unpublished work. Translations and previously self-published books are not eligible.

Mail to: The Kathryn A. Morton Award for Poetry

Address: Sarabande Books, Inc., P.O. Box 4999, Louisville, KY 40204

Phone: (502) 458-4028   **Fax:** (502) 458-4065

Category: Poetry

Contest results announced: July

Past Winners: *The Gatehouse Heaven*, James Kimbrell, 1997; *When*, Baron Wormser, 1996; and *The Lord and the General Din of the World*, Jane Mead, 1995

Past Judges: Charles Wright, 1997; Alice Fulton, 1996; and Philip Levine, 1995.

Advice: All MSS must be accompanied by the entry form, which contains all the necessary information. Do not send MS without this form. Retain a copy of MS. MSS are not returned. Submissions of more than one MS is permissible if each MS is accompanied by an entry form and handling fee. Simultaneous submission to other publishers permitted, but Sarabande Books must be notified immediately if MS is accepted elsewhere. MS must be postmarked between 1/1 and 2/15. Do not send MS via UPS, Federal Express, or by overnight mail. "We strongly advise that you send your manuscripts first class." Sarabande books will consider all finalists for publication. Send SASE for complete guidelines.

SARABANDE BOOKS

Contest/Award Name:
Mary McCarthy Award for Short Fiction

*SF

Award Director: Sarah Gorham, Editor in Chief

Prize: $2,000 and publication

Entry Fee: $15

Deadline: 2/15   **Postmarked:** 2/15

Open to: Any writer of English who is a citizen of the United States, except employees of Sarabande Books, Inc. Submitted manuscript must be an unpublished work. Translations and previously self-published books are not eligible.

Mail to: The Mary McCarthy Prize in Short Fiction

Address: Sarabande Books, Inc., P.O. Box 4999, Louisville, KY 40204

Phone: (502) 458-4028   **Fax:** (502) 458-4065

Category: Short Fiction

Contest results announced: July

Past Winners: *A Gram of Mars*, Becky Hagenston, 1997; *Sparkman in the Sky & Other Stories*, Brian Griffin, 1996; and *The Least You Need to Know*, Lee Martin, 1995

Past Judges: A. M. Holmes, 1997; Barry Hanna, 1996; and Amy Bloom, 1995

Advice: All MSS must be accompanied by the entry form, which contains all the necessary information. Do not send MS without this form. Retain a copy of MS. MSS are not returned. Submissions of more than one MS is permissible if each MS is accompanied by an entry form and handling fee. Simultaneous submission to other publishers permitted, but Sarabande Books must be notified immediately if MS is accepted elsewhere. MS must be postmarked between 1/1 and 2/15. Do not send MS via UPS, Federal Express, or by overnight mail. "We strongly advise that you send your manuscripts first class." Sarabande books will consider all finalists for publication. Send SASE for complete guidelines.

St. Martin's Press

Contest/Award Name:
The Best First Private Eye Novel Contest and
The Malice Domestic Best First Novel Contest

---

*F

Award Director: Thomas Dunne Editors

Prize: $10,000 advance and publication

Entry Fee: $0

Deadline: Private Eye: 8/1; Malice: 11/15   **Postmarked:** 8/1; 11/15

Open to: Anyone who has not yet published a Private Eye or Mystery novel

Number of applications last year: 250

Award has been in existence: Private Eye since 1986; Malice award since 1989

Mail to: Thomas Dunne Books

Address: St. Martin's Press, 175 Fifth Ave., New York, NY 10010

Phone: (212) 674-5151

Category: Fiction—Private Eye or Mystery Novel

Contest results announced: First week of November

Past Judges: Editorial staff at Thomas Dunne

Publication and Promotion: Contest announced in press releases and monthly newsletters. Award-winning book published in both hardback and paperback. Number of copies printed varies.

Advice: Patience. SASE a must. Not looking for excessive violence or overt sex.

STORY LINE PRESS
Contest/Award Name:
Nicholas Roerich Poetry Prize

*P

Award Director: Robert McDowell

Prize: $1,000, publication, and reading at the Nicholas Roerich Museum

Entry Fee: $15

Deadline: 10/15

Open to: All U.S. poets

Number of applications last year: 600 to 1,000

Award has been in existence: since 1987

Mail to: Story Line Press

Address: Three Oaks Farm, Brownsville, OR 97327

Phone: (541) 466-5352

Category: Poetry

Contest results announced: January

Past Winners: David Mason, Kate Light, Amy Yucmatsu, Jane Ransom, and Greg Williamson

Past Judges: Dana Gioia, Robert McDowell, and George Hitchcock

Publication and Promotion: Contest is announced in *Poets & Writers, AWP Chronicle, American Poetry Review, Hudson Review,* and various ads.

Tri-Quarterly Books/
Northwestern University Press

Contest/Award Name:
Terence Des Pres Prize for Poetry

*P

Prize: $1,000 and publication

Deadline: 4/30

Open to: All U.S. Poets

Mail to: Tri-Quarterly, Northwestern University

Address: 2020 Ridge Ave., Evanston, IL 60208-4302

Phone: (847) 491-5313

Category: Poetry

Advice: Submission period from 10/1 to 4/30

University of Arkansas Press

Contest/Award Name: Arkansas Poetry Award

*P

Prize: Publication

Entry Fee: $15

Deadline: 5/1

Open to: A U.S. poet whose work has never been previously published in book form. Chapbooks, self-published books, limited editions, and books produced with the author's subsidy are not considered previously published books. Translations are not acceptable.

Mail to: University of Arkansas Press, Arkansas Poetry Award

Address: 201 Ozark Ave., Fayetteville, AR 72701

Phone: (501) 575-3246

Category: Poetry

Contest Results Announced: August

Past Winners: *News From Where I Live*, Martin Lammon, 1997; *The Listening Chamber*, William Aberg, 1996; *Anne & Alpheus*, Joe Survant, 1995; *The Man on the Tower*, Charles Rafferty, 1994; and *At Every Wedding Someone Stays Home*, Dannye Romine Powell, 1993

Past Judges: Samuel Hazo, 1997; John Stone, 1996; Rachel Hadas, 1995; Susan Ludvigson, 1994; and Jo McDougall, 1993

Publication and Promotion: The winning book will be published in paperback, on which the author will receive a royalty of 7.5% of net receipts.

Advice: Submission period from 1/1 to 5/1. Send SASE for guidelines.

UNIVERSITY OF GEORGIA PRESS

Contest/Award Name:
Flannery O'Connor Award for Short Fiction

*SF

Award Director: Jane Kobres and Charles East

Prize: (2) $2,000 and publication for each

Entry Fee: $10

Deadline: 7/31

Open to: All fiction writers—published and unpublished

Number of applications last year: 330

Award has been in existence: since 1982

Mail to: University of Georgia Press

Address: 330 Research Drive, Suite B-100, Athens, GA 30602-4901

Phone: (706) 369-6130

Category: Short Fiction

Contest results announced: November

Past Winners: *Sky Over El Nido*, C. M. Mayo; *Large Animals in Everyday Life*, Wendy Brenner; *How Far She Went*, Mary Hood; *Winter Money*, Andy Plattner; *Under the Red Flag*, Ha Jin; *No Lie Like Love*, Paul Rawlins; *The Quarry*, Harvey Grossinger; *The Nature of Longing*, Alyce Miller; *Nervous Dancer*, Carol Lee Lorenzo; *All My Relations*, Christopher McIlroy; *A Brief History of Male Nudes in America*, Dianne Nelson; and *Mother Rocket*, Rita Ciresi

Past Judges: One of the early judges was Raymond Carver. Charles East is the final judge after MSS have been screened by an anonymous panel of screeners.

Advice: Please send SASE for guidelines. Collections that include long stories or novellas are acceptable. Novels or single novellas will not be considered. Simultaneous submissions are acceptable. Please notify the press immediately if MS has been accepted elsewhere after it has come under the review process. Submission period from 6/1 to 7/1.

UNIVERSITY OF IOWA PRESS

Contest/Award Name:
Iowa Short Fiction Award and
John Simmons Short Fiction Award

*F/SF

Prize: Publication (first print run approximately 2,500 copies)

Entry Fee: $0

Deadline: 9/30

Open to: Any writer who has not previously published a volume of prose fiction

Number of applications last year: 400

Award has been in existence: since 1970

Mail to: University of Iowa Press

Address: Iowa Short Fiction Award, Iowa Writer's Workshop, 102 Dey House, Iowa City, IA 52242-1000

Phone: (319) 235-2665

Category: Fiction and Short Fiction

Contest results announced: January to early February

Past Winners: David Borofka, 1996; Robert Boswell, 1985; and Susan Dodd, 1984

Past Award-Winning Books: *Dancing in the Movies*, Robert Boswell; and *Old Wives Tales*, Susan Dodd

Past Judges: Ann Beaty, Oscar Hijuelos, and Frederick Bush

Publication and Promotion: Award-winning books will be published by the University of Iowa Press under the Press's standard contract. The awards are announced in *Poets and Writers* and *AWP*.

Advice: The MS must be a collection of short stories of at least 150 word-processed, double-spaced pages. A SASE must accompany MS. Send SASE and follow guidelines.

University of Massachusetts Press

Contest/Award Name:
Juniper Prize (in odd-numbered years for first books)

*P

Award Director: Chris Hammel

Prize: $1,000 and publication

Entry Fee: $10

Deadline: 9/30

Open to: All U.S. writers

Number of applications last year: 800

Award has been in existence: since 1975

Mail to: University of Massachusetts

Address: P.O. Box 429, Amherst, MA 01004

Phone: (413) 545-0111/2217

Category: Poetry

Contest results announced: April

Past Winners: *The Double Task*, Gray Jacobik, 1997; *At the Sight of Inside Out*, Anna Rabinowitz, 1996; *Cities and Towns*, Arthur Vogelsang, 1995; *The Postal Confessions*, Max Garland, 1994; *Child in Amber*, Stephen McNally, 1992; and *Tasker Street*, Mark Halliday, 1991

Publication and Promotion: Announcements in *Poets and Writers* and *AWP*

Advice: Alternates annually between first-time authors and previously published authors. "Go to bookstores and find out what we have published and who has won the award."

University of Pittsburgh Press

Contest/Award Name: Agnes Lynch Starrett Prize

*P

Award Director: Ed Ochester

Prize: $2,500 and publication

Entry Fee: $15

Deadline: 4/30   **Postmarked:** 4/30

Open to: Any writer who has not had a full-length poetry book published

Number of applications last year: approximately 1,000

Award has been in existence: since 1981

Mail to: University of Pittsburgh Press

Address: 127 North Bellefield Ave., Pittsburgh, PA 15260

Phone: (412) 624-4141

Category: Poetry

Contest results announced: varies

Past Winners: *Red Peony Night*, Helen Conkling, 1996; *Pears, Lake, Sun*, Sandy Solomon, 1995; *Mad River*, Jan Beatty, 1994; *Red Under the Skin*, Natasha Saje, 1993; *The Domestic Life*, Hunt Hawkins, 1992; *Sleeping Preacher*, Julia Kasdorf, 1991; *Walking Distance*, Debra Allbery, 1990; *The Face in the Water*, Nancy Vieira Couto, 1989; *Toluca Street*, Maxine Scates, 1988; *Torque*, David Rivard, 1987; *Kingdoms of the Ordinary*, Robley Wilson, 1986; *The Fire Music*, Liz Rosenberg, 1985; *Elegy on Independence Day*, Arthur Smith, 1984; *The White Wave*, Kate Daniels, 1983; *Shouting at No One*, Lawrence Joseph, 1982; and *Heart of the Garfish*, Kathy Callaway, 1981

Past Judges: Ed Ochester is the final judge after work has been screened by an anonymous panel.

Publication and Promotion: Announcements in several poetry magazines including *Poets & Writers* and *AWP.*

Advice: Write good poetry and follow the guidelines' instructions.

UNIVERSITY OF TEXAS PRESS

Contest/Award Name:
American Short Fiction Prizes

---

*SF

Award Director: Joseph Kruppa

Prize: $1,000 and publication to $200 and possible publication

Entry Fee: $20 (includes one-year subscription to *ASF*)

Deadline: 5/31

Open to: All U.S. writers

Number of applications last year: 400

Award has been in existence: since 1996

Mail to: Joseph Kruppa, Editor

Address: Parlin Hal 108, University of Texas, Austin, TX 78712-1164

Phone: (512) 471-4531

Category: Short Fiction

Contest results announced: August

Past Winners: *The Novelty of Flight*, Sabina Murray, 1996 (first place); *Choices*, Sussanne Davis, 1996 (second place); and *Mutuality*, Candida Lawrence, 1996 (third place)

Past Judges: Joseph Kruppa, Caitlin Wood, and Robert Tateum

Publication and Promotion: Award announced in *AWP Chronicle, Poets & Writers*, and in distributed flyers

Advice: MS must be 7,000 words or less, original, unpublished, and not submitted elsewhere. Multiple entries are allowed. Submission period from 9/1 to 5/31. Send SASE for further information.

UTAH STATE UNIVERSITY

Contest/Award Name: May Swenson Poetry Prize

*P

Prize: $750 and publication

Entry Fee: $20

Deadline: 9/30

Open to: All U.S. poets. Translations are not eligible.

Mail to: May Swenson Poetry Award

Address: Utah State University, Logan, UT 84322-7800

Category: Poetry

Publication and Promotion: Award is announced in *Poets & Writers*.

Advice: Send SASE for guidelines.

WHITE PINE PRESS

Contest/Award Name: White Pine Poetry Prize

*P

Award Director: Dennis Maloney

Prize: $500 and publication

Entry Fee: $15

Deadline: 10/15

Open to: All U.S. poets. Translations are not eligible.

Number of applications last year: 500

Award has been in existence: since 1992

Mail to: White Pine Press, Poetry Prize Contest

Address: 10 Village Square, Fredonia, NY 14063

Phone: (716) 672-5743

Category: Poetry

Contest results announced: June or July

Past Winners: *Bodily Course*, Deborah Gorlin, 1996; and *Zoo and Cathedral*, Nancy Johnson, 1995

Past Judges: David St. John, Mekeel McBride, and Maurice Kenny

Publication and Promotion: Contest is announced through news releases and ads in several literary journals.

Advice: Submission period is from 7/15 to 11/15. "Get the guidelines." Guidelines change from year to year.

WRITERS AT WORK

Contest/Award Name:
Fellowship Competition for Fiction,
Poetry, Screenplay/Teleplay

*F/P/SP

Prize: $1,500, publication in *Quarterly West*, featured reading, tuition for afternoon session of the '98 conference

Entry Fee: $12 reading fee each entry

Deadline: 3/15

Open to: Open to all U.S. writers—screenwriters must be Utah residents.

Number of applications last year: 1,300 to 1,600

Award has been in existence: since 1983

Mail to: Writers at Work c/o (specifiy genre)

Address: P.O. Box 1146, Centerville, UT 84014-5146

Phone: (801) 292-9285

Category: Fiction, Poetry, Screenplay/Teleplay

Contest results announced: 5/31

Past Winners: Mark Wonderlich (Poetry), 1996; and Shelly Hunt Kamoin (Fiction), 1996.

Advice: Eligibility for fiction and poetry include any writer who has not yet published a book-length volume of original work. Short story/novel excerpts 5,000-word maximum, double-spaced. Poetry MSS: six poems, 10-page maximum. Please send SASE for complete guidelines.

YALE UNIVERSITY PRESS

Contest/Award Name:
Yale Series of Younger Poets

---

*P

Award Director: Richard Miller

Prize: Publication

Entry Fee: $15

Deadline: 2/28

Open to: Poets under 40 years of age

Number of applications last year: 696

Award has been in existence: since 1919

Mail to: Yale University Press

Address: P.O. Box 209040, New Haven, CT 06520-9040

Phone: (203) 432-0960

Category: Poetry

Contest results announced: June

Past Winners: Brigit Pegeen Kelly, Olga Broumas, Carolyn Forche, James Tate, Alan Dugan, John Hollander, James Wright, John Ashbery, W. S. Merwin, Adrienne Rich, Muriel Rukeyser, James Agee, and Paul H. Engle

Past Judges: James Dickey, 1990–1996; James Merrill, 1983–1989; Richard Hugo, 1977–1982; Stanley Kunitz, 1969–1976; Dudley Fitts, 1959–1968; W. H. Auden, 1946–1958; Archibald MacLeish, 1942–1945; Stephen Vincent Benet, 1933–1942; William Alexander Percy, 1925–1932; Edward Bliss Reed, 1923–1924; Frederick E. Pierce, 1923; and Charlton M. Lewis, 1919–1920

Publication and Promotion: Award is announced in *Poets & Writers, American Poetry Review, Poetry Magazine,* and other publications.

Advice: Submission period is the month of February. Send SASE to obtain guidelines and application.

AWARDS EXCLUSIVELY FOR UNPUBLISHED FIRST-BOOK MANUSCRIPTS

BY PRIZE

Award Name	Prize
Arkansas Poetry Award	Publication
Iowa Short Fiction Award and John Simmons Short Fiction Award	Publication
Yale Series of Younger Poets	Publication
National Fiction Competition	Publication and a reading
Bakeless Literary Publication Prizes	Publication by Middlebury College/University Press of New England and fellowship to attend Bread Loaf Writer's Conference
NWA Novel Contest	$500 and Clearinghouse representation (first place); $250 (second place); $150 (third place)
Peregrine Smith Poetry Competition	$500 and publication
White Pine Poetry Prize	$500 and publication
Children's Book Award	$500 for each of three prizes for first and second book
First Book Awards	$500 and publication (poetry)
North American Native Authors First Book Awards	$500, publication by Greenfield Review Press, and standard royalties

Award Name	Prize
May Swenson Poetry Prize	$750 and publication
Owl Creek Poetry Prize	$750 and publication
QRL Poetry Book Series	$1,000 and 100 copies of publication
Hemingway First Novel Contest	$1,000 and literary representation for 1 year by top New York literary agent
Poetry and Fiction Awards (formerly the Bobst Award)	$1,000 and publication
Terence Des Pres Prize for Poetry	$1,000 and publication
Willa Cather Fiction Prize	$1,000 and publication
Marianne Moore Poetry Prize	$1,000 and publication
First Book Awards (fiction, short fiction, and nonfiction)	$1,000 and publication
Walt Whitman Award	$5,000 and publication
Barnard New Women Poets Prize	$1,000 and publication by Beacon Press
Juniper Prize (in odd-numbered years for first books)	$1,000 and publication
Intro Series in Poetry	$2,500 and publication
Nicholas Roerich Poetry Prize	$1,000, publication, and reading at the Nicholas Roerich Museum
American Short Fiction Prizes	$1,000 and publication
Delacorte Press Prize for a First Young Novel	$1,500 cash prize, $6,000 advance against royalties, and book contract

Award Name	Prize
Fellowship Competition for Fiction, Poetry, Screenplay/Teleplay	$1,500, publication in *Quarterly West*, featured reading, tuition for afternoon session of the '98 conference
Marguerite de Angeli Contest	$1,500, $3,500 advance against royalties, and book contract
Flannery O'Connor Award for Short Fiction	(2) $2,000 and publication for each
AWP Award Series in Poetry	$2,000, publication, and standard royalties
AWP Award Series in Short Fiction	$2,000, publication, and standard royalties
AWP Award Series in Creative Nonfiction	$2,000, publication, and standard royalties
Kathryn A. Morton Award for Poetry	$2,000, publication, and standard royalties
The Stan and Tom Wick Poetry Prize	$2,000 and publication by Kent State University Press
Mary McCarthy Award for Short Fiction	$2,000 and publication
AWP/St. Martin's Press Young Writer's Award	$2,000 against royalties, publication, and standard royalties
The James Jones First Novel Fellowship	$2,500
Agnes Lynch Starrett Prize	$2,500 and publication
PEN/Norma Klein Award	$3,000 biennially
Honickman First Book Prize	$3,000 and publication
Renato Poggioli Translation Award	$3,000
The Best First Private Eye Novel Contest and The Malice Domestic Best First Novel Contest	$10,000 advance and publication

Awards Exclusively for Unpublished First-Book Manuscripts

by Genre

3

Awards Favorable to Unpublished First-Book Manuscripts

American-Scandinavian Foundation
Contest/Award:
ASF Translation Prize for Fiction

*F/TR

Prize: $2,000, plus publication in the *Scandinavian Review*

Entry Fee: $0

Deadline: 6/1

Open to: Authors of published translations

Mail to: Adrienne Gyongy

Address: American-Scandinavian Foundation, Publishing Division, 725 Park Avenue, New York, NY 10021

Category: Fiction

Description of Award: The award is offered for the best translations of fiction written in Danish, Finnish, Icelandic, Norwegian, or Swedish. Honorable mention (Inger Sjoberg Prize) is awarded $500, a bronze medallion, and an excerpt of his or her work published in the *Scandinavian Review*. Send SASE for complete guidelines.

The Center Press

Contest/Award:
Center Press Masters Literary Awards

*F/NF/P

Prize: $1,000

Entry Fee: $15

Deadline: varies

Open to: No restrictions

Mail to: Gabriella Stone

Address: Center Press, Masters Literary Awards, P.O. Box 16452, Encino, CA 91416-6452

Category: Fiction, Nonfiction, and Poetry

Description of Award: The Masters Literary Awards, sponsored by Center Press, are offered annually and quarterly for both published work (published within the preceding two years) and unpublished fiction, poetry, and nonfiction. Five quarterly honorable mentions are made, from which one annual Grand Prize is selected for the $1,000 prize. Fiction should be 15 pages or less; poetry should be no more than five pages or 150 lines; and nonfiction should be 10 pages or less. Quarterly deadlines are 3/15, 6/15, 8/15, and 12/15. "A selection of all winning entries will appear in our national literary publication." Send SASE for complete guidelines.

Centro Studi G. Donati

Contest/Award:
Giorgio La Pira Literary Prize for Fiction

*F

Prize: from $291 to $873 (U.S. dollars)

Entry Fee: 25 lire (approximately 25 cents)

Deadline: 5/31

Open to: No restrictions

Mail to: Secretary, G. La Pira International Literary Prize

Address: Centro Studi G. Donati, Piazza S. Francesco, 60, 51100 Pistoia, Italy

Category: Fiction

Description of Award: For a reading fee of 25 lire, authors may submit up to three short stories. Prizes vary. Send SASE for guidelines. Include International Response Coupons (IRC).

CHELSEA AWARD COMPETITION

Contest/Award: Chelsea Award for Fiction

*F

Prize: $500, plus publication in *Chelsea*

Entry Fee: $10

Deadline: 6/15

Open to: No restrictions

Mail to: Richard Foerster, Editor

Address: Chelsea Award Competition, P.O. Box 1040, York Beach, ME 03910

Category: Fiction

Description of Award: A cash prize is awarded for a work of short fiction (7,500 words or less). Work must not have been published previously. Entry fee of $10 gives entrant a subscription to *Chelsea*. Make checks payable to Chelsea Associates, Inc. All works entered will be considered for publication in the magazine. Send SASE for guidelines.

COLORADO STATE UNIVERSITY

Contest/Award: Colorado Prize

*P

Prize: $1,500, plus publication of award-winning manuscript by University of Colorado Press

Entry Fee: $20

Deadline: 1/12

Open to: No restrictions

Mail to: Director

Address: c/o Colorado Review, Dept. of English, Colorado State University, Ft. Collins, CO 80523

Category: Poetry

COLUMBIA PACIFIC UNIVERSITY

Contest/Award:
Columbia Pacific University Literary Fiction Contest

*SF

Prize: Ranges from $35 to $200, plus publication in the *CPU Review*

Entry Fee: $5

Deadline: varies

Open to: No restrictions

Mail to: Mariam Baker

Address: CPU Office of the President, 1415 Third Street, San Rafael, CA 94901

Category: Short Fiction

Description of Award: Columbia Pacific University Literary Fiction Contest offers awards in original, unpublished short stories. The submissions should be no more than 2,500 words in length. Send SASE for complete guidelines.

IDAHO COMMISSION ON THE ARTS

Contest/Award: Idaho Fellowships in Fiction

*F

Prize: $5,000

Entry Fee: $0

Deadline: varies

Open to: Idaho residents

Mail to: Artist's Services Director

Address: Idaho Commission on the Arts, 304 West State Street, Boise, ID 83720

Category: Fiction

Description of Award: Fellowship grants of $5,000 are awarded to individual artists in fiction. Grants are available to Idaho residents of one year prior to application, ages 18 and up. Send SASE for guidelines and application forms.

IDAHO COMMISSION ON THE ARTS
Contest/Award:
Idaho Sudden Opportunity Awards for Fiction

---

*F

Prize: $1,000

Entry Fee: $0

Deadline: varies

Open to: Idaho residents

Mail to: Artist's Services Director

Address: Idaho Commission on the Arts, 304 West State Street, Boise, ID 83720

Category: Fiction

Description of Award: Sudden Opportunity Awards offer up to $1,000 to support activities relevant to an artist's work and/or career, especially professional opportunities uniquely available during a limited time. Awards are available to Idaho residents of one year prior to application, ages 18 and up. Send SASE for guidelines and deadlines.

IDAHO COMMISSION ON THE ARTS
Contest/Award:
Idaho Worksites Awards for Fiction

---

*F

Prize: $5,000

Entry Fee: $0

Deadline: varies

Open to: Idaho residents

Mail to: Artist's Services Director

Address: Idaho Commission on the Arts, 304 West State Street, Boise, ID 83720

Category: Fiction

Description of Award: Worksites Awards offer up to $5,000 for artists wishing to work as apprentices with a master or artists seeking a residence at an artist colony. Awards are available to Idaho residents of one year prior to application, ages 18 and up. Send SASE for guidelines and deadlines.

INSTITUTE OF INTERNATIONAL EDUCATION

Contest/Award:
Binational Commission (Fulbright)
Scholarships in Denmark

*F/NF/P

Prize: varies

Entry Fee: $0

Deadline: varies

Open to: U.S. citizens who are university graduates

Mail to: Fulbright Scholarships in Denmark, Director

Address: Institute of International Education, 809 United Nations Plaza, New York, NY 10017

Category: Fiction, Nonfiction, and Poetry

Description of Award: Candidates for the Binational Commission (Fulbright) Scholarships for study and research in Denmark should be university graduates with a specific research program in mind. Creative writers are eligible. Grants are designed to cover the maintenance and travel expenses for graduate students as well as for postdoctoral or advanced research candidates. Deadlines vary: 10/31 for predoctoral students; 6/15 for postdoctoral candidates. Send SASE for complete guidelines and required application forms.

KENTUCKY ARTS COUNCIL

Contest/Award:
Kentucky Artist's Fellowships in Fiction (in even-numbered years)

*F

Prize: $5,000

Entry Fee: $0

Deadline: 6/1

Open to: Kentucky writers who are residents

Mail to: Irwin Pickett

Address: Kentucky Arts Council, 31 Fountain Place, Frankfort, KY 40601

Category: Fiction

Description of Award: In even-numbered years, Kentucky writers in fiction may win awards up to $5,000 to assist in the continued development of their creative work. The actual deadline for this fellowship is 9/1, but the Kentucky Arts Council asks that applicants send for guidelines three months before the deadline. Send SASE for application forms and guidelines.

LITERARY ARTS PROGRAMS, ARTS BRANCH

Contest/Award:
Arts Branch Literary Arts Awards & Creation Grants

*F/NF/P

Prize: $8,500 (Canadian), approximately $6,115 (U.S. dollars)

Entry Fee: $0

Deadline: varies

Open to: New Brunswick–resident writers (for two of the last four years)

Mail to: Bruce Dennis, Literary Arts Officer

Address: Literary Arts Programs, Arts Branch, Department of Municipalities, Culture & Housing, P.O. Box 6000, Frederickton, New Brunswick E3B 5H1

Category: Fiction, Nonfiction, and Poetry

Description of Award: The Arts Branch, Literary Awards Program offers several awards and grants to New Brunswick–resident writers. Arts Awards are available up to C$2,500, and Creation Grants up to C$6,000 (a total of C$8,500). The deadline for the Arts Awards is 3/15. The deadline for the Creation Grants are 1/15 and 7/15. The Literary Awards Programs also offers Development Travel, Promotional Travel, Excellence Awards, Artists-in-Residence, Arts Scholarships, and the New Brunswick Arts Abroad Programs. Send SASE for complete guidelines or call (506) 453-2555.

LUDWIG VOGELSTEIN FOUNDATION

Contest/Award:
Ludwig Vogelstein Foundation Grants

*D/F/J/NF/P

Prize: $2,500

Entry Fee: $0

Deadline: varies

Open to: Artists and writers

Mail to: Ludwig Vogelstein Foundation Grants Director

Address: Ludwig Vogelstein Foundation, P.O. Box 4924, Brooklyn, NY 11240-4924

Category: Drama, Fiction, Journalism, Nonfiction, and Poetry

Description of Award: The Ludwig Vogelstein Foundation provides individuals in the arts and humanities grants up to $2,500. The foundation offers fewer than 50 grants a year and the deadline varies. These grants are not for student aid. Send SASE for complete guidelines and application forms.

MACDOWELL COLONY FELLOWSHIPS

Contest/Award: MacDowell Colony Fellowships

*D/F/NF/P

Prize: varies

Entry Fee: $0

Deadline: varies

Open to: No restrictions

Mail to: MacDowell Colony Fellowship Director

Address: 100 High Street, Peterborough, NH 03458

Category: Drama, Fiction, Nonfiction, and Poetry

Description of Award: The MacDowell Colony Fellowships were created to help support residencies at the Colony in Peterborough, New Hampshire for literary writers in all genres and other artists to concentrate on their personal creative endeavors without interruption. Studios, room, and board are provided. Residencies are up to eight weeks. The deadlines vary: 1/15 for May to August residencies; 4/15 for September to December residencies; and 9/15 for January to April residencies. Send SASE for complete guidelines.

MARYLAND STATE ARTS COUNCIL

Contest/Award:
Maryland State Individual Artist
Award for Fiction

***F**

Prize: $6,000

Entry Fee: $0

Deadline: 6/1

Open to: Adult Maryland residents

Mail to: James Backas

Address: Maryland State Arts Council, 601 North Howard Street, 1st Floor, Baltimore, MD 21201

Category: Fiction

Description of Award: Individual Artist Awards for fiction writers of $1,000, $3,000, and $6,000 are available in odd-numbered years to Maryland residents over the age of 18 who are not students. The awards are chosen solely on excellence of previous work. Write for information in December. Send SASE for guidelines and applications.

The Mentor Newsletter

Contest/Award: Mentor Award

*F/J/NF

Prize: $100

Entry Fee: $4

Deadline: varies

Open to: No restrictions

Mail to: Maureen Waters, Award Director

Address: The Mentor Award, Mentor Newsletter, P.O. Box 4382, Overland Park, KS 66204-0382

Category: Fiction, Journalism, and Nonfiction

Description of Award: Established in 1989, the Mentor Award, sponsored by the *Mentor Newsletter*, offers a $100 cash prize to promote and encourage mentoring through feature articles, book reviews, movie reviews, interviews, and short stories about mentoring-related subjects. The applicant must be at least 16 years old. The deadlines vary: 12/31, 3/31, 6/30, and 9/30. Send SASE for complete guidelines.

Money for Women/ Barbara Deming Memorial Fund

Contest/Award: Fannie Lou Hamer Award

*F/NF/P

Prize: $1,000

Entry Fee: $0

Deadline: varies

Open to: Women writers

Mail to: Pam McAllister, Administrator

Address: Money for Women/Barbara Deming Memorial Fund, P.O. Box 40-1043, Brooklyn, NY 11240-1043

Category: Fiction, Nonfiction, and Poetry (women and gay/lesbian)

Description of Award: The Fannie Lou Hammer Award is sponsored by Money for Women/The Barbara Deming Memorial Fund and is given to a woman "whose work combats racism and celebrates women of color." The fund provides grants up to $1,000 to feminists active in the arts "whose work speaks for peace and social justice and in some way sheds light upon the condition of women or enhances self-realization." Grants are offered twice a year. Deadlines are 6/30 and 12/31. Send SASE for complete guidelines.

Money for Women/ Barbara Deming Memorial Fund

Contest/Award:
Gerty, Gerty, Gerty in the Arts, Arts, Arts Award

*F/NF/P

Prize: $1,000

Entry Fee: $0

Deadline: varies

Open to: Lesbian writers

Mail to: Pam McAllister, Administrator

Address: Money for Women/Barbara Deming Memorial Fund, P.O. Box 40-1043, Brooklyn, NY 11240-1043

Category: Fiction, Nonfiction, and Poetry (Women, Gay/Lesbian)

Description of Award: The Gerty, Gerty, Gerty in the Arts, Arts, Arts Award is sponsored by Money for Women/Barbara Deming Memorial Fund and named after Gertrude Stein. The award is given for an "outstanding work by a lesbian whose work gives voice to a lesbian sensibility or confronts homophobia." The fund provides grants up to $1,000 to feminists active in the arts "whose work speaks for peace and social justice and in some way sheds light upon the condition of women or enhances self-realization." Grants are offered twice a year. Deadlines are 6/30 and 12/31. Send SASE for complete guidelines.

The New Delta Review

Contest/Award: Eyster Prize—New Delta Review

*F/P

Prize: $50

Entry Fee: $0

Deadline: varies

Open to: Authors published in *The New Delta Review*

Mail to: Nicola Mason

Address: The New Delta Review, Louisiana State University, English Department, Baton Rouge, LA 70803-5001

Category: Fiction and Poetry

Description of Award: The Eyster Prize is offered to the best piece of poetry or fiction published in each issue of *The New Delta Review*. Thus, you first need to submit your work for publication in this journal and become accepted before becoming eligible for this particular prize. What *The New Delta* is looking for: "We at *The New Delta Review* are most interested in promoting new writers and exploring new directions in poetry and fiction. We have no thematic or stylistic biases; we simply want pieces with raw energy behind them." Deadlines are 3/15 for the spring/summer issue and 10/15 for the fall/winter issue. Send SASE for the return of your MS and/or acceptance letter.

Ohio University Press

Contest/Award:
Hollins Summers Poetry Prize Contest

*P

Prize: $500, plus publication of award-winning manuscript by University of Ohio Press

Entry Fee: $15

Deadline: 10/31

Open to: No restrictions

Mail to: Director

Address: Ohio University Press, Athens, OH 45701

Category: Poetry

Oregon Institute of Literary Arts

Contest/Award:
Oregon Institute of Literary Arts Fellowship for Fiction

---

*F

Prize: varies

Entry Fee: $0

Deadline: 5/30

Open to: Writers and publishers living in Oregon for at least one year

Mail to: Oregon Institute of Literary Arts, Director

Address: Oregon Institute of Literary Arts, P.O. Box 10608, Portland, OR 97210

Category: Fiction

Description of Award: The Oregon Institute of Literary Arts offers fellowships for fiction writers that are designed to assist the writer and is given to fiction writers who have lived in Oregon. The prize amount varies from $500 to $2,000 for individual fiction writers and $500 to $3,000 for publishers. Send SASE for complete guidelines and application forms.

Oregon Institute of Literary Arts

Contest/Award: H. L. Davis Award for Fiction

---

*F

Prize: $1,000

Entry Fee: $0

Deadline: 5/30

Open to: Published works by Oregon residents

Mail to: Davis Award for Fiction, Director

Address: Oregon Institute of Literary Arts, P.O. Box 10608, Portland, OR 97210

Category: Fiction

Description of Award: The H. L. Davis Award for Fiction is offered for published books from the Oregon Arts Commission. The fellowship is designed to assist writers in furthering their careers and is given every two years. Applicants must have lived in Oregon at least one year and their work may be nominated by publishers, authors, or friends. This award is given to outstanding authors. Write and send SASE for guidelines.

PARIS REVIEW

Contest/Award: Aga Kahn Prize

*F/TR

Prize: $1,000, plus publication in the *Paris Review*

Entry Fee: $0

Deadline: 6/1

Open to: No restrictions

Mail to: Fiction Editor

Address: *Paris Review*, 541 East 72nd Street, New York, NY 10021

Category: Fiction and Translation

Description of Award: The editors of the *Paris Review* look for the best unpublished story (1,000 to 10,000 words) submitted. Submission period is from 5/1 to 6/1. Translations are also accepted when accompanied by original text. One submission per envelope. Send SASE for return of MS or response. Send SASE for complete guidelines.

THE PUBLISHING TRIANGLE

Contest/Award: Bill Whitehead Award in Fiction

*F

Prize: $1,000, plus publication

Entry Fee: $0

Deadline: Ongoing—no deadline

Open to: Gay and lesbian authors

Mail to: Bill Whitehead Award, Director

Address: The Publishing Triangle, P.O. Box 114, New York, NY 10012

Category: Fiction

Description of Award: The Bill Whitehead Award for Fiction offers $1,000 to a fiction writer for lifetime achievement in gay and lesbian literature. This award has no application process. In-house nomination only.

Quality Paperback Book Club

Contest/Award: New Voices Awards in Fiction

---

*F

Prize: $5,000

Entry Fee: $0

Deadline: Ongoing—no deadline

Open to: See description of award

Mail to: New Voices Awards, Director

Address: Quality Paperback Book Club, 1271 Avenue of the Americas, New York, NY 10017

Category: Fiction

Description of Award: The New Voices Awards offer a $5,000 cash prize to the most distinctive and promising work of fiction. This award is offered by the Quality Paperback Book Club. A panel of editors chooses the winner from work already selected as Book Club offerings. This award has no application process. In-house nomination only.

The Southern Anthology

Contest/Award:
Southern Prize for Fiction and Poetry

---

*F/P

Prize: $600, and publication

Entry Fee: $10

Deadline: 5/30

Open to: No restrictions

Mail to: The Southern Prize Director, The Southern Anthology

Address: The Southern Prize, 2851 Johnson Street, #321, Lafayette, LA 70503

Category: Fiction and Poetry

Description of Award: The grand prize is $600 and publication awarded to the best short story or novel excerpt submitted (7,500 words or less), or poem. Each short story applicant should submit one manuscript; poets may submit up to three poems. All MSS must be original and unpublished. No MSS are returned. Send SASE for complete guidelines.

UNION DES ECRIVAINS QUEBECOIS

Contest/Award:
Le Prix Molson de l'Academie des Lettres du Quebec

---

*F

Prize: $5,000 (Canadian)

Entry Fee: $0

Deadline: 6/10

Open to: French-Canadian nationals

Mail to: Union des Ecrivains Quebecois

Address: 1030 rue Cherrier, Bureau 510, Montreal, Quebec H2L 1H7

Category: Fiction

Description of Award: Le Prix Molson de l'Academie des Lettres du Quebec is offered for a published novel that has been submitted to the Union des Ecrivains. The cash prize of $5,000 (Canadian) is awarded to the chosen novel.

UTAH ARTS COUNCIL

Contest/Award:
Utah Arts Council Publication Prize

---

*C/F/NF/YA

Prize: $5,000

Entry Fee: $0

Deadline: 6/15

Open to: Utah residents

Mail to: G. Barnes, Literary Coordinator

Address: Utah Arts Council, 617 East South Temple Street, Salt Lake City, UT 84102-1177

Category: Children, Fiction, Nonfiction, and Young Adult

Description of Award: The Publication Prize offers one prize of $5,000 to one of the book-length first-place winners of the Utah's Original Writing Competition in the following categories: autobiography/biography, fiction novel, short story collections, or the young adult book. Applicant must be a resident of Utah. The prize is designed specifically to expedite publication and to ensure a high-quality presentation and wide publicity for the chosen work. The prize money may be used only to assist a reputable publisher with the production and distribution of the work. Any eligible MS accepted for publication during the year before the prize is awarded cannot be considered for the prize. Send SASE for complete guidelines and application forms.

UTAH ARTS COUNCIL
Contest/Award:
Utah's Original Writing Competition for a Short Story

*F/SF

Prize: $300

Entry Fee: $0

Deadline: 6/15

Open to: Utah residents

Mail to: G. Barnes, Literary Coordinator

Address: Utah Arts Council, 617 East South Temple Street, Salt Lake City, UT 84102-1177

Category: Fiction and Short Fiction

Description of Award: The Utah's Original Writing Competition for a Short Story offers a first-place cash award of $300 and a second-place cash award of $200 for the best unpublished short story written by a Utah resident. "MSS need not be bound but should at least be contained in a box. No part of the work may have been published or accepted for publication at time of entry. Every year the winners of the Annual Utah Original Writing Competition, one of country's oldest such competition for writers, draws more attention to the state of Utah. Winners of the competition regularly go on to garner national prizes, national publications, and national acclaim. Working with the Utah State Legislature to provide prizes and judges worthy of our best writers, the Utah Arts Council applauds those who achieve literary excellence and who, through their efforts, bring prestige and honor to the state." Send SASE for guidelines and application forms.

UTAH ARTS COUNCIL

Contest/Award:
Utah's Original Writing Competition for a Young Adult Book

---

*F/YA

Prize: $1,000

Entry Fee: $0

Deadline: 6/15

Open to: Utah residents

Mail to: G. Barnes, Literary Coordinator

Address: Utah Arts Council, 617 East South Temple Street, Salt Lake City, UT 84102-1177

Category: Fiction and Young Adult

Description of Award: The Utah's Original Writing Competition for a Young Adult Book offers a first-place cash award of $1,000 and a second-place cash award of $750 for the best unpublished young adult book (readers 12 to 18) written by a Utah resident. "MSS need not be bound but should at least be contained in a box. No part of the novel may have been published or accepted for publication at time of entry. Every year the winners of the Utah Original Writing Competition, one of country's oldest such competitions for writers, draws more attention to the state of Utah. Winners of the competition regularly go on to garner national prizes, national publications, and national acclaim. Working with the Utah State Legislature to provide prizes and judges worthy of our best writers, the Utah Arts Council applauds those who achieve literary excellence and who, through their efforts, bring prestige and honor to the state." Send SASE for guidelines and application forms.

Utah Arts Council

Contest/Award:
Utah's Original Writing Competition in the Fiction Novel

*F

Prize: $1,000

Entry Fee: $0

Deadline: 6/15

Open to: Utah residents

Mail to: G. Barnes, Literary Coordinator

Address: Utah Arts Council, 617 East South Temple Street, Salt Lake City, UT 84102-1177

Category: Fiction

Description of Award: The Utah's Original Writing Competition in the Fiction Novel offers a first-place cash award of $1,000 and a second-place cash award of $750 for the best unpublished novel written by a Utah resident. "MSS need not be bound but should at least be contained in a box. No part of the work may have been published or accepted for publication at time of entry. Every year the winners of the Utah Original Writing Competition, one of country's oldest such competitions for writers, draws more attention to the state of Utah. Winners of the competition regularly go on to garner national prizes, national publications, and national acclaim. Working with the Utah State Legislature to provide prizes and judges worthy of our best writers, the Utah Arts Council applauds those who achieve literary excellence and who, through their efforts, bring prestige and honor to the state." Send SASE for guidelines and application forms.

Utah Arts Council

Contest/Award:
Utah's Original Writing Competition;
Short Story Collections

*SF

Prize: $1,000

Entry Fee: $0

Deadline: 6/15

Open to: Utah residents

Mail to: G. Barnes, Literary Coordinator

Address: Utah Arts Council, 617 East South Temple Street, Salt Lake City, UT 84102-1177

Category: Short Fiction

Description of Award: The Utah's Original Writing Competition in a book-length collection of short stories offers a first-place cash award of $1,000 and a second-place cash award of $750 for the best unpublished work written by a Utah resident. "MSS need not be bound but should at least be contained in a box. No part of the work may have been published or accepted for publication at time of entry. Every year the winners of the Utah Original Writing Competition, one of country's oldest such competitions for writers, draws more attention to the state of Utah. Winners of the competition regularly go on to garner national prizes, national publications, and national acclaim. Working with the Utah State Legislature to provide prizes and judges worthy of our best writers, the Utah Arts Council applauds those who achieve literary excellence and who, through their efforts, bring prestige and honor to the state." Send SASE for guidelines and application forms.

UTAH STATE UNIVERSITY

Contest/Award: May Swenson Poetry Award

*P

Prize: $750, plus publication

Entry Fee: $20 (which includes a copy of the winning book)

Deadline: 9/30

Open to: No restrictions

Address: Utah State University, Logan, UT 84322-7800

Category: Poetry

Description of Award: Submitted collections must be original poetry in English; 50 to 100 pages; no restrictions on form or content. Name/address on cover sheet only; SASE for announcement of winner; manuscripts will not be returned. Most recent judge: John Hollander.

WEST VIRGINIA COMMISSION ON THE ARTS

Contest/Award:
West Virginia Literature Fellowship in Fiction

*F

Prize: $3,500

Entry Fee: $0

Deadline: 6/1

Open to: West Virginia residents

Mail to: Tod Ralstin, Fellowship Awards

Address: West Virginia Commission on the Arts, Cultural Center, 1900 Kanawha Boulevard East, Charleston, WV 25305-0300

Category: Fiction

Description of Award: The West Virginia Literature awards cycle every three years. Playwrights, poets, writers of fiction, nonfiction, and children's literature are offered the fellowships. Literature fellowships were offered in 1996. Suggestions by the Commission on how the writer should use the award money are given, but it's really up to the winner on how he or she chooses to utilize the funds. Send SASE for guidelines.

Awards Favorable to Unpublished First-Book Manuscripts

by Prize

Award Name	Prize
Giorgio La Pira Literary Prize for Fiction	varies
Binational Commission (Fulbright) Scholarships in Denmark	varies
MacDowell Colony Fellowships	varies
Oregon Institute of Literary Arts Fellowship for Fiction	varies
Eyster Prize—New Delta Review	$50
Mentor Award	$100
Columbia Pacific University Literary Fiction Contest	$200
Utah's Original Writing Competition for a Short Story	$300
Chelsea Award for Fiction	$500
Hollins Summers Poetry Prize Contest	$500
Southern Prize for Fiction and Poetry	$600
May Swenson Poetry Award	$750, plus publication
Aga Kahn Prize	$1,000
Utah's Original Writing Competition for a Young Adult Book	$1,000
Utah's Original Writing Competition in the Fiction Novel	$1,000
Utah's Original Writing Competition; Short Story Collections	$1,000

Award Name	Prize
Center Press Masters Literary Awards	$1,000
Fannie Lou Hamer Award	$1,000
Gerty, Gerty, Gerty in the Arts, Arts, Arts Award	$1,000
Idaho Sudden Opportunity Awards for Fiction	$1,000
Bill Whitehead Award in Fiction	$1,000
H. L. Davis Award for Fiction	$1,000
Colorado Prize	$1,500
ASF Translation Prize for Fiction	$2,000
Ludwig Vogelstein Foundation Grants	$2,500
West Virginia Literature Fellowship in Fiction	$3,500
Kentucky Artist's Fellowships in Fiction	$5,000
Le Prix Molson de l'Academie des Lettres du Quebec	$5,000 (Canadian)
Utah Arts Coucil Publication Prize	$5,000
Idaho Fellowships in Fiction	$5,000
Idaho Worksites Awards for Fiction	$5,000
New Voices Awards in Fiction	$5,000
Maryland State Individual Artist Award for Fiction	$6,000
Arts Branch Literary Arts Awards & Creation Grants	$8,500 (Canadian)

Awards Favorable to Unpublished First-Book Manuscripts

by Genre

Young Adult

4

FIRST BOOK AMERICAN CLASSICS

━━━━━━━━━━━━━━━━━━━━━━━━━━━━━━━━━━━━

❧◉❧

Edgar Allan Poe

Tamerlane and Other Poems. By a Bostonian
Boston: Calvin F. S. Thomas, Printer, 1827

*T*he publication of *Tamerlane* was an obscure event of an obscure period of Poe's life. When the young man's career at the University of Virginia closed in December 1826, with debts and dissipations, Mr. Allan failed to understand how his own attitudes might have contributed to his foster son's excesses, nor did he help him find suitable work. After three months in Richmond, Poe ran away from home. He went to Boston, drawn perhaps by the accident that his parents had been performing there when he was born. Little is known of his first two months in Boston. Possibly he tried to follow in his parents' footsteps and obtain work in the theater. On May 26, 1827, he enlisted in the U. S. Army as Private Edgar A. Perry. By August he had arranged for the publication of *Tamerlane* with Calvin Thomas, a nineteen-year-old printer. Not many copies were printed, perhaps as few as forty, perhaps as many as two hundred. Certainly, the book dropped quickly out of sight.

A forty-page pamphlet, *Tamerlane* was originally covered in paper wrappers. It was discovered in Maine by Andrew McCance, another Boston bookseller. Mr. McCance sold it to the collector W. T. H. Howe for $3,700 in 1938. Howe's library was purchased by Albert A. Berg in 1941. In 1990, at the sale of the library of collector H. Bradley Martin, a copy (with wrappers) of the pamphlet sold for $150,000.

Nathaniel Hawthorne

Fanshawe, a Tale
Boston: Marsh & Capen, 1828

*W*hen Hawthorne entered Bowdoin in 1821, it was a small college of 114 students on the edge of the Maine wilderness. There, in his senior year, 1824–1825, he may have begun *Fanshawe*. There, too, he observed incidents and personalities that he used in the novel to illustrate those ideas of good and evil that he was to develop so forcefully in later work. Hawthorne paid one hundred dollars for the publication of the novel, and the greatest return on his investment was the interest *Fanshawe* aroused in Samuel Griswold Goodrich, the Boston publisher. For the next fourteen years, Goodrich provided an outlet for Hawthorne's stories in his annual, *The Token*, and in the *New England Magazine*, to which he introduced Hawthorne. He also employed Hawthorne to compile *Peter Barley's Universal History*, a compendium for children, for him in 1837. Though Goodrich was tardy in paying for such hack work as the latter, his interest kept Hawthorne writing.

Walt Whitman

Franklin Evans; or The Inebriate. A Tale of the Times
In the *New World*, Vol. 2, No. 10, Extra Series No. 34,
November, 1842

*T*he first forty years of Walt Whitman's life are intimately associated with Brooklyn. Of English and Dutch blood, Whitman (1819–1892) was born on a farm on Long Island and brought to the city as a child. There he attended school until he was eleven or thirteen. His first real job was as a printer's devil, and for the next three decades he was primarily associated with newspapers and magazines as printer or editor, in Brooklyn, New York, or New Orleans.

While working as a compositor for the *New World* in 1842, he produced *Franklin Evans; or The Inebriate* for an extra issue of the paper.

Influenced by the melodramatic and sentimental side of Dickens, this "original temperance novel" gave no promise of what would follow. It was *Leaves of Grass*, first published in 1855 in Brooklyn, that brought Whitman fame, first in England and later in America, and made him a subject of violent controversy during the latter part of his life. He died, an enigmatic idol, in his shrine in Camden, New Jersey.

Henry David Thoreau

A Week on the Concord and Merrimack Rivers
Boston and Cambridge: James Munroe; New York:
George P. Putnam; Philadelphia: Lindsay and Blackiston;
London: John Chapman, 1849

Thoreau and his brother John, his devoted companion, spent the first half of September 1839 in a dory equipped with sails on the Concord and Merrimack Rivers. Ten years later, Henry published an account of this expedition, into which he fitted sections dealing with his reading and his philosophy taken from the journals that he had kept since he was at Harvard. He could not find a publisher for *A Week on the Concord and Merrimack Rivers*, so he paid for publication himself.

Despite the outlets suggested by the imprint, the book was a failure. Of the 1,000 copies printed, Munroe sold 219; another 75 were given away; and 706 were returned to Thoreau in 1853. "I have now a library of nearly nine hundred volumes," he wrote in his journal, "over seven hundred of which I wrote myself."

Louisa May Alcott

Flower Fables
Boston: George W. Briggs, 1855

Louisa May Alcott (1832–1888) was the second of the four daughters of Amos Bronson Alcott, called the most transcendental of the Transcendentalists, a lovable, gifted, and entirely impractical man. Something of the poverty and struggles of the Alcotts, but softened and idealized, can be found in her *Little Women*. The privations of her early life—which even included a stint of democratic service—were brightened by the interest taken in her by such friends of her father's as Theodore Parker, Thoreau, and Emerson. The little fairy stories which make up *Flower Fables* were written when its author was sixteen to entertain Emerson's daughter Ellen, to whom Alcott later dedicated the book.

Flower Fables waited six years for publication. It was brought out in time for Christmas 1854, in an edition of 1,600 copies that was paid for by a friend, the appropriated named Miss Wealthy Stevens. Though the author received only $32—not the "money and fame" that she confided to her journal she hoped for—she was delighted with what she called her "first born."

Mark Twain

The Celebrated Jumping Frog of Calaveras County, and Other Sketches
New York: C. H. Webb, 1867

The actual event upon which this story and the beginning of Clemens's fame are based occurred in 1849 and had been written up briefly in a California newspaper as early as 1853. Clemens remembered that he had told the anecdote, which he had jotted down in his notebook, to Atremus Ward, the professional humorist, and that Ward had urged him to write it out and send it to G. W. Carleton, the New York publisher. Carleton turned the manuscript over to a magazine called the *Saturday Press*, which published "Jim Smiley and His Jumping Frog" in its final issue, November 18, 1865. Charles Henry Webb, whom Clemens had known first in San Francisco, brought out the story with other newspaper sketches by the humorist. Clemens was already using the pseudonym Mark Twain, which he had derived from the Mississippi River term for two fathoms. He got a 10 percent royalty on his first book.

The Jumping Frog himself is celebrated among book collectors for the numerous positions he assumes on the front cover.

Edith Wharton

Verses
Newport, RI: C. E. Hammett, Jr., 1878
The Pierpont Morgan Library. Gift of Mr. Louis S. Auchincloss, 1986

 Novelist Edith Wharton's (1862–1937) first publication is a thin book of delicate poetry, looking for all the world like the product of a debutante daughter of Longfellow. It was printed in haste and in few copies (only nine are now known to exist), as a gift for the sixteen-year-old Edith Newbold Jones of 14 West 23rd Street, New York City. The poems included in it had been written by young Miss Jones in her fourteenth and fifteenth years, and were full of the weather and flowers.

Miss Jones, like her first book, was a product of Old New York wealth, gentility, and repression. Born in the enclave of New York's fashionable and aristocratic society, she was baptized at Grace Church, spent summers in elegant Newport, Rhode Island, and came out into society at a Fifth Avenue mansion near 42nd Street. Although her first book was published when she was sixteen, Edith Wharton would have to wait twenty years until she could "come out" into literary society with *The Greater Inclination*, a book of short stories published in 1899 by Scribner's. In the ensuing years, she published some of the finest novels of the century, including *House of Mirth* (1905), *Ethan Frome* (1911), *The Custom of the Country* (1913), and *The Age of Innocence* (1920). Each of these novels was first published in a printing of over 40,000 copies, testifying to the remarkable popularity of her work.

A woman of accomplishment in other areas as well, Edith Wharton introduced Henry James to the charms of the automobile and Paris on a three-week trip, or "motor flight," in 1907.

PART 3

LESS IS OFTEN MORE: AWARDS FOR CHAPBOOKS

Introduction

Ruth Greenstein

What is a chapbook?

A chapbook is a short, booklet-style publication of a work that can
be encapsulated in a short form. Chapbooks are well known in the
worlds of poetry and small press publishing. Many chapbooks are
only twenty-four to twenty-eight pages, and are printed in runs of
no more than five hundred copies. While chapbooks are unlikely
to make their way into the neighborhood superstore in the same
way that full-sized books might, for many authors—Ezra Pound,
A. R. Ammons, and Denis Johnson, to name a few—they offer an
excellent opportunity for getting your work into print.

You may want to set aside a period of time, two years or so, for
submitting your work to first-book contests and publishers, after
which, if you have had no luck, you could pursue the chapbook
option.

Bear in mind, however, that in some cases, publishing a chapbook
will disqualify you from later submitting your work for certain first-
book awards. For example, chapbooks that are over twenty-four
pages long or are printed in editions of over five hundred copies are
considered to be first books by certain contests. So if you have
published a chapbook and want to submit your work for first-book
awards, it is critical that you review the guidelines for each award
you are considering to find out if any such restrictions apply.

When considering the chapbook option, it's up to you to weigh
the pros and cons. While you do not want to jeopardize your
chances of entering first-book competitions, you may also feel that
publishing a chapbook at this point in your career is your best
opportunity for publication.

5
Awards for Chapbooks

Alice James Books and The Jane Kenyon Memorial Fund

Contest/Award:
Jane Kenyon Chapbook Award Series

*P

Address: 98 Main Street, Farmington, ME 04938

Prize: $250 prize and publication

Entry Fee: $5

Deadline: 6/15

General Information: Open to New England residents only

Anabiosis Press

Contest/Award:
Annual Poetry Chapbook Competition

*P

Address: P.O. Box 7787, North Port, FL 34287-0787

Prize: $100 prize and 25 copies

Entry Fee: $7

Deadline: 5/31

Anamnesis Press

Contest/Award: Chapbook Competition

*P

Address: P.O. Box 581153, Salt Lake City, UT 84158-1153

Prize: $500 first prize, publication, and 10 copies; $200 second prize, publication, and 10 copies

Entry Fee: $10

Deadline: 6/15

General Information: Submission period: 1/1 to 6/15. Poems of intellectual and emotional depth that give full rein to the imagination, whether free verse or formalist.

Bacchae Press

Contest/Award: Annual Chapbook Contest

*P

Address: c/o Brown Financial Group, 10 Sixth Street, Astoria, OR 97103

Prize: 25 copies of professionally printed chapbook

Entry Fee: $8

Deadline: 4/15

General Information: MSS must not exceed 16 to 24 pp.

Bear Star Press

Contest/Award: Chapbook Contest

*P

Address: 185 Hollow Oak Drive, Cohasset, CA 95973

Prize: $50 prize and 50 copies

Entry Fee: $5

Deadline: 12/15

General Information: MSS must not exceed 16 to 24 pp.

Bright Hill Press

Contest/Award: Poetry Chapbook Competition

*P

Address: P.O. Box 193, Treadwell, NY 13846

Prize: $100 prize and publication

Entry Fee: $8

Deadline: 5/31

Center for Book Arts

Contest/Award:
Annual Poetry Chapbook Competition

*P

Address: 626 Broadway, New York, NY 10012

Prize: $500 prize, $500 reading honorarium, and a limited edition letterpress chapbook publication

Entry Fee: $10

Deadline: 12/31

General Information: MSS must not exceed the 500-line limit.

Dead Metaphor Press

Contest/Award: Chapbook Contest

*P

Address: Dead Metaphor Press, P.O. Box 2076, Boulder, CO 80306-2076

Prize: 10% press run

Entry Fee: $8

Deadline: 10/31

DEVIL'S MILLHOPPER PRESS

Contest/Award: Annual Chapbook Contest

*P

Address: University of South Carolina at Aiken, English Department, 171 University Parkway, Box 26, Aiken, South Carolina 29801-6309

Prize: $50 prize, publication, and 50 copies

Entry Fee: $10 (includes one-year subscription to magazine)

Deadline: 2/28

General Information: Submission period: 1/1 to 2/28

EXCURSIS MAGAZINE

Contest/Award: Poetry Chapbook Competition

*P

Address: P.O. Box 1056, Knickerbocker Station, New York, NY 10002

Prize: 50 copies and wide-distribution prize (chapbook is inserted in every copy of literary journal and distributed to bookstores throughout country in December)

Entry Fee: $20

Deadline: 2/28

General Information: MSS must not exceed 15 pp.

FLOATING BRIDGE PRESS

Contest/Award: Annual Chapbook Contest

*P

Address: P.O. Box 18814, Seattle, WA 98118

Prize: $100 prize, 50 copies, and reading in Seattle area

Entry Fee: $10

Deadline: 1/15

General Information: Submission period: 9/1 to 1/15. Contest open to Washington residents only.

FLUME PRESS

Contest/Award: Annual Chapbook Contest

*P

Address: 773 Sierra View, Chico, CA 95926

Prize: $50 prize and 50 books

Entry Fee: $7

Deadline: 5/30

FRANK CAT PRESS

Contest/Award: Poetry Chapbook Contest

*P

Address: 1008 Ouray Avenue, Grand Junction, CO 81501

Prize: $25 cash prize, publication, and copies

Entry Fee: $7

Deadline: 3/1

HELLAS/THE ALDINE PRESS, LTD

Contest/Award: Lyidas Award

*P

Address: Lyidas Award, Lyrica Chapbook Series, 304 S. Tyson Avenue, Glenside, PA 19038

Prize: Publication only

Deadline: Please inquire.

General Information: Metrical Poetry Chapbooks

Illinois State University

Contest/Award:
Frank O'Hara Chapbook Competition

---

*P

Address: c/o Jim Elledge, Thorngate Rd., Campus Box 4241, Unit for Contemporary Literature, Illinois State University, Normal, IL 61790-4241

Prize: $200, publication, and 25 copies of MS

Entry Fee: $10

Deadline: 2/1

General Information: Contest open to gay, lesbian, and bisexual authors. MS cannot exceed 20 pp of poetry—free verse, traditional form, postmodern, prose poems, and cross-genre texts.

Laverne E. Frith, Publishing

Contest/Award: Chapbook Competition

---

*P

Address: P.O. Box 161236, Sacramento, CA 95816-1236

Prize: $50 cash prize and 50 books, 14 to 22 pp

Entry Fee: $8

Deadline: 9/30

General Information: MS must be between 14 and 22 pages.

The Ledge

Contest/Award:
Ledge Poetry Chapbook Competition

---

*P

Address: The Ledge, c/o Timothy Monaghan, 78-08 83 Street, Glendale, NY 11385 (718) 456-5255

Prize: $500, publication, 50 free copies

Entry Fee: $10

Deadline: 10/31

MIDDLE TENNESSEE STATE UNIVERSITY

Contest/Award:
Annual Tennesse Chapbook Contest

*P/PL

Address: Gay Brewer, Editor, English Dept., Middle Tennessee State University, Murfreesboro, TN 37132

Prize: 50 copies of printed MS

Entry Fee: $10

Deadline: 1/15

General Information: Poems and/or short plays considered

OWL CREEK PRESS

Contest/Award: Green Lake Chapbook Prize

*P

Address: 1620 N. 45th Street, Seattle, WA 98103

Prize: $500 advance against royalties and publication

Entry Fee: $10

Deadline: 8/15

General Information: MSS should not exceed 40 pp.

PAINTED BRIDE QUARTERLY

Contest/Award: Chapbook Contest

*P

Address: Painted Bride Art Center, 230 Vine Street, Philadelphia, PA 19106

Prize: Publication only

Entry Fee: $10

Deadline: 7/31

PANHANDLER

Contest/Award: Poetry Chapbook Contest

*P

Address: Laurie O' Brien, Editor, English Dept., University of West Florida, Pensacola, FL 32514-5751

Prize: Inquire about prize

Entry Fee: $7

Deadline: 1/15

General Information: Submission period: 10/15 to 1/15

PAVEMENT SAW PRESS

Contest/Award: Poetry Chapbook Contest

*P

Address: Tara Pauliny, Editor, 7 James Street, Scotia, NY 12302

Prize: $500

Entry Fee: $7

Deadline: 12/15

General Information: MSS must not exceed the 32 pp limit.

PERMAFROST

Contest/Award:
Midnight Sun Poetry Chapbook Contest

*P

Address: English Dept., P.O. Box 755720, University of Alaska Fairbanks, Fairbanks, AK 99775

Prize: Inquire about prize.

Entry Fee: $10 (includes subscription to magazine)

Deadline: 3/15

Poetry Society of South Carolina

Contest/Award:
Annual Kinloch Rivers Chapbook Competition

*P

Address: Rivers Chapbook, 2204 Forest Lakes Blvd, Charleston, SC 29141

Prize: $100 and 50 copies

Entry Fee: $6

Deadline: 10/31

Poet's Journey

Contest/Award: Chapbook Contest

*P

Address: P.O. Box 9873, The Woodlands, TX 77387-6873

Prize: $100 and five copies of MS

Entry Fee: $10

Deadline: 7/13

General Information: Entries must be between 25 to 38 pp.

Pudding Magazine

Contest/Award:
National Looking Glass Poetry
Chapbook Competition

*P

Address: 60 N. Main Street, Johnstown, OH 43031

Prize: Publication of book, 20 copies, and wholesale rights

Entry Fee: $10

Deadline: 6/30

General Information: Contest open to collections of poems that represent the magazine's editorial slant: popular culture, social justice, psychology, etc.

Pyx Press

Contest/Award:
Annual Magic Realism Magazine's
Short Fiction Award

*SF

Address: P.O. Box 922648, Sylmar, CA 91392-2648

Prize: $50 prize and chapbook contract

Entry Fee: $0

Deadline: 7/15

Riverstone Press

Contest/Award:
Annual Poetry Chapbook Competition

*P

Address: 1184-A MacPherson Drive, West Chester, PA 19380

Prize: $100 prize and 50 copies of MS

Entry Fee: $8

Deadline: 6/30

Saddle Mountain Press

Contest/Award: Annual Chapbook Contest

*P

Address: Saddle Mountain Press, 1434 6 Street, Astoria, OR 97103

Prize: 25 copies of professionally printed chapbook

Entry Fee: $9

Deadline: 10/1

General Information: MSS must not exceed 12 to 16 pp.

Sarasota Poetry Theatre

Contest/Award: Annual Chapbook Competition

*P

Address: P.O. Box 48955, Sarasota, FL 34230-6955

Prize: $100 prize and 50 copies of MS

Entry Fee: $10

Deadline: 8/31

Sheila-Na-Gig

Contest/Award: Annual Chapbook Contest

*P

Address: 23106 Kent Avenue, Torrance, CA 90505

Prize: $100 prize and 10 copies of MS

Entry Fee: $10

Deadline: 6/30

Shenango River Books

Contest/Award: Prose Chapbook Contest

*NF/SF

Address: P.O. Box 631, Sharon, PA 16146

Prize: $100 prize and 100 copies of MS. All entrants receive copy of winning chapbook.

Entry Fee: $10

Deadline: 2/28

General Information: Contest open to 40 to 60 pp of prose, short stories, and creative nonfiction.

Slapering Hol Press

Contest/Award: Chapbook Competition

*P

Address: Stephanie Strickland, The Hudson Valley Writer's Guild, P.O. Box 366, Tarrytown, NY 10591

Prize: $200 cash prize and 10 copies of MS

Entry Fee: $10

Deadline: 4/15

General Information: "Slapering Hol" means Sleepy Hollow.

Slipstream

Contest/Award: Annual Chapbook Competition

*P

Address: Dept. C-10, P.O. Box 2071, Niagra Falls, NY 14301

Prize: First Place: $500 cash prize, 50 copies of MS, and distribution to subscribers; Second Place: $100; Third Place: $100

Entry Fee: $10

Deadline: 4/30

General Information: Submission period is March through April.

St. Louis Poetry Center

Contest/Award: Hanks Chapbook Award

*P

Address: Jason Sommer, Fontbonne College, 6800 Wydown Blvd, St. Louis, MO 63105

Prize: $500 cash prize and 100 chapbooks as well as a St. Louis poetry reading

Entry Fee: $0

Deadline: 4/1

General Information: MS cannot exceed 24 to 30 pp.

STILL WATERS PRESS

Contest/Award: Winter Poetry Competition

*P

Address: Shirley A. Warren, Contest Director, 459 S. Willow Ave., Galloway Township, NJ 08201

Prize: Inquire about prize

Entry Fee: $10

Deadline: 9/30

WEST TOWN PRESS

Contest/Award: Chapbook Competition

*P

Address: 717 N. Paulina #2, Chicago, IL 60622

Prize: $50 and 50 copies of MS

Entry Fee: $10

Deadline: 6/15

WHITE EAGLE COFFEE STORE PRESS

Contest/Award:
Spring Poetry Chapbook Contest

*P

Address: P.O. Box 383, Fox River Grove, IL 60021

Prize: $150 cash prize and 25 copies of MS

Entry Fee: $10

Deadline: 3/30

White Eagle Coffee Store Press

Contest/Award: Long Fiction Contest

*F

Address: P.O. Box 383, Fox River Grove, IL 60021

Prize: $200 cash prize and 25 copies of MS

Entry Fee: $10

Deadline: 12/15

Wick Poetry Chapbook Series

Contest/Award: Student Competition

*P

Address: The Wick Poetry Program, Dept. of English, Kent State University, P.O. Box 5190, Kent, OH 44242-0001

Prize: Publication (750 copies printed)

Entry Fee: $0

Deadline: 10/31

General Information: Open to poets currently enrolled in an Ohio college or university who have not previously published a full-length book of poems 48 pp or more, with a 500 or more print run.

Awards for Chapbooks

by Prize

Award Name	Prize
Panhandler Poetry Chapbook Contest	Inquire about prize
Permafrost Midnight Sun Poetry Chapbook Contest	Inquire about prize
Still Waters Press Winter Poetry Competition	Inquire about prize
Hellas/The Aldine Press, Ltd Lyidas Award	Publication
Painted Bride Quarterly Chapbook Contest	Publication
Wick Poetry Chapbook Series Student Competition	Publication
Bacchae Press Annual Chapbook Contest	25 copies of professionally printed chapbook
Saddle Mountain Press Annual Chapbook Contest	25 copies of professionally printed chapbook
Middle Tennessee State University Annual Tennessee Chapbook Contest	50 copies of MS
Excursis Magazine Poetry Chapbook Competition	50 copies and wide distribution prize (chapbook is inserted in every copy of literary journal and distributed to bookstores throughout country in December)
Dead Metaphor Press Chapbook Contest	10% of press run

Award Name	Prize
Pudding Magazine National Looking Glass Poetry Chapbook Competition	Publication of book, 20 copies, and wholesale rights
Frank Cat Press Poetry Chapbook Contest	$25 cash prize, publication, and copies
Bear Star Press Chapbook Contest	$50 prize and 50 copies
Devil's Millhopper Press Annual Chapbook Contest	$50 prize, publication, and 50 copies
Flume Press Annual Chapbook Contest	$50 prize and 50 books
Laverne E. Frith, Publishing Chapbook Competition	$50 cash prize and 50 books
West Town Press Chapbook Competition	$50 and 50 copies of MS
Pyx Press Annual Magic Realism Magazine's Short Fiction Award	$50 prize and chapbook contract
Bright Hill Press Poetry Chapbook Competition	$100 prize and publication
Poet's Journey Chapbook Contest	$100 and 5 copies of MS printed
Sheila-Na-Gig Annual Chapbook Contest	$100 prize and 10 copies of MS
Anabiosis Press Annual Poetry Chapbook Competition	$100 prize and 25 copies of MS
Poetry Society of South Carolina Annual Kinloch Rivers Chapbook Competition	$100 and 50 copies of MS
Sarasota Poetry Theatre Annual Chapbook Competition	$100 prize and 50 copies of MS
Riverstone Press Annual Poetry Chapbook Competition	$100 prize and 50 copies of MS

Award Name	Prize
Floating Bridge Press Annual Chapbook Contest	$100 prize, 50 copies, and reading in Seattle area
Shenango River Books Prose Chapbook Contest	$100 prize and 100 copies of MS. All entrants receive copy of winning chapbook.
White Eagle Coffee Store Press Spring Poetry Chapbook Contest	$150 cash prize and 25 copies of MS
Slapering Hol Press Chapbook Competition	$200 cash prize and 10 copies of MS
Frank O'Hara Chapbook Competition	$200, publication, and 25 copies of MS
White Eagle Coffee Store Press Long Fiction Contest	$200 cash prize and 25 copies of MS
Alice James Books and The Jane Kenyon Memorial Fund Jane Kenyon Chapbook Award Series	$250 prize and publication
Pavement Saw Press Poetry Chapbook Contest	$500
Anamnesis Press Chapbook Competition	$500, publication, and 10 copies (first prize); $200, publication, and 10 copies (second prize)
The Ledge Poetry Chapbook Competition	$500, publication, and 50 free copies
Slipstream Annual Chapbook Competition	$500 cash prize, 50 copies of MS and distribution to subscribers (first place); $100 (second place); $100 (third place)
St. Louis Poetry Center Hanks Chapbook Award	$500 cash prize and 100 chapbooks as well as a St. Louis poetry reading

Award Name	Prize
Center for Book Arts Annual Poetry Chapbook Competition	$500 prize, $500 reading honorarium, and a limited edition letterpress chapbook publication
Owl Creek Press Green Lake Chapbook Prize	$500 advance against royalties and publication

PART 4

MORE LIGHT: PUBLISHERS

INTRODUCTION

Ruth Greenstein

There are thousands of publishers in the United States, from huge corporate media giants to university presses to small family-style operations. Some are only looking to publish blockbuster books with the widest possible appeal, while others specialize in books aimed at very narrow markets. One of the primary jobs of a literary agent is to match the right publisher and editor with the right book project. If you are working without an agent, you will need to become familiar with these various kinds of publishers to determine where your work is most likely to be well received. Here are some questions to ask yourself in your search to locate publishers who will consider your work.

Have I familiarized myself with the field?

The library, the bookstore, and your own bookshelves are the best places to begin. Look at books by writers you admire and whose work seems similar to your own. Who published their first books? Then read the listings here as well as those found in other reference guides (see the Resources section of this book, page 281) to find out more about the publishers that interest you. Request catalogs from publishers of interest to look more closely at what they do.

What kind of publisher is the best for me?

That depends on the type of book you have written and the kind of readers you hope to attract. Is it a specialized book that will only appeal to gardeners, mutual fund investors, gay men, parents of children with learning disabilities? If so, a specialized publisher may be your best bet. If you've written a novel with broad appeal, a large or small general publisher is probably the right place to begin.

What is an unsolicited manuscript?

Many publishers use the term *unsolicited* to refer to manuscripts that are sent to them unagented. Such manuscripts are generally given the lowest priority and are read by junior staff if and when time allows. More generally, an unsolicited manuscript can be any project a publisher receives—agented or not—without having expressed interest in it beforehand.

What is a simultaneous or multiple submission?

Most agents and writers send out manuscripts to several publishers simultaneously. As with awards, this is the best way to maximize your time and your chances of finding a publisher. However, when a writer or agent has a special relationship with a publisher and has reason to believe the publisher is very likely to be interested in the work a submission may be made exclusively to one publishing house.

How should I approach the publisher?

Find out exactly how the publisher wants to be approached and, if possible, an appropriate contact name. Staff changes at publishing houses happen fast and frequently, so be sure your contact information is current. Most publishers are extremely busy and cannot spend time answering questions by phone. If you need to request information by phone, be succinct. The first step in approaching a publisher is usually to write a brief query letter. There is an art to writing a compelling letter about yourself and your work, without which you may never receive the kind of serious consideration you are looking for. So take the time to write your best letter, and if possible, have a professional look at it before you send it out.

How should I follow up on my submission?

Most publishers need at least two or three months to evaluate and respond to a submission. Give them the time they need. If you haven't received an answer after several months, follow up with a brief letter, fax, or phone call. Don't be a pest. The surest way to put off a publisher is to phone every week to check on the status of your manuscript.

What should I do when my manuscript has been returned?

Most publishers do not have time to respond to projects they are not interested in with more than a form letter. If you are fortunate enough to receive a rejection letter that addresses the particulars of your project, send a thank-you note to the person who wrote to you and give serious consideration to what he or she has said. Has he or she suggested that you approach a different kind of publisher, or that you need to revise your manuscript? If so, you may want to redirect your efforts accordingly. Again, bear in mind that rejections are an inevitable part of the submissions process, and are often invaluable in helping you reach your goal.

CHRONOLOGY OF A
FIRST BOOK, 1981–1993

Anna Monardo

I spent ten years writing my first novel, *The Courtyard of Dreams*.
When the book was published in August 1993 by Doubleday, many
good things happened. It was reviewed well. There were three
foreign sales. Most of the first printing was sold. Then, after the book
had been on the market for fifteen months, I got word from my
agent that it was being remaindered. What did this mean? It meant
that my baby would show up on the discount tables of bookstores
for a while, and then disappear. The novel would no longer be in
print; it could not be ordered. Remaindering meant it was time for
me to come to terms with what had not happened—no extra
printings, no paperback sale. Secretly, I had always hoped the novel
would give me a chance to meet Johnny Carson. Remaindering
meant it was time to move on. Before I could do that, though, I had
to figure out exactly what I'd been doing during the decade it took
me to give birth to this book. I sketched the following chronology:

> **July 1981.** I spend a month in New Jersey. I am living in a
> damp cottage near a gritty beach. At night, from the back
> porch, I see the A & P parking lot stretched out flat and soul-
> less. From the front porch, I see the thinnest slice of ocean.
> But there's the smell of salt water every morning and the feel
> of sand when I walk barefoot in the house. That's all it
> takes—I begin thinking wildly, obsessively, of summers I
> spent on a beach with my relatives in southern Italy. Giulia,
> the young American girl who will be my main character,
> appears on the pages of my sandy legal pad. Giulia is talking
> to her young cousin Lina, and Lina is talking to me, telling
> the story of a time when Giulia was in Italy. Every sunset
> they talk about Italy. I take notes. New Jersey disappears.

> **September 1981.** Back home in New York City, I have a few
> notebooks full of Giulia and the Italian beach. I'm caught in
> an extended "hallucination." When I walk down Broadway,

the fruit stands remind me of markets in Calabria. And the fat old buildings on West End Avenue remind me of Rome. Parallel to my life—and more compelling—is Giulia's life. I am in a workshop at this time, and I try to manipulate my notes into a short story. People in workshop see right through it. "This is a novel, isn't it?" Oh God, now what? I know nothing about writing a novel.

October 1981. My grandmother, whom I am very close to, is dying. One of the last times I see her she says to me, slowly, "You know what I want? I want to write the story of my life." The story I've begun is not her life, and it's not my life, but, whatever it is, I have no way out now. My grandmother has just told me that a story's urgency never fades, with time it gets sharper.

Spring 1982. I have a chance to hear Gail Hochman, an agent, give a talk about how to find an agent. She's young, energetic, warm; she suggests you look for an agent who is, above all, enthusiastic, someone with a particular interest in your kind of book. "Me, for example," she says, "I love Italy."

I am thrilled. And terrified. I've been paralyzed by shyness about approaching editors, agents, and established writers when I go to hear them speak. This time, though, I will have to do it. At the end of Gail's talk, I introduce myself and tell her I'm writing a novel set in Italy.

"Great," she says. "Whenever you're ready, let me see it."

May 1982. My workshop ends. I decide I've had enough workshopping for a while. All I want is to sit and get this novel done. What I need is space. I move to a big apartment in Brooklyn.

March 1984. I move out of Brooklyn.

Summer 1984. It has been almost three years. I have arranged my world to have time for "the n-word." I want a published novel, of course; but more than that, the material is important to me: a young woman's separation from her family, and an Italian immigrant family's separation from their culture. I work night shifts as a *Time* proofreader. Social life? Less is not more. For all this commitment, I have very little to show—only messy piles of notes, lists, scenes, dialogues.

So far I see the book in three parts: Part One is Giulia's childhood in Ohio. In Part Two she's seventeen, goes to Italy, some big stuff (still not sure what) happens. Part Three is ten years later and we see the consequences of the big stuff that happened when she was seventeen. I'm still on Part One. Lina, the young cousin, is still the Nick Carraway–like, involved-uninvolved narrator.

I've shown Gail a few batches of pages. She's interested in reading more. I'm encouraged. But also sad and afraid. Here's this wonderful agent, yet I can't come up with a finished novel. What if she loses interest, what if I blow it?

March 1985. I spend a month in northern California, at the Djerassi Foundation, a relatively new artists' colony. No one I know has ever heard of it, but I'm desperate to make headway on this novel. I go there, half afraid it will be a Moonie ranch. It is not. It is heaven. I have a room with a view of the hills (there is even a view from my shower). I don't have to do anything but write all day and show up for dinner at 6:00. I get to the end of Part One. I plunge into Part Two, which takes place in Italy. It's clear to me that I need a stretch of time in Rome. One day, I stand in the hills and vow to the cows grazing in the fields of the Djerassi Foundation that I will go to Italy.

September–December 1985. I live in Rome. I have my uncle's Olivetti manual. But now that I'm in Italy there seems little point to sitting inside writing about Italy. Rome is a city for walking. I am in love with this city. I walk and take notes. One hot afternoon I step off a busy street, into a monastery, and find myself in a courtyard. It is small, quiet, ancient, and perfect. It comes to me this way: To be a woman in an Italian family is to live in a courtyard, an enclosed world—it is safety, confinement, beauty, deprivation, fulfillment, wretched, wonderful, inescapable. I can't stop writing about courtyards. By the time I leave Rome I haven't finished the novel, but I do have my central metaphor. This will organize everything.

April 1987. I've been working on the novel for six years. I've been to Italy and back and still don't have a finished manuscript. I've been trying to give Part One a dramatic focus, but Lina, the narrator, is like a wind-up doll, going over and over the same scenes. When I sit to work I can barely look at the pages. I can't write unless I have a box of Dutch Mill doughnuts (the ones in the blue box) next to me. Usually I have powdered sugar or cinnamon. On very bad days, chocolate-dipped.

Something is not happening. Writing is not fun any more. The story is lead. The day before my thirty-first birthday, I sit at the desk and think, Is there any way on God's good earth for Lina to tell this story and make it halfway interesting? Wait a minute. Why is Lina telling this story? It's Giulia's story. Giulia has to speak. This thought is light and heavy at the same time; it comes to me with the unmistakable weight and flight of truth. This is it. I write on a sheet of paper: Giulia must tell her own story.

Why did I waste so much time with Lina? Years later I will realize that the Lina drafts were crucial. The novel deals with autobiographical issues, and writing the story through Lina's eyes has helped me to make Giulia a character who is different from me. But I don't understand this yet. Feeling completely defeated, I put the whole manuscript in a drawer and lock it. I don't have to write.

I get a job teaching English as a Second Language, I read *War and Peace,* I prepare to be audited by the IRS in June. I am not writing; I am living in the world. I'm not happy, but I'm not tortured.

November 1987. On a train going to a friend's for Thanksgiving, I hear an older Giulia begin talking about when she was young, living in Rome. I take notes. At home, I write scenes. This feels good, but I refuse to consider I may be working on the you-know-what again. It is not long, though, before Giulia is telling the story of her childhood. And I am writing Part One. Again.

But I am smarter this time. I find a group of writers. We meet monthly; this gives me deadlines. We read each other's work and talk. Writing begins to feel more like a way of life, a good thing, and less like prison.

December 1987. I get a Christmas card—simple, elegant, no return address, signed Gail. I get tears in my eyes. She still believes in me. Strengthened by this, I set a deadline. I will get her a manuscript in six months.

I make and break many deadlines, but through spring, summer, and fall, Gail's Christmas card is on my desk. It gives me courage. It gives me hope.

December 1988. I'm talking with a friend in the copy room at *Time*. She is saying she wishes she were organized enough to send Christmas cards. She mentions a woman from a different department of the magazine who last year sent cards to everyone, even people in our department. I say, "She didn't send me a Christmas card."

"Of course she did. At first I wasn't sure who it was from. There was no return address, no note. She just wrote her name."

The woman's name is Gail.

June 1989. I get together Part One, Part Two, and a summary of Part Three, all written in Giulia's voice. I send this to Gail Hochman, who writes back, "I think you cover way too much ground." She suggests I cut Part One, make Part Two the body of the novel, skip Part Three. I do it.

November 1989. The novel is condensed; Gail has a completed manuscript. She sends it to three or four editors, who all reject it. A few say, "This seems kind of Young Adult." I am upset, not because I have anything against YA novels, but because I didn't mean to write one. I've failed to do what I set out to do.

January 1990. At the Virginia Center for the Creative Arts (another heaven-sent haven, more cows; do all artists' colonies have cows?), I begin the novel again. This time Giulia is twenty-eight and very depressed, so depressed there is no mistaking this for a YA novel. She's in mid-crisis, which forces her to look back over her childhood, Italy, the whole shebang. When Gail sees this new rough draft, she says, "You have a lot of work to do here."

"I'll be done in a few months."

"It may take longer," she warns. I try to ignore that.

February 1991. Fourteen months after I began the new draft, I am finished. The manuscript is 660 pages. It takes an entire weekend to print out. At one point, my super knocks on my door and asks if everything is all right.

June 10, 1991. I come home from teaching. There is a message from Gail. Sit down, she says. I have news. Deb Futter, a great young editor, has accepted the manuscript. We all agree the novel is too long. But the next morning I wake up happy, thinking, I don't have to write that novel anymore! This happiness is completely false.

July 10, 1991. Lunch with Deb. We agree on which parts of the manuscript need to be cut. A cinch, I say.

August 14, 1991. I sign the contract at Gail's office. That week, half my advance arrives in the mail—a check for real money, for words I wrote myself. Problem is, I wrote way too many words. And what if I can't pull this unruly thing together? That night I have a horrific dream. I wake, sit bolt upright in the dark. I am still not done rewriting. I am Sisyphus. I have been put on this earth to do nothing but write and rewrite this one novel. Mountains will crumble. Oceans will dry up. Children will grow old. But I will never be released from this task.

August–December 1991. I cut and revise. I cry daily.

December 1991. The manuscript has been to Weight Watchers, lost 200+ pages. I deliver it to Deb. This is the first Christmas in nine years that I am not writing the novel. My family rejoices.

January 1992. Deb and I meet for the first of many working sessions in her office at Doubleday. In the lobby of the building is a newsstand that sells penny candy. I fill up my purse. Upstairs, I dump small Mounds bars and Hershey's kisses onto Deb's round glass-top work table. There's lots of work ahead. We go over this and that. Then Deb says, "I have a really wild idea. Tell me what you think. It occurred to me, Chapter 1 begins with this woman who's twenty-eight, depressed. I've read this kind of story before. Chapter 2, on the other hand, starts with the childhood scenes, and they seem fresh. So I'm thinking, Why not start with Chapter 2?"

I am thinking, I just spent three months writing Chapter 1. I feel sick to my stomach; it's not the chocolate. "But if we cut Chapter 1, we'll have to cut all the chapters of Giulia at twenty-eight."

Deb's eyes widen. "Good idea!" she says. "Excellent!"

She made me say it. What's worse, I know she is right—the new material is not strong enough yet. I also see two years of work pass before my eyes.

April 1992. I deliver the newest condensed version to Deb. She accepts it. We have several glasses of wine. They taste good.

August 1992. Deb calls. Time to write catalog copy. It's a sales tool, and it's important. Years of work and thousands of sheets of paper reduced to three paragraphs that describe the novel and make it a must-buy. This is exciting—the book is more real now—but it's in other people's hands, becoming a thing outside of me. I feel nervous. Or sad. Or something.

November 1992. Several afternoons Deb and I meet over her glass-top table to line edit. More candy.

January 1993. A few people read the edited, cut-down story. Two readers tell me, "I couldn't put it down. I spent the whole weekend reading it." This equation—ten years to write equals one weekend to read—is, I tell myself, better than its converse.

February 1993. Loose galleys are in. I'm to read them and make corrections. Last chance for changes. No more "work-in-progress." When I release the galleys, the novel will be done. I have two problems: (1) I am afraid it is not perfect yet; and (2) I do not want to read this novel again. I can't look at it any more. A sunny cold Sunday afternoon; my friends go ice skating and I cannot go. Poor me.

By nighttime, though, I've reached the middle—Giulia is in Italy, in love. I have the music on—Italian pop I listened to all the years I was writing; schmaltzy music, but it always had the power to transport me. It's just me and the music and this story and we're lost in the night, like so many nights and weekends and years we spent together. I realize that during all those years I was doing exactly what I wanted to do.

July 1993. Deb calls me. "Come down to my office as soon as you can." When I get there, she puts a copy of *The Courtyard of Dreams* in my hands. I cry.

October 1994. I get the letter from Doubleday informing me that the book is being remaindered. I have a month to send in my order to buy copies at discount. "Buy as many as you can afford," Gail tells me, "as many as you have room for."

I've needed a table in the hallway—you know, a place to put mail, to plop down my purse when I come in the door. I order two hundred copies of my novel. They arrive in little boxes of ten. Twenty boxes, as neat and manageable as Legos. Piled up against the wall in the hallway, covered with a bright cloth, the boxes of my novel make a perfect narrow table. Having them there makes my day-to-day life better, a little easier.

6

PUBLISHERS FAVORABLE TO UNPUBLISHED FIRST-BOOK MANUSCRIPTS

ALFRED A. KNOPF

*F/NF

Address: 201 East 50th Street, New York, NY 10022

Phone: (212) 751-2600

Category: Fiction and Nonfiction

General Information: Publishes hardcover and paperback originals. Royalties and advances vary. Publishes book one year after acceptance of MS. Accepts simultaneous submissions if informed. Reports in three months on MSS. Knopf publishes 200 titles each year and won three Pulitzer Prizes in 1995. Recent titles include *I Was Amelia Earhart*, Jane Mendelsohn.

ALYSON PUBLICATIONS

*F/NF

Contact: Julie K. Trevelyan

Address: P.O. Box 4371, Los Angeles, CA 90078-4371

Phone: (213) 871-1225   **Fax:** (213) 467-6805

Category: Fiction and Nonfiction

Publisher's Notes on First Books: Published five first books, out of 35 total books, last year. Scheduled to publish two first books in 1997, as well as six in 1998 and six in 1999. Recent first-book titles include *Lucy on the West Coast*, Mary Beth Caschetta, 1996; *Fast Ride With the Top Down*, Harper Gray, 1996; and *Dancing with Two Dogs and Mozart*, Michael Freiberg, 1996. "Our first books sell moderately. Some of the benefits to publishing first books are giving new authors publishing recognition, exposing readers to their work and possibly discovering a very good writer we can publish again in the future. The difficulties we encounter are dealing with new authors who are not familiar with the publishing procedures in addition to the unknown selling strength of the author."

Advice to new authors: "Send us an original, dynamite proposal—typed and double-spaced. Don't forget to include a SASE. Please do not call us."

ARCADE PUBLISHING
*F/NF/P

Contact: Richard Seaver

Address: 141 Fifth Ave., New York, NY 10010

Phone: (212) 353-8148

Category: Fiction, Nonfiction, and Poetry

Publisher's Notes on First Books: Arcade Publishing published 10 to 12 first books, out of 40 total books, last year. Accepts agented submissions only. Recent first-book titles include *The Secret Diary of Anne Bolan*, Robin Maxwell, 1997; and *Elvis in the Twilight Memory*, June Juanico, 1996.

General Information: Publishes hardcover originals, trade paperback originals, and reprints. Pays royalty on retail price. Offers $1,000 to $100,000 advance. Publishes book 18 months after acceptance. Reports in three months on queries. "We do not publish poetry as a rule; since our inception we have published only a few volumes of poetry." Recent fiction titles include *Trying to Save Piggy Sneed*, John Irving.

AVON BOOKS
*F/NF

Contact: Alice Webster-Williams

Address: 1350 Avenue of the Americas, New York, NY 10019

Phone: (212) 261-6800   **Fax:** (212) 261-6895

Category: Fiction and Nonfiction

General Information: Publishes trade and mass market paperback originals and reprints. Royalty and advance negotiable. Publishes MS two years after acceptance. Accepts simultaneous submissions. Reports in three months on MSS. Avon Books publishes 400 titles each year. Send SASE for guidelines. Recent titles include *Memoir from Antproof Case*, Mark Helprin.

BALLANTINE BOOKS, DIVISION OF RANDOM HOUSE, INC.

*F/NF

Address: 201 East 50th Street, New York, NY 10022

Phone: (212) 572-4910   **Fax:** (212) 572-2676

Category: Nonfiction and Fiction

General Information: Receives 3,000 submissions per year. Pays royalty on retail price. Accepts simultaneous submissions. Reports in two months on MSS. Publishes 120 titles each year. Book catalog free. Send SASE for MS guidelines. Recent fiction titles include *Weighed in the Balance*, Anne Perry.

BEACON PRESS

*F/NF/P

Contact: Amy Caldwell

Address: 25 Beacon Street, Boston, MA 02108-2800

Phone: (617) 742-2800

Category: Fiction, Nonfiction, and Poetry

Publisher's Notes on First Books: Beacon Press publishes nonfiction, political, anthropology, and gender studies. Also publishes historical, religious, and spirituality subjects if book is an academic treatment of these subjects. Does not accept unsolicited MSS. Beacon publishes approximately 60 books per year. Recent first-book titles include *Here and No Where Else: Late Seasons of a Farm and Its Family*, Jane Brox; *The Very Rich Hours*, Emily Hiestand; and *The Power of Their Ideas*, Deborah Myer. New authors are generally referred to the press from other Beacon writers or agents.

General Information: Receives 6,000 MSS and query submissions each year. Letter of query (with SASE) and sample chapter should precede MS. Responds to MS and query submissions in six to eight weeks. Returns MSS with SASE. MS should be on 8^1/$_2$ × 11-inch paper, single-sided, typed, double-spaced, letter-quality.

BLACK HERON PRESS

*F

Contact: Jerry Gold

Address: P.O. Box 95676, Seattle, WA 98145

Phone: (206) 363-5210

Category: Fiction

General Information: Publishes hardcover and trade paperback originals. Pays 8 to 10% royalty on retail price. Reports in three months on queries, six months on proposals and MSS. Black Heron Press publishes four titles per year. Press is looking for high-quality, innovative fiction. Query with outline, three sample chapters and SASE should precede MS. Recent titles include *Terminal Weird*, Jack Remick (surrealistic short stories).

BLUE MOON BOOKS, INC.

*F/NF

Contact: Barney Rosset

Address: North Star Line, 61 Fourth Ave., New York, NY 10003

Phone: (212) 505-6880   **Fax:** (212) 673-1039

Category: Nonfiction and Fiction

Publisher's Notes on First Books: Blue Moon Books published four first books, out of 15 total books, last year. They are scheduled to publish at least three first books this year.

General Information: Publishes trade paperback and mass market paperback originals. Receives 700 queries and 500 MSS each year. Pays $7^1/_2$ to 10% royalty on retail price. Offers $500 or more as advance. Publishes book one year after acceptance of MS. Accepts simultaneous submissions. Reports in two months on MSS. Book catalog free on request. Send #10 SASE for MS guidelines. Recent titles include *Patrong Sisters: An American Woman's View of the Bangkok Sex World*, Cleo Odzer.

BLUE STAR PRODUCTIONS,
A DIVISION OF BOOKWORLD, INC.
*F/NF

Contact: Barbara DeBolt

Address: 9666 E. Riggs Rd., #194, Sun Lakes, AZ 85248

Phone: (602) 895-7995   **Fax:** (602) 895-6991

Category: Fiction and Nonfiction

General Information: Publishes trade and mass market paperback originals. Receives 500 queries and 400–500 MSS per year. Pays 10% royalty on either wholesale or retail price. Reports in one month on queries, two months on proposals, six months on MSS. Publishes 10 to 12 titles per year. Book catalog free. Send #10 SASE for MS guidelines. "Know our no-advance policy beforehand and know our guidelines. No response ever comes without a SASE. No phone queries. We have absolutely restricted our needs to those MSS whose focus is metaphysical, ufology, time travel and North American." Recent fiction includes *Dance on the Water*, Laura Leffers.

BRANDEN PUBLISHING CO., INC.
*F/NF

Contact: Adolf Caso

Address: 17 Station Street, Box 843, Brookline Village, MA 02147

Phone: (617) 734-2045   **Fax:** (617) 734-2046

Category: Fiction and Nonfiction

General Information: Publishes hardcover and trade paperback originals, reprints, and software. Receives 1,000 submissions each year. Pays 5 to 10% royalty on net. Offers $1,000 maximum advance. Publishes book 10 months after acceptance. Reports in one month. Publishes 15 titles per year. Average first print run for a first book is 3,000 copies. Branden publishes MSS that are determined to have a significant impact on modern society. "Our audience is a well-read general public of professionals, college students, and some high school students.

"If I were a writer trying to market a book today, I would thoroughly investigate the number of potential readers. We like books by or about women." Recent fiction titles include *The Straw Obelisk*, Adolf Caso. Recent nonfiction titles include *From Trial Court*, Diane Wakowski.

BROOKLINE BOOKS

*F/NF

Contact: Sadi Ranson

Address: P.O. Box 1047, Cambridge, MA 02238

Phone: (617) 868-0360   **Fax:** (617) 868-1772

Category: Fiction and Nonfiction

Publisher's Notes on First Books: Brookline Books published five to six first books, out of 20 total titles, last year. "We will not read any MSS that do not include return postage. Also, we are not open to publishing science fiction, horror, or pornography—though we are open to anything else." Recent first-book titles include *Silk*, Grace Dane Mazur, 1996; and *Urban Oracle*, Mayar Santos Febref, 1997. "Publishing first books gives us the opportunity to provide a fresh perspective and new language. It is difficult dealing with the unknown element in a person and in a new MS. You have to push first books harder than work written by someone previously published and sold."

Advice to new authors: "Call for a catalog and push your own work. New authors *have* to push their own work."

CALYX BOOKS

*F/NF/P

Contact: Margarita Donnelly

Address: P.O. Box B, Coravallis, OR 97339

Category: Women's Fiction, Nonfiction, and Poetry

Publisher's Notes on First Books: Calyx Books only publishes first books. Last year they published three first books. Recent first book titles include *Into the Forest*, Gene Heglend. The average first print run for first books is 1,500 copies for poetry, and usually 5,000 copies for fiction. "Publishing first books and discovering emerging writers is our mission."

General Information: Receives 400 MSS and query submissions each year. Letter of query should precede MS submission. Responds to queries in one month. Responds to MS submissions in one year. Accepts simultaneous submissions. Offers advances; pays royalties.

Advice to new authors: "Find out our deadlines, accept that we are slow, and be patient."

CENTER PRESS

*F/NF/P

Contact: Gabriella Stone

Address: P.O. Box 16452, Encino, CA 91416-6452

Category: Fiction, Nonfiction, and Poetry

Publisher's Notes on First Books: The Center Press is no longer accepting unsolicited MSS. Through 1/1/98, they will only read MSS received from agents and those received through direct solicitation, in addition to their sponsored literary contest.

General Information: Publishes hardcover and trade paperback originals. Receives 600 queries and 300 MSS per year. Pays 10 to 30% royalty on wholesale price or makes outright purchase of $500 to $5,000. Publishes book 10 months after acceptance. Accepts simultaneous submissions. Reports in three months on MSS. Publish four to six titles per year. Offers $200 to $2,000 advance. Publishes book 10 months after acceptance. Accepts simultaneous submissions. Reports in three months on MSS. Send a #10 SASE for MS guidelines. "Our readers are typically well educated, tending to urban, creative, middle income (mostly), eclectic, and well intended."

CHAMPION BOOKS

*F/NF/P/SF

Contact: Rebecca Rush

Address: P.O. Box 636, Lemont, IL 60439

Phone: (800) 230-1135

Category: Fiction, Nonfiction, Poetry, and Short Fiction

Publisher's Notes on First Books: All titles are first books. Champion publishes approximately five titles each year. Recent first-book titles include *Warning This is Not a Book*, Pete Babones; *Simple Shrine*, Jim Vetter; and *My Gradual Demise & Honeysuckle*, Douglas A. Martin.

General Information: Imprint is the New Shoes Series. Publishes trade paperback originals. Pays 8 to 10% royalty on retail price. Publishes book five months after acceptance of MS. Accepts simultaneous submissions. Reports in four months on MSS. Send a SASE for book catalog and MS guidelines. Submissions may include ethnic, feminist, gay/lesbian, literary, poetry, and short story collections. Any finished or unfinished fiction work will be considered. "We are seeking work that applies to or deals with contemporary American society with an emphasis on counterculture and alternative lifestyles." Average first print run is 500 copies.

Advice to new authors: "Do a lot of self-promotion. It's best if authors have heavily promoted their own writing in the form of publishing chapbooks, self-publication, and doing a lot of readings."

CHRONICLE BOOKS

*F/NF/SF

Address: 85 Second Street, San Francisco, CA 94105

Phone: (415) 777-7240

Category: Fiction, Nonfiction, and Short Fiction

General Information: 20% of books from first-time authors. Publishes book 18 months after acceptance. Accepts simultaneous submissions and reports in three months on queries for nonfiction. For fiction and short fiction send complete MSS—do not query. Nonfiction submissions may include coffee-table books, cookbooks, regional California, architecture, art & design, gardening, gifts, health, nature, nostalgia, photography, recreation, and travel. Fiction submissions may include novels, novellas, and short story collections. Submissions may also include children's books. Recent titles: *LaParilla: The Mexican Grill*, Reed Hearon (cookbook); and *The Lies of the Saints*, Erin McGraw (short story collection).

CLEIS PRESS

*F/NF

Contact: Frederique Delacoste

Address: P.O. Box 14684, San Francisco, CA 94114

Fax: (415) 575-4705

Category: Proactive Fiction and Nonfiction books by women "(and a few men)"

Publisher's Notes on First Books: Cleis Press published six first books, out of 15 total titles, last year. Recent book titles include *Memory Mumble*, Achy Obejas. "Niche books (lesbian, gay, Hispanic, African American), sell much better than general fiction. Authors must believe in what we do. We are known for doing risky books."

General Information: Receives 300 MSS and query submissions each year. Responds to queries in four to six weeks. Responds to MS submissions in four weeks. MS should be on $8^1/_2 \times 11$-inch paper, typed, double-spaced. Pays royalties.

Advice to new authors: "Have enough experience as a writer. Develop your craft. Be clear and have a function for your work. Also, have a sense of who we are."

CONFLUENCE PRESS INC.

*F/NF/P/SF

Address: Lewis-Clark State College, 500 Eighth Ave., Lewiston, ID 83501-1698

Phone: (208) 799-2336   **Fax:** (208) 799-2324

Category: Fiction, Nonfiction, Poetry, and Short Fiction

General Information: Receives 500 queries and 150 MSS each year. Pays 10 to 15% royalty on net sales price. Offers $100 to $2,000 advance. Publishes book 18 months after acceptance. Accepts simultaneous submissions. Reports in one month on proposals, two months on queries, and three months on MSS. Publishes an average of four to five titles each year. Book catalog and MS guidelines free upon request. Nonfiction submissions may include reference books and bibliographies. Fiction submissions may include ethnic, literary, mainstream/contemporary, and short story collections. Send six sample poems for poetry submissions. Recent titles include *Even in Quiet Places*, William Stafford; and *Cheerleaders Grom Gomorrah*, John Rember.

COPPER CANYON PRESS

*P

Address: P.O. Box 271, Port Townsend, WA 98368

Phone: (360) 385-4925

Category: Poetry

Publisher's Notes on First Books: Copper Canyon published two first books, out of 10 to 12 total books, last year. Recent first-book titles include *Country of Air*, Richard Jones, 1996; *Leaving a Shadow*, Heather Allen, 1996; *Infanta*, Erin Belieu, 1995; *Terra Firma*, Thomas Centolella, 1992; and *The Island*, Michael White, 1992. The average first print run for first books is approximately 3,000 copies.

General Information: Receives 1,500 queries and 500 MSS each year (95% of books from unagented authors). Publishes book 18 months after acceptance. Reports in one month on MSS. MS guidelines and book catalog free on request. Query must accompany by five to seven sample poems. Recent poetry titles include *Collected Poems*, Hayden Carruth.

Advice to new authors: "In some ways it is easier to sell first books because our culture is predicated on the next new thing. We are always looking for new authors. The best thing an author can do is be familiar with Copper Canyon's work. Know our books. What we publish is governed individual taste. It also helps to have an understanding of the classics, as well as to be published in journals and magazines—already have your name out there."

COUNTERPOINT

*F/NF/SF

Contact: Jack Shoemaker, Editor-in-Chief

Address: 1627 I St., NW, Suite 850, Washington DC 20006

Fax: (202) 887-0562

Category: Fiction, Nonfiction, and Short Fiction

General Information: Publishes hardcover and trade paperback originals and reprints. Receives 10 queries per week and 250 MSS each year. Pays $7^1/_2$ to 15% royalties on retail price. Publishes book 18 months after acceptance. Accepts simultaneous submissions. Reports in two months on MSS. Publishes an average of 20 to 25 titles each year. Nonfiction submissions may include biography, and coffee table and gift books. Agented submissions only for nonfiction. Recent nonfiction titles include *The Invention of Television*, David E. Fisher and Marshall John Fisher. Fiction submissions may include historical, humor, literary, mainstream/contemporary, religious, and short story collections. Agented submissions only. Recent fiction titles include *Women in Their Beds*, Gina Berriault (short stories).

DANCING JESTER PRESS
*F/NF/P/SF

Contact: Glenda Daniel, Publisher/ Editor

Address: 3411 Garth Rd., Suite 208, Baytown, TX 77521

Phone: (281) 427-9560

Category: Fiction, Nonfiction, Poetry, and Short Fiction

General Information: Publishes hardcover and trade paperback originals and reprints. 100% of books from unagented authors. Pays 4 to 12% royalties on retail price or makes outright purchase. Does not pay advances. Publishes book 18 months after acceptance. Accepts simultaneous submissions. Reports in three months on proposals, six months on MSS. Publishes an average of 16 titles each year. Also sponsors the "One Night in Paris Should Be Enough" prize. Nonfiction submissions may include autobiography, children's/juvenile, coffee table, cookbooks, how-to, humor, illustrated, multimedia, reference, self-help, and textbooks. Fiction submissions may include adventure, erotica, ethnic, experimental, feminist, gay/lesbian, historical, humor, juvenile, mainstream/contemporary, mystery, picture books, plays, short story collections, suspense, thrillers, westerns, and young adult. Send complete MS when submitting poetry. Recent fiction titles include *Twin Blue Slipper of Swan Lake*, Lillian Cagle (children's mystery series). Recent poetry titles include *Sex Lives of Animals*, Jason Love (annotated limmericks).

DANTE UNIVERSITY OF AMERICA PRESS, INC.

*F/NF/P

Contact: Adolf Caso, President

Address: P.O. Box 843, Brookline Village, MA 02147-0843

Fax: (617) 734-2046

Category: Fiction, Nonfiction, and Poetry

General Information: Publishes hardcover and trade paperback originals and reprints. Receives 50 submissions each year. 50% of books published from unagented authors. Average print run for a first book is 3,000 copies. Pays royalties. Advances are negotiable. Publishes book 10 months after acceptance of MS. Query with a SASE. Reports in two months on MSS. Published an average of five titles each year. Nonfiction submissions may include biography, reference, reprints, and translations from Italian and Latin. Fiction submissions may include translations from Italian and Latin. Send query with a SASE. "There is a chance that we would use Renaissance poetry translations." Recent fiction titles include *Rogue Angel*, Carol Damioli. Recent poetry titles include: *Italian Poetry 1950–1990*.

DAVID R. GODINE, PUBLISHER

*F/NF

Contact: Lissa Warren, Publicity Director (ext. 11)

Address: P.O. Box 9103, Lincoln, MA 01773

Phone: (617) 259-0700   **Fax:** (617) 259-9198

Category: Fiction and Nonfiction

Publisher's Notes on First Books: David R. Godine published two first books, out of 25 total books, in 1996. They do not accept unsolicited MSS. MSS must be submitted through an agent. Recent first-book titles include *Little Jordan*, Marly Youmans, 1995; *The Empty Creel*, Geraldine Pope, 1995; and *Eliza's Carousel Lion*, Lynn Strough, 1994.

Of the three books above (two children's books and one novel) they sold 2,000 to 3,000 copies of each (3,000 for *Little Jordan*). Returns were high for both children's books.

Advice to new authors: "We find new authors via suggestions from authors we have previously published. Have your agent contact us, or have a published author who knows your work write us on your behalf."

THE ECCO PRESS

*F/NF/P

Contact: Daniel Halpern

Address: 100 W. Broad Street, Hopewell, NJ 08525

Phone: (609) 466-4748   **Fax:** (609) 466-4706

Category: Fiction, Nonfiction, and Poetry

Publisher's Notes on First Books: Ecco Press published five to 10 first books, out of a total of 60 books, last year. Recent first book titles include: *One Day as a Tiger*, Anne Haverty, 1997; *The Killer*, Patricia Melo, 1997. The average first print run for first books is 5,000 to 7,500 copies.

General Information: Publishes hardcover and trade paperback originals, reprints, and trade paperback reprints. Receives 1,200 queries each year. Publishes book one year after acceptance of MS. Reports in two months on queries.

Advice to new authors: "Writers should be published in journals and/or participate in a writing program. Somehow they need to show us that they are committed writers, that this is a career."

EIGHTH MOUNTAIN PRESS

*F/NF/P

Contact: Ruth Gundle

Address: 624 SE 29th Ave., Portland, OR 97214

Phone: (503) 233-3936

Category: Fiction, Nonfiction, and Poetry by women

Publisher's Notes on First Books: Eighth Mountain published one first book (a second edition), out of two total books published, last year. Recent first book titles include *A Journey of One's Own: Uncommon Advice for the Independent Woman Traveler*, Thalia Zepatos. The average final print run for all books ranges from 15,000 to 35,000 copies (nonfiction selling more).

General Information: Eighth Mountain has an annual contest for book-length poetry MSS. Contest prize is $1,000 cash and publication in the prize series. Receives 500 to 1,000 MS and query submissions each year. Letter of query should precede MS submission. Responds to queries in two to eight weeks. Responds to MS submissions in one to four months. Does not accept simultaneous submissions. Has an average overall marketing budget of $5,000 to $6,000. Has an average per-book marketing budget of $2,000 to $3,000. Pays royalties.

Advice to new authors: "Submit a query that is as clear as possible and a MS that fits what Eighth Mountain is doing. Eighth Mountain Press publishes high-quality feminist literature written by women, in beautifully designed and produced editions."

FABER & FABER INC

*F/NF

Address: 53 Shore Rd., Winchester, MA 01890

Phone: (617) 721-1427

Category: Fiction and Nonfiction

Publisher's Notes on First Books: Faber and Faber, Inc. published two first books, out of 30 total books, last year. Recent first-book titles include *A Child Out of Alcatraz*, Tara Ison, 1997; and *Offseason*, Niomi Haloch, 1997.

General Information: Publishes hardcover and trade paperback originals. Receives 1,200 submissions each year. 25% of all books by unagented authors. Pays royalty on retail price. Advance varies. Publishes book one year after acceptance of MS. Accepts simultaneous submissions. Reports in three months on queries. Send a #10 SASE for guidelines. Nonfiction submissions may include anthologies, biographies, contemporary culture, screenplays and film, history and natural history, cooking, and popular science. Faber & Faber is not open to mysteries, thrillers, or children's fiction. Recent nonfiction titles include *Uncommon Voyage: Parenting a Special Needs Child in the World of Alternative Medicine*, Laura Shapiro Kramer. Recent fiction titles include *Empire Under Glass*, Julian Anderson.

Advice to new authors: "Please send us *quality literary fiction* that is unique."

FIREBRAND BOOKS

*F/NF/P

Contact: Nancy K. Bereano

Address: 141 The Commons, Ithaca, NY 14850

Phone: (607) 272-0000

Category: Publishes lesbian and feminist Fiction, Nonfiction, Poetry, Erotica, News, and political subjects

General Information: Receives 500 MSS and query submissions per year. 50% of books published from first-time authors and 90% from unagented authors. Book catalog free upon request. Responds to queries in two weeks. Responds to MS submissions in two months to two weeks. Accepts simultaneous submissions (with notification only). No handwritten submissions except from institutionalized women. Pays royalties. Firebrand Books publishes eight to 10 books per year. Recent first-book titles include *Stone Butch Blues*, Leslie Feinberg. Other titles include *S/HE*, Minnie Bruce Pratt; *Good Enough to Eat*, Leslea Newman; *The Women Who Hate Me*, Dorothy Allison; *Presenting . . . Sister NoBlues*, Hattie Gossett; and *A Burst of Light*, Audre Lorde.

FOUR WALLS EIGHT WINDOWS

*F/NF/P

Contact: John Oakes

Address: 39 West 14th Street, #503, New York, NY 10011

Phone: (212) 206-8965

Category: Fiction, Nonfiction, and Poetry

Publisher's Notes on First Books: Four Walls Eight Windows published three first books, out of 18 total books, last year. Recent first-book titles include *Slaughtermatic*, Steve Aylett, 1998; *Simple Annals*, Robert Howard Allen, 1997; and *The Renunciation*, Edgardo Rodriguez Julia, 1997. The average first print run for first books is 3,000 to 5,000 copies.

General Information: Does not accept unsolicited MSS. However, 50% of books published come from unagented authors. Receives 2,000 MS and query submissions per year. Letter of query (with SASE) should precede MS submission. Responds to queries in three weeks. Responds to MS submissions in three months. Accepts simultaneous submissions. Pays advances. Other recent titles include *Bike Cult*, David Perry and *Ribo Funk*, Paul Di Filippo.

Advice to new authors: "We are always looking for good strong fiction. We often write to people we read. Be familiar with our list and have a reason for publishing the thing you submit."

FREDERIC C. BEIL, PUBLISHER, INC.
*F/NF

Contact: Mary Ann Bowman

Address: 609 Whitaker Street, Savannah, GA 31401

Phone: (912) 233-2446   **Fax:** (912) 233-2446

Category: Fiction and Nonfiction

Publisher's Notes on First Books: Frederic C. Beil published four first books, out of nine total books in 1996. They are scheduled to publish five more in 1997.

Recent first-book titles include *The Red Blackboard: An American Teacher in China*, Ruth Koenig, 1997; *A Butler's Life: Scenes From the Other Side of the Silver Salver*, Christopher Allen, with Kimberly K. Allen, 1997; and *A Master of the Century Past*, Robert S. Metzger, 1997.

General Information: Does not accept unsolicited MSS. Publishes hardcover originals and reprints. Receives 700 queries and nine MSS each year. Pays 7¹/₂% royalty on retail price. Publishes book 20 months after acceptance. Reports in one month on queries. Book catalog free on request. Submissions may include: biography, general trade, illustrated book, juvenile, and reference. Subjects may include: art/architecture, history, language/literature, and book arts. Recent fiction titles include *A Woman of Means*, Peter Taylor.

GRAYWOLF PRESS
*F/NF/P

Contact: Jeffrey Shotts

Address: 2402 University Avenue, Suite 203, St. Paul, MN 55114

Phone: (612) 641-0077   **Fax:** (612) 641-0036

Category: Fiction, Nonfiction, and Poetry

Publisher's Notes on First Books: Graywolf Press published four first books, out of 16 total books, in 1996. They are scheduled to publish three to four each year for the next three years. While they do not accept unsolicited MSS, they do accept unsolicited queries. Recent first-book titles include *Wild Kingdom*, Vijay Seshadri, 1996; *Jack & Rochelle*, Jack & Rochelle Sutton, Edited Lauren Sutton, 1996; *Rainey Lake*, Mary F. Rockcastle, 1996; and *The Apprentice*, Louis Libbey. The average first print run is approximately 4,000 copies.

Advice to new authors: "Sometimes we seek out new authors—those who seem promising in journals and magazines. It is important that you are familiar with the press. Create a really professional query and sample of your writing. Read other Graywolf books. There is a real rush to be published. Slow down and be clear—be professional."

HANGING LOOSE PRESS

*F/P/SF

Contact: Bob Hershon

Address: 231 Wyckoff, Brooklyn, NY 11217

Phone: (212) 206-8465

Category: Fiction, Poetry, and Short Fiction

Publisher's Notes on First Books: Hanging Loose Press published one first book, out of six total books, last year. Recent first-book titles include *Familiar*, Carole Bernstein; and *American Guise*, Elinor Nauen. The average first print run for first books is 1,200 to 1,500 copies.

General Information: "We have a habit of keeping all of our books in print—eventually they *do* find their audience. We are committed to certain people—as well as staying open to new writers."

Advice to new authors: "Work hard on your book. We read MSS by invitation and we request MSS from writers we read in magazines. The best way to be considered for publication is to first send work to the magazine and let us get to know your work through that."

HARD PRESS INC.

*F/P/SF

Contact: Jonathan Gams

Address: P.O. Box 184, West Stockbridge, MA 01266

Phone: (413) 232-4690

Category: Fiction, Poetry, and Short Fiction

Publisher's Notes on First Books: Hard Press Inc. published four first books last year and is scheduled to publish five this year. Recent first-book titles include *Little Men*, Kevin Killian, 1996 (won the PEN Oakland Award); *Solow*, Lynn Crawford, 1995; and *The Geographics*, Albert Mobilio, 1995.

Advice to new authors: "Anything that has a niche market (African American, Hispanic, lesbian, and gay), is easier to sell and market. First, find yourself an editor who is not your friend and who is willing to work on your MS. Also, a phone call is good. Read what we publish and see if your work fits or is close/similar to what we publish. Finally, your synopsis and cover letter should be clear and engaging as only 10% of received MSS are completely read."

MILKWEED EDITIONS

*C/F/NF/P

Address: 430 First Ave. N., Suite 400, Minneapolis, MN 55401-1743

Phone: (612) 332-3192   **Fax:** (612) 332-6248

Category: Children's, Fiction, Nonfiction, and Poetry

Publisher's Notes on First Books: Milkweed Editions publishes an average of five to six first books, out of 12 to 15 total books, each year. Recent first-book titles include *Confidence of the Heart*, David Schweidel; *The Tree of Red Stars*, Tessa Bridal; *Rescuing Little Roundhead*, Syl Jones; and *Homestead*, Annick Smith.

General Information: Pays $7^{1}/_{2}$% royalty on list price. Advance varies. Publishes work one year after acceptance. Accepts simultaneous submissions. Send SASE for MS guidelines. Reports in six months on MSS. Returns unsolicited MS if SASE provided. No longer accepting children's biographies.

Advice to new authors: "We are looking for unpublished authors. 30% of books published are from first-time authors. We find them in magazines, journals, through other writers, writing programs, our own unsolicited MSS, and agents. Read our catalog. Understand what we publish. If it seems to be a good fit, send the MS with an intelligent letter explaining why this book should be published."

NAIAD PRESS, INC.

*F/NF

Contact: Barbara Grier

Address: P.O. Box 10543, Tallahasse, FL 32302

Phone: (904) 539-5965

Category: Lesbian Fiction, Nonfiction, Erotica, Academic, and Historical Subjects

Publisher's Notes on First Books: Naiad published nine first books, out of 30 total books, last year. Recent first-book titles include *Dream Lover*, Lynn Denison; *The Color of Winter*, Lisa Shapiro; and *First Impressions*, Kate Calloway. The average first print run for first books is approximately 6,000 copies in the first year and approximately 12,000 in the second year. "Being a lesbian press we have a very specific audience."

General Information: One of the largest and oldest lesbian presses in the country (their 25th anniversary was in January 1998). Receives 1,100 query and MSS submissions each year. Letter of query should precede MS submission. Does not accept simultaneous submissions. Fiction MS should not exceed 50,000 words. Responds to MS submissions in three to six months. MSS should be on $8^1/_2 \times 11$-inch paper, typed, double-spaced, consecutively numbered pages with $1^1/_2$-inch top and bottom margins. Has an average annual marketing budget of $200,000. Pays royalties.

Advice to new authors: "Send one page, with three paragraphs, about the book. Make it simple. Also send a brief history and explanation of why you can write."

NEW VICTORIA PUBLISHERS

*F/NF/P

Contact: Beth Dingham

Address: P.O. Box 27, Norwich, VT 05055

Phone: (802) 649-5297 **Fax:** (802) 649-5297

Category: Lesbian Biography, Fiction, History, Nonfiction, and Poetry

Publisher's Notes on First Books: New Victoria published five first books, out of eight books total last year. Recent first-book titles include *No Daughter of the South*, Cynthia Webb; and *Orlando's Sleep*, Jennifer Spry. The average first print run for first books is 4,000 to 5,000 copies (mysteries sell much better and therefore have a larger first print run).

General Information: Receives 150 to 200 MSS and query submissions each year. Letter of query should precede MS submission. Responds to queries in two weeks. Responds to MS submissions in one month. Prefers not to receive simultaneous submissions. Pays royalties. "If you want a response, always send a SASE."

Advice to new authors: "First books tend to pile up on our desk. Be active in promoting your own work. Be daring and adventurous in your work. Don't be too subtle, and try to successfully write tension."

OWL CREEK PRESS

*F/P/SF

Address: 1620 North 45th Street, Seattle, WA 98103

Phone: (360) 387-6101

Category: Fiction, Poetry, and Short Fiction

Publisher's Notes on First Books: Owl Creek Press published four first books last year. Recent first-book titles include *Broken Darlings*, Ellen Watson. The average first print run for first books is approximately 1,000 copies and 500 copies for chapbooks. "We are totally nonprofit so the benefit of publishing first books is that everyone we publish is totally dedicated."

Advice to new authors: "We do accept unsolicited MSS but poetry MSS must come through our contest (*The Owl Creek Poetry Prize*)."

PRESS GANG PUBLISHERS

*F/NF/P

Contact: Barbara Kuhne

Address: 603 Powell Street, Vancouver, British Columbia, V6A 1H2 Canada

Phone: (604) 876-7892

Category: Feminist and Lesbian Fiction, Nonfiction, Erotica, and Political Subjects

General Information: Receives 150–200 submissions and MS queries per year. Book catalog free upon request. Letter of query (with SASE) should precede MS submission. Responds to queries in two months. Responds to MS submissions in three to four months. Accepts simultaneous submissions. Publishes approximately five total titles each year. MSS should be double-spaced. Prefers letter-quality submissions. Pays royalties. U.S. writers should send postal coupons—not U.S. stamps—on SASE. "We give priority to Canadian women's writing."

SEVEN STORIES PRESS

*F/NF

Contact: Daniel Simon

Address: 140 Watts Street, New York, NY 10013

Phone: (212) 226-8760   **Fax:** (212) 226-1411

Category: Fiction and Nonfiction

Publisher's Notes on First Books: Seven Stories Press published five first books, out of 25 total books, last year.

General Information: Does not accept unsolicited MSS. Publishes hardcover and trade paperback originals. Pays 7 to 15% royalty on retail price. Publishes book one to three years after acceptance. Accepts simultaneous submissions. Reports in three months on MSS. Book catalog and MS guidelines free upon request. Recent titles include *Parable of the Sower*, Octavia E. Butler (feminist fiction). Audience is well educated, progressive, and mainstream.

Advice to new authors: "Publish anywhere you can. Read the books we publish. Submit MSS only when you feel your own work resonates with a publisher's list."

St. Martin's Press

*F/NF

Contact: Calvert Morgan

Address: 175 Fifth Ave., New York, NY 10010

Phone: (212) 674-5151   **Fax:** (212) 674-9314

Category: Fiction and Nonfiction

Publisher's Notes on First Books: St. Martin's Press publishes approximately 150 first books, out of 600 total books, each year. "St. Martin's finds that we can support authors early in their career who—even if not with their first title—have success in their future. The most difficult thing about publishing first books is convincing retailers to give space to unknown writers—finding publicity for first-time novelists."

Advice to new authors: "Write a smart, concise cover letter."

W. W. Norton

*F/NF/P

Contact: Jill Bialosky

Address: 500 Fifth Ave., New York, NY 10110

Phone: (212) 354-5500   **Fax:** (212) 869-0856

Category: Fiction, Nonfiction, and Poetry

Publisher's Notes on First Books: W. W. Norton published one first book last year. Recent first-book titles include *Piaceso Effects*, Jeanie Marie Beaumont.

General Information: General trade publisher of fiction and nonfiction, educational and professional books. Subjects include biography, history, music, psychology, and literary fiction. Do not submit juvenile or young adult, religious, occult or paranormal, genre fiction (formula romances, science fiction, or westerns), or arts and crafts MSS. Send query with an outline, the first three chapters, and a SASE.

Advice to new authors: "Be published in distinguished literary journals."

WHITE PINE PRESS

*F

Contact: Bree Bishop

Address: 10 Village Square, Fredonia, NY 14063

Phone: (716) 672-5743

Category: Fiction

Publisher's Notes on First Books: White Pine Press published one first book last year through the *White Pine Press New American Voices Series*. Recent first-book titles include *Where This Lake Is*, Jeff Lodge.

Advice to new authors: "Do a standard query along with a biography and sample writing (two to three chapters). The *White Pine Press New American Voices Series* was established in 1996 in response to dramatic changes in the book industry that made it more difficult for first-time novelists to find a publisher. We believe that our literary heritage must continue to grow and that it must be vast enough to encompass the tremendous variety of writing from the Americas. Readers must be given the opportunity to hear vibrant, new voices. It is the intent of the series to present first novels that not only entertain but also offer insights into our world and ourselves."

PUBLISHERS FAVORABLE TO UNPUBLISHED FIRST-BOOK MANUSCRIPTS

BY GENRE

Short Fiction

PRESSES AND PUBLISHERS
BY PERCENTAGE OF FIRST BOOKS*

Publisher	% First Books	#First Books	Total Titles
Calyx Books	100%	3	3
Champion Books	100%	5	5
Branden Publishing Inc. Co.,	80%	10–12	15
Blue Star Productions, a Division of Bookworld, Inc.	75%	9	10–12
Confluence Press Inc.	50%	2–3	5
Dante University of America Press, Inc.	50%	2–3	5
Eighth Mountain Press	50%	1	2
Firebrand Books	50%	5	10
New Victoria Publishers	40%	3–5	9
Cleis Press	35%	5–6	15
Blue Moon Books, Inc.	30%	4	20–40
Naiad Press Inc.	30%	9	30
Brookline Books	25%	5–6	20
Center Press	25%	1–2	6
Graywolf Press	25%	4	16
St. Martin's Press	20–30%	150	600
Chronicle Books	20%	40	200
Milkweed Editions	20%	3	15

*Figures are approximate

Publisher	% First Books	#First Books	Total Titles
Hanging Loose Press	16%	1–2	6
Alfred A. Knopf	15%	30	200
Dancing Jester Press	15%	2–3	16
The Ecco Press	15%	8–9	60
Four Walls Eight Windows	15%	3	18
Frederic C. Beil, Publisher, Inc.	15%	4	7
Seven Stories Press	15%	5	15
Alyson Publications	10–15%	5	35
Copper Canyon Press	10%	2	10–12
Faber & Faber Inc.	10%	2	30
David R. Godine, Publisher	5–10%	2	25
Arcade Publishing	5%	10–12	40
Counterpoint	2%	1	25

FIRST BOOK RECOMMENDATIONS
BY PUBLISHERS

First Books	Recommended By
The Necessary Angel, Nina Revoyr	Alyson Publications
The Power of Their Ideas, Deborah Myer; *The Very Rich Hours*, Emily Hiestand	Beacon Press
Brazen, Ghislaine Dunant (translated by Rosette Lamont)	Blue Moon Books, Inc.
Silk, Grace Dane Mazur; *Little Jordan*, Marly Youmans	Brookline Books
Second Sight, Richey Garddiam; *Into the Forest*, Gene Hegland; *The Violet Shyness of Their Eyes*, Barbara Scott	Calyx Books
The Broken World, Marcus Cafagna; *The Legend of Light*, Bob Hicok	David R. Godine, Publisher
Returning to A, Dorien Ross; *A Drink Before the War*, Dennis Lehane; *In the Garden of the North American Martyrs*, Tobias Wolff	The Ecco Press
Angela's Ashes, Frank McCourt	Eighth Mountain Press
Leaves of Grass, Walt Whitman; *Simple Annals*, Robert Howard Allen	Four Walls Eight Windows
Wild Kingdom, Vijay Seshadri; *Reading in the Dark*, Samas Dean	Graywolf Press
Delores: The Alpine Years, Pansy Maurer-Alvarez; *The Business of Fancy Dancing*, Sherman Alexie; *The Very Stuff*, Stephen Beal; *Air Pocket*, Kimiko Hahns	Hanging Loose Press

Basement of the Cafe Rilke, Rafael Rubenstein; *Star Fiction*, Eric Belgium	Hard Press, Inc.
Swimming in the Congo, Margaret Meyers; *A Keeper of Sheep*, William Carpenter	Milkweed Editions
Color of Winter, Lisa Shapiro; *Wild Wood Flowers*, Julia Watts; *Benediction*, Diane Salvatore	Naiad Press, Inc.
I, Rigahenta Meushu; *Never Come Morning*, Nelson Algren; *In Dreams Begin Responsibilities*, Delmore Schwartz	Seven Stories Press
Generation X, Douglas Coupland; *All Creatures Great and Small*	St. Martin's Press
The Christmas Show, Harriet Levin; *The End of Desire*, Jill Bialosky	W. W. Norton
Body of This Death, Louise Bogan; *Sea Garden*, H.D.; *Too Bright to See*, Linda Gregg; *To Put the Mouth To*, Judith Hall; *Letters to a Stranger*, Thomas James; *The Evolution of the Flightless Bird*, Richard Kenney; *The Lord & the General Din of the World*, Jane Mead; *Nothing in Nature is Private*, Claudia Rankine; *United Artists*, S. X. Rosenstock	Academy of American Poets
Be Properly Scared, M. Wyrebek; *Corporal Works*, Lynn Domina	Four Way Books

7

FIRST BOOK AMERICAN CLASSICS

❧❦❧

Emily Dickinson

Poems
Boston: Roberts Brothers, 1890

The poems of Emily Elizabeth Dickinson (1830–1886) suggest hidden meanings that are never baldly revealed, and her life, appropriately, holds at its heart a mystery that has never been plucked out. Her world was Amherst, Massachusetts, where her father, who dominated his family, was a man of considerable importance. She was well educated for her time and locality, and for the first twenty-four years of her life enjoyed the usual social activity of a small college town.

In 1854, she visited Washington and Philadelphia, where she may possibly have fallen in love with a married man. Certainly thereafter she drifted further and further into seclusion. Her time was occupied with family duties and with the writing of poetry. Although she wrote hundreds of poems, she published only a handful during her lifetime. The first collection of them was brought out after her death, by two friends, Mabel Loomis Todd and Thomas Wentworth Higginson, to whom she had showed them. Although this and the second volume they edited finally brought Dickinson the public she had never known during her lifetime, Higginson's editing seriously misrepresented her art: in an effort to tame what he considered to be unorthodoxies of rhyme, meter, and even language, Higginson had altered Dickinson's texts.

Jack London

The Son of the Wolf. Tales of the Far North
Boston: Houghton Mifflin, 1900

$\mathcal{N}$o other American man of letters crowded into forty years so much adventure and activity as Jack London (1876–1916). The illegitimate son of an Irish astrologer named Chaney, the boy received his early education primarily on the waterfront of Oakland, California. At age sixteen he owned his own sloop and was the hard-drinking Prince of the Oyster Pirates, a dangerous profession. On his seventeenth birthday, he signed on to a sealer as able-bodied seaman for a year's cruise in the North Pacific. Ashore again he took to the road as a hobo and toured the eastern states.

Thirty days in a New York State jail gave London time to realize that he was too smart to spend his life that way. He returned to Oakland, went to high school, and read widely, especially in the socialist philosophers. In August 1896, he entered the University of California—and left it five months later.

Next he went to the Klondike in the Gold Rush of 1897, and nearly died of scurvy. Unable to find work on his return to California, he turned to writing. *The Son of the Wolf*, drawn from his Alaskan experiences, was published within two years, and thereafter he had no trouble selling as much as he could write—fifty volumes in eighteen years. The brutality of his material, the vividness of his stories, the socialist dream he followed, won him wide popularity. He is said to have earned over a million dollars, all of which he spent.

Always restless, London visited Europe and was a correspondent for the Russo-Japanese and the Mexican wars. His first marriage ended in divorce. With his second wife he traveled in the West Indies and the South Pacific islands. He then settled in California, where he poured money and energy into his ranch. His health began to crack, and in November 1916, he died of an overdose of morphine.

Theodore Dreiser

Sister Carrie
New York: Doubleday, Page, 1900

$\mathcal{L}$ong before his death, Theodore Dreiser (1871–1945) had become one of the legendary figures of American letters and a center of controversy. Born in Indiana of German parents, he was brought up in an atmosphere of religious intolerance. The future novelist attended Indiana University for a year and then went into business in Chicago. When he was twenty-one, he decided to become a journalist and worked, off and on, on newspapers and magazines in Chicago, St. Louis, New York, and Philadelphia from 1892 to 1934.

The struggle that Dreiser waged for acceptance of his realistic depiction of life began with his first book, *Sister Carrie*. Declined by Harper's, the manuscript was accepted by Doubleday, Page. Mrs. Doubleday is said to have insisted that it not be published, and Dreiser to have demanded that the firm honor its contract. The book *was* published, in an edition of some 1,000 copies: 129 were sent out for review; 465 were sold; and 423 copies were remaindered.

Dreiser's fight for freedom of expression and of opinion did not end with *Sister Carrie*. In 1914 *The Genius* and in 1925 *An American Tragedy* met with attack and censorship. Dreiser's pro-Russian and anti-British point of view was also subject to intense criticism. Nevertheless, his insistence upon independence for the writer was an important factor in the development of twentieth-century literature.

Willa Cather

April Twilights
Boston: Richard G. Badger, The Gorham Press, 1903

Cather published her first poem, a derivative effort entitled "Shakespeare," while she was a freshman at the University of Nebraska. The early and exploratory poetry of the young, star-struck devotee of literature included translations of Horace, Anacreon, and Heine. Some of her early work was published with the pseudonyms John Esten, John Charles Asten, or Clara Wood Shipman. These last names were used for poems published in *The Library*, a Pittsburgh literary magazine that Cather edited; the poems were perhaps written to fill white space in the magazine.

Most of the poems included in *April Twilights* were written from 1900 to 1902 when she was solidifying her relationship with Isabella McClung (from 1901 until her move to New York in 1906, Cather lived in the McClung household, discomforting Isabella's parents, brothers, and sisters). Although she began to come into her own as an authentic writer during this period, Cather found most of her early poetry (and her first stories) irredeemable, and republished little of it. She brought out a new edition of *April Twilights* in 1923, removing thirteen poems from the original edition and adding twelve new ones. In fact, she so disliked her first book that at one point she bought up all the copies she could find and destroyed them. In 1925 she said, "I do not take myself seriously as a poet."

William Carlos Williams

Poems
Rutherford, NJ: [Printed for the Author by Reid Howell], 1909
The Lily Library, Indiana University, Bloomington, Indiana

*P*oems is a delicate, pseudo-Victorian pamphlet, lovingly designed by William's beloved older brother Edgar. Its twenty-two pages were published locally by the job printer Reid Howell of Rutherford, NJ, a friend of William's father, and the first printing was a disaster, full of typographical and spelling errors. It was destroyed (except for two copies; one of them, annotated by Williams and his father, is now housed at the University of Pennsylvania). Williams later reminisced about this first printing and the Penn copy:

The local journeymen must have had a tough time of it, never having set up anything of the sort in their lives, because when I saw the first finished volume I nearly passed out. I've still got the thing in my trunk in the attic: about half errors—like the Passaic River in its relationship to the sewage of that time. I notice, by looking over the disastrous first issue (which never appeared), that it bears the markers of Pop's corrections and suggestions all over it—changes most of which I adopted. Poor Pop, how he must have suffered.

The second printing sold for twenty-five cents (only four of the one hundred copies printed were sold at Garrison's stationary store in Rutherford). Williams gave nine or ten copies to friends and relatives; the rest were stored by the stationer and "inadvertently burned after they had reposed ten years or more on a rafter under the eaves of his old chicken coop." As of 1968, only nine copies had been located by Williams's bibliographer, Emily Mitchell Wallace. In publishing his first volume himself, Williams joined a long list of self-publishers, which included his friend Ezra Pound, who had published his own first book, *A Lume Spento*, in Venice the previous year. The original printer's estimate for *Poems* was $32.45. Williams also paid Elkin Matthews for the publication in London of his second volume, *The Tempers* (1913), which was introduced by Pound with this prophetic line: "God forbid that I should introduce Mr. Williams as a cosmic force."

Gertrude Stein

Three Lives. Stories of the Good, Melanctha, and the Gentle Lena
New York: The Grafton Press, 1909

Gertrude Stein (1874–1946), the most controversial writer of her generation, was born in Pennsylvania and grew up in California. During her youth in San Francisco, Stein read voraciously in Mechanics Library's collection of seventeenth- and eighteenth-century English literature. (As for the dawning twentieth-century literature, Gertrude Stein helped invent it.) At Radcliffe, which she left in 1897 without taking a degree, she studied psychology with William James. She next studied medicine for four years at Johns Hopkins, again without taking a degree. Her distaste for examinations may not be without bearing upon the state of mind that produced her mature literary style.

Gertrude Stein really found herself when in 1903 she went with Alice B. Toklas to live in Paris. There she made friends, enemies, and disciples among artists and literary men, natives and expatriates. Her collection of paintings by contemporary artists who were not yet popular with collectors was astutely gathered. Young American writers, including Hemingway, were inspired by her encouragement. Except for a lecture tour of the United States in 1934, she remained in France, even during the dangerous days of World War II.

In writing *Three Lives,* the most traditional of her books, Stein said she was influenced by Flaubert a little, and "Because the realism of the people who did realism before was a realism of trying to make people real. I was not interested in making people real, but in the essence, or as a painter would call it a value. One cannot live without the other. . . the Cezanne thing I put into words came in *Three Lives.*" *Three Lives* does not look much like anything else Gertrude Stein wrote. She financed its publication herself, and it was very much just the beginning. Her writing has been hailed as fundamental to an understanding of advanced contemporary art, praised as a fertilizing influence on more intelligent writers, and denounced as a racket. *Three Lives,* her first book, presents the reader with no problem in communication.

Robert Frost

A Boy's Will
London: David Nutt, 1913

The thirty-nine-year-old Robert Frost's first book, *A Boy's Will* (1913), was published not in New York, but in England, and by the first publisher he approached. The first copy from the press of David Nutt was spirited off by Ezra Pound, who used it to advance Frost's career, writing a long and positive review of the book for Harriet Monroe's *Poetry* magazine, and passing the book and a copy of his review on to Yeats, who was later to entertain the two with stories by candlelight.

A Boy's Will was actually Frost's second publication: it had been preceded by a twenty-page pamphlet, *Twilight*, containing five poems, which Frost had had printed in 1894 by a job printer in Lawrence, Massachusetts. Only two copies were printed: Frost destroyed one of them after his marriage proposal had been rebuffed by his eventual wife, Elinor White. The surviving copy, originally given to Mrs. Frost, is now owned by the Clifton Waller Barrett Library of the University of Virginia.

Frost chose to reprint only one of the five poems, "The Butterfly," twenty years later in *A Boy's Will*. Probably a little more than 1,000 copies were printed of *A Boy's Will*, but of the original first issue and first binding of pebbled cloth there were under 300 copies.

PART 5

"WHAT LOVEST WELL REMAINS,
WHAT LOVEST WELL IS THY TRUE HISTORY":
MORE WRITERS ON THEIR FIRST BOOKS

FAITH AND FIRST FICTION

Sadi Ranson

The offices of Condé Nast where I began my career in publishing are long, curving hallways, with offices off to the side, where editors sit fashionably dressed, moody and always overworked. The usual hours, when I worked there at seventeen years old, were something like 7:30 A.M. to late at night, depending on the day. Moments of respite came when we left at five.

My first assignment was to read the "slush," the unsolicited manuscripts that hopeful writers had sent (kissing the envelope before popping it in the post box) addressed to the features editors.

I remember those summers, reading slush, trying to determine what was "good." It struck me then that almost everything had some redeeming quality. I was too much of a socialist in my youth, and I found the Good in everything. So what if it wasn't original, it was well crafted, it was something new, and so on. To my knowledge, during my time there, we did not accept a single unsolicited manuscript. If memory serves, the manuscripts we did publish were always solicited or "agented," sent in by aggressive New York agents who pushed hard for their clients. As a young writer, it was depressing to think that a writer of talent would receive nothing more than a curt form letter in return for years of work. Still, I realize now that it is unreasonable, impossible, for every manuscript to get a personal response. This is the domain of MFA programs in Creative Writing; this is the job of a teacher.

Years later, I read fiction for C. Michael Curtis at the *Atlantic Monthly*. On average, I suppose we received somewhere between thirty and forty unsolicited manuscripts each day. If you factor in the agents, then there were more. The difference here was, it was my job to read a manuscript, and return it to the editor with a two-paragraph report detailing:

What is it about?

Should we/should we not publish it and why?

These reports, of which I kept copies, are brief and to the point. What I learnt from C. Michael Curtis, and what I retain, is that if I am still thinking about a manuscript—its images, phrasing, characters, plot—if these are still with me a month from now, then indeed the manuscript merits serious consideration. Few were this affecting. But some were. And those that lodged in my temporal lobe, teasing me with their words, their snapshot images, were published.

Unlike so many publishers, the *Atlantic Monthly* does publish work that comes in over the transom—unsolicited— and often, there were gems amongst this work. Writers who would later become well known: John Sayles, Joyce Carol Oates, E. S. Goldman, Tobias Wolf, and Heidi Jon Schmidt have all published at the *Atlantic Monthly*. There were "Atlantic Firsts." It is remarkable when one considers that the Atlantic receives some 15,000 manuscripts annually, all of which do get read.

Two years ago I started a publishing imprint that I named Lumen Editions. The name Lumen, a measure of light, derived from what I determined to be the mission of the house—to shed light on formerly unexplored corners of the world, to present things in a new way, to shine a brilliant light on new, younger, previously unpublished authors. To illuminate, and how brightly. This was not a philosophical ideal; we did not see it as a public service. But rather, as something that needed to be done.

We publish first fiction, first collections of short stories, and, yes, even poetry (gosh!). In the beginning, I was told this could never work. The naysayers who said, "it won't sell. Stories don't sell. Translations—who cares? And poetry?" Perhaps I was crazy, but it has served me well.

Presently, we publish between ten and fifteen new titles each year. At least three or four of these titles are by writers who have never been published, or have never been published in the English language. The media—the *New York Times Book Review*, the *Washington Post*, *Publishers Weekly*, all of the usual suspects—have given us tremendous support, allotting full-page reviews for our modest soft covers by first-time authors, and selecting one of them as among the best books of 1996. Three of our books went back to press within the first seven months of publication. We sold out our initial print run.

Those naysayers should sit back down and rethink their bleak vision of first fiction.

Publishing first fiction and succeeding is not about arrogance and being able to say "I told you so." It is about reading a book, having it affect you as an editor—so much so that you think about it for days, weeks, months after you first read it. Trust that instinct. Trust that if it impacted you, no matter how "unknown" the author that this books merits being published. This is how I make publishing decisions. There's no science to it. It is instinctual, elemental and pure. And in large part, it's about faith.

I once told someone that publishing is a ministry of sorts—the salaries are pitiful when one factors in the amount of time and work, yet it is a passion one cannot stay away from. Every project, every new book, becomes an obsessive love affair that you are determined to make work. You think about it late at night. You convince others of its worth. It often (though not always) changes your life. You hope it affects other readers the same way. You go to work, you read, you look for something good. Inspiring. The book that presents the elusive Other. Like a Jesuit or a nun, you wear too much black, you flog yourself, and you despair when a book doesn't make its mark and is instead pulled into the vortex of thousands of other books published each year. You pray. You keep your faith. You know there is undiscovered talent out there and you know that you will find it. The reward is in that First Fiction. It is the hope that we hold out that not all talent has been discovered—because we know there is more than this.

8

WRITERS ON THEIR
OWN FIRST BOOKS

"Try Even Those Places You're Doubtful About"

Roberta Allen

Roberta Allen, whose new book, *Certain People,* was published in 1997 by Coffee House Press in their Coffee-To-Go Short Short Series, spent a year sending around her first story collection, *The Traveling Woman,* to small presses before it was accepted by Vehicle Editions, a one-woman press. She'd been aware of Vehicle for several years and submitted to them because they had beautiful books and had published Alex Katz and some poetry books. She was introduced to her Vehicle editor at a party for Gregory Corso's photographs. "She'd already decided to take my book but hadn't told me, yet. When he introduced me, she had this big smile," Ms. Allen says, and adds, "She's the one who convinced me to put drawings in the book. I wasn't going to do it—this was my first literary experience and I wanted it to be pure." She laughs, "I drew fifty-two little drawings in one weekend and we used some of those. Now, I always include drawings." Ms. Allen says that the hardest part was organizing the stories: "It took me a year to find the sequence."

Ms. Allen advises writers to keep trying since editors change. "Try even the places that you're doubtful about. It's important to keep the book around. There are certain times for certain books and this moment may not be your book's moment."

Clarice LeSpector and Marguerite Duras are Ms. Allen's favorite authors, "but I don't know what was their first book or their tenth," she says.

Roberta Allen's first book was a collection of stories, The Traveling Woman *(Vehicle Editions). In addition to* Certain People, *her latest books include* Fast Fiction: Creating Fiction in Five Minutes *(Storyline Press). She teaches at NYU, The Writer's Voice, and The New School in New York City.*

"Spend All the Time You Can"

Andrea Barrett

Andrea Barrett reveals that *Lucid Stars* really wasn't her first book. Largely self-taught, she'd spent seven years on a novel. "I couldn't write a sentence or a paragraph when I got started. I just kept scribbling and scribbling away," she says.

In 1984 or '85, she went to Bread Loaf Writer's Conference with "a story for class and a novel in my purse." Nicholas Delbanco asked her if she had anything else and out came the novel. He told her she was a pretty good writer but that she should throw it out and move on, because she'd been learning to write with that novel. "As a teacher, I realize how hard it is to say that," Ms. Barrett says. But it was a relief to get rid of it and after that, "*Lucid Stars* came quickly and happily." Up at Bread Loaf, she'd met the literary agent, Wendy Weil, who had asked Ms. Barrett to send something when she was finished. In 1987, *Lucid Stars* went to Jane Rosenman, who was then at Delacorte. The publisher was one of the first to start a paperback originals series, which they called Delta, and *Lucid Stars* was one of their launch books. So even though it was never in hardcover, "it had a little better chance," she says. "It was a pleasant experience, the book was pretty, and it had its little moment out in the world."

Ms. Barrett's all-time favorite first book is *Housekeeping*, by Marilyn Robinson. "*Learning By Heart,* by Margot Livesey Areally stuck with me." She also likes Brian Kitely's *Still Life With Insects* and Virginia Woolf's *The Voyage Out.* Kim Edward's collection of short stories, *Tales of the Fire King,* "is really strong. The stories are mature, assured, and finished," Ms. Barrett says, adding that many collections have only a handful of great stories because writers have rushed to get published. "But every story in Kim Edward's collection is great; the stories are devastating."

"It's hard advice, but spend all the time you can," Ms. Barrett says to the writers composing their novels and story collections. "It's easy to be frantic with the first book because it marks the transition between being known and being taken seriously. But, it's the last really secretive time with no one looking over your shoulder. As a teacher, it makes me sad to see them rushing," she says.

Andrea Barrett teaches in the MFA Program for Writers at Warren Wilson College. Her first novel was Lucid Stars, *published with Delacorte in 1988, and her current collection of stories,* Ship Fever & Other Stories *won the National Book Award in 1996.*

❦

"Wait Until the Last Minute"

Sophie Cabot Black

Sophie Cabot Black's first book of poetry, *The Misunderstanding of Nature,* published by Graywolf, took a long while—two years—to be accepted and in that time, she'd already started on her second book. She agonized over whether she should combine the two and decided she would. The agony was over how to make the arc work, since the first book had a distinct arc. Graywolf accepted the changed manuscript, which found its own structure—two-thirds of the old manuscript and one-half of the new that she'd already finished.

"I do believe in waiting and not worrying about the book not being taken. I know that's hard when you want to teach, but I'm glad I waited. I believe in waiting to the last minute to start, when the book has a strong, new, authoritative voice, a life without you," Ms. Cabot Black says. "When I teach first books, I choose breakthrough books that show the personality of the poet rather than just a collection of poems. Basically, keep putting the best poems in there."

Ms. Cabot Black took out twelve poems that were in the book originally and that had been published in magazines that she'd have loved to have listed in the beginning of the book, but they just didn't fit. Her favorite first books are *Sleeping with One Eye Open,* by Mark Strand; *The Lost Pilot,* by James Tate; *The Colossus,* by Sylvia Plath; *Too Bright to See,* by Linda Gregg; and *Death of a Naturalist,* by Seamus Heaney.

Sophie Cabot Black's first collection of poems, The Misunderstanding of Nature, *received The Norma Farber Award for a first book by the Poetry Society of America. She was recently a fellow at The Bunting Institute.*

"Read, Read, and Read"

T. C. Boyle

The three best first novels that come to T. C. Boyle's mind, Thomas Pynchon's *V.*, John Fowles's *The Collector,* and Louise Erdrich's *Love Medicine,* certainly match the wild textures of his own fiction. "Read, read, and read," Mr. Boyle advises. "My first book was a collection of seventeen stories, *Descent of Man.* All the stories had been published in magazines little and big. My agent, Georges Borchardt, who took me on the basis of these stories and a recommendation from one of his clients, sold the book to Peter Davison at Atlantic-Little, Brown. The first printing was 3,500. There was a second printing of 2,500. I was paid considerably less than $10,000. The year was 1979," Mr. Boyle says. After the success of two printings of his first book, Atlantic-Little, Brown & Co. as it was known then, published Mr. Boyle's first novel, *Water Music,* in 1982. "And for that, I was paid less than $10,000, but have recouped a bit of money since. Both books remain in print, both here and abroad."

T. C. Boyle's most recent novel is River Rock *(Viking, 1997). He teaches at the University of Southern California.*

⋘◉⋙

"Do It"

Susan Cheever

"Without question, my favorite first book is Genesis, God's first book," Susan Cheever says, laughing, while serious, having alighted upon a favorite book that is indeed that author's first. "Then, *War & Peace,* by Tolstoy," she adds, amazed and delighted to confirm that this epic was his first.

Ms. Cheever wrote her first book, *Looking For Work,* in France in 1978. "I never wanted to be a writer, it was my vow," she says. "I avoided it and at thirty-five, I ended up at *Newsweek.* Then I quit and ran off to the south of France with somebody else's husband and sat down and wrote it. Nobody else spoke English." With all that pent-up energy and isolation writing in a French resort town in winter, Ms. Cheever wrote the book in a month, or two. It had been germinating without her knowing. "I felt so disoriented by it in those circumstances, I didn't believe I had written a novel," although she was in love with the story she wrote. "I went around counting the words in all the books to see if I had one," she says. They only had about twenty English books. fortunately, they were mostly James M. Cain novels, which are short. "I was sophisticated in many ways, but innocent."

When asked what advice she'd give to writers approaching the publication of their first book, she says "Duck." But, for those approaching the writing of their first books? "Do it."

Susan Cheever's nine books include Home Before Dark, Looking for Work, *and her forthcoming memoir,* Note Found in a Bottle: My Life as a Drinker. *All of her books have been published by Simon & Schuster. She teaches in the MFA program at Bennington College.*

"A Worthy Book Will Eventually Find a Publisher"

Stephen Dunn

Mr. Dunn's advice to writers is threefold. "One, try not to send out your manuscript as soon as you have enough poems for it to be considered a manuscript. Wait awhile. As long as you can bear it. Your manuscript is likely to get better. Two, try not to get discouraged. I believe that a worthy book will eventually find a publisher. Three, write very good poems. Your poems, no one else's. Always be more concerned with furthering your work as opposed to furthering your reputation."

Mr. Dunn's experience with his first book, *Looking For Holes in the Ceiling*, best illustrates his advice. "It took me two years to realize that none of the poems I had written in graduate school (though I was a successful graduate student poet) should be in the manuscript. About three years of work went into the poems that eventually constituted the book. It was rejected several times over a two-year period. It should have been. When finally I wrote a longish poem that became the book's centerpiece, the book was accepted by The University of Massachusetts Press. I believe I received a $500 advance. I was thirty-five when it was published in 1974."

Stephen Dunn's selected poems were published by W. W. Norton in 1996. He directs the writing program at Stockton State College.

❧

"You Can't Just Sit Home"

Elaine Equi

"Book contests have the function of independent films, today," says Elaine Equi, since they tend to support writers with a different view than the mainstream. The author of nine books of poetry, Ms. Equi says to try a lot of different things. Try contests and presses that don't have contests but who you think might like your work. Many think *Surface Tension* (Coffee House Press) is her first book since that brought her more widespread attention, but *Federal Woman*, in 1978, started the ball rolling.

A group of friends that were printers and visual artists interested in poetry, visual, and performing arts decided to put together chapbooks under the name Danaidus Press. They went around to readings in Chicago to hear what was being written. Ms. Equi had seen their chapbooks of Harry Crosby, which she loved, and, in turn, they liked her work. They told her they were tired of doing dead people, and asked her for *Federal Woman*.

"You can't just sit home and decide you have the gift of poetry," Ms. Equi says. "Get readings, be a known quantity. Build a résumé with work in many different kinds of magazines, just get it out there and get your name around." She is sure that Allen Kornblum at Coffee House decided to look at her manuscript because he knew her name, not because he just started reading the poems. "Also, don't be afraid to change your manuscript, to polish and fine-tune the poems. It's one to two years between the time that Coffee House accepts my manuscript and publishes it, and in that time, the book will change."

She also recommends the wisdom of Harold Bloom in his book *The Anxiety of Influence,* who states a case for all poems coming from other poems, "so poets shouldn't be worried that reading other poets will make them copy a style," Ms. Equi says.

Ms. Equi highly recommends the work of Lee Ann Brown, a poet in New York City, whose work has been published in magazines and who gives many readings. She's anticipating Brown's first book, which won a contest sponsored by Sun & Moon Press two years ago.

Elaine Equi's first book, Federal Woman, *was published by Danaidus Press. Her ninth collection,* Voice Over, *is forthcoming in 1998 from Coffee House Press.*

"The Most Deeply Private Joy"

Carolyn Forche

A few of Carolyn Forche's list of impressive first books arrived on the scene without benefit of winning awards, including, *Disfortune,* by Joe Wenderoth; *The Tulip Sacrament,* by Annah Sobelman; and *Candy Necklace,* by Calvin Bendient, all recently published by Wesleyan. *Cities of Memory,* by Ellen Hinsey, which won the 1996 Yale Series of Younger Poets, and *The New Intimacy,* by Barbara Cully, which Ms. Forche selected for the National Poetry Series (Penguin, 1997) are the two standouts from award books. She was impressed, as well, by Ray DiPalma's National Poetry Series selection of *The Little Door,* by Jeff Clark, Sun & Moon, 1997) and remarks that a few of these writers are in their thirties and their manuscripts have made the rounds. "I'm reminded of the old adage: it takes years to become an overnight success."

Ms. Forche's first book, *Gathering the Tribes,* was the Yale Series of Younger Poets winner in 1975 when she was twenty-five. "I had entered the manuscript in the previous year's competition, and when I received a handwritten, encouraging letter of rejection from the judge, Stanley Kunitz, I was naive enough to feel resigned rather than jubilant. I continued to revise the manuscript, but consigned it to a drawer. At the strong insistence of a friend, I typed a clean copy on my Smith Corona and sent it again on the deadline date. In the following months, I somehow forgot that I had entered, and so was worried when I received a telephone massage from New Haven, as I didn't know anyone there, and associated Connecticut with insurance companies that I very nearly did not return the call.

"Stanley Kunitz, who has perhaps done more for young poets than any other living poet, was immensely kind to me during the publication process, which I found interesting but also terrifying. I remember the day my Yale editor, Cathy Iino, accompanied me to a book-signing at the Grolier in Cambridge. Copies of the book were stacked in the windows. Inside, people were leafing through the book, people I didn't know—readers, most beloved of poets—but it was my first experience of having my poems read by people other than those to whom I had given them. Cathy Iino sensed my anguish, but told me that it was too late. I protested that I could buy all the copies and take them home. She laughed. 'We'll print more.'

"The most deeply private joy of my life had become, irrevocably, public."

Carolyn Forche's most recent book, The Angel of History, *was published by HarperCollins in 1994. She teaches at George Mason University.*

"A Pursuit of Art as Ruthless as the Pursuit of Experience"

Edward Hirsch

"I, myself, have a sense of a book as a journey, a pilgrimage," says the poet, Edward Hirsch, whose first book, *For the Sleepwalkers*, also had a long journey to publication. His favorite first books are *White Buildings*, by Hart Crane, and *Harmonium*, by Wallace Stevens. "The process of the first book is long, moving though so many stages of progression and development," he says. "It covers a period of entire apprenticeship."

Mr. Hirsch first wrote poems in high school, but in 1976, at age twenty-six, he wrote two poems that were better than any he'd written before, and that "sounded a note that I wanted to sound," he says. "Everything that went into *For the Sleepwalkers* came from that and stayed. It was the soil for the organic growth of poems that emerged in my thirties." A book should not be just the best hits, not just the best poems of poetic apprenticeship. "The process of maturation is putting together the poems you like, but also, fused into a sum larger than its parts," he says, adding that Robert Frost said that if a book has twenty-nine poems that the book, itself, is the thirtieth. "What one *wants* with a first book is a continual expansion and a radical coherence," he says.

Mr. Hirsch had a number of poems in magazines when, in 1978, he sent *For the Sleepwalkers* to Knopf, over the transom. Although it was easier back then to send an unsolicited manuscript of poetry to a major house, "it was not like it was wildly open," he contends. "They held it for a very long time, kept it for a year and a half, but they were enthusiastic about it. They reassured me many times that they wanted it. Alice Quinn was starting a poetry series there and said she wanted it. It was published as the fifth book of that series in 1981," he says. Knopf remains his publisher, although Alice Quinn moved on to edit poetry for the *New Yorker. For the Sleepwalkers* won both the Peter I. B. Lavan Younger Poet Prize from the Academy of American Poets and the Delmore Schwartz Award from New York University and was nominated for the National Book Critics Circle, an award Mr. Hirsch won for his second book, *Wild Gratitude.*

As for advice, Mr. Hirsch says, "Poetry comes out of poetry, not just from self-expression. Your experience in life is the gift of your material, but it's only a beginning. One needs to honor that material like your life because poetry is a vocation, a calling. Most books seem terrifically marred by inadequate means. What one wants from a first book is a pursuit of art as ruthless as the pursuit of experience, and intensity that shines."

Edward Hirsch teaches at the University of Houston. His first book, For The Sleepwalkers, *was published in 1981 with Knopf and reprinted in 1997 with Carnegie Mellon University Press. His newest collection,* The Lectures On Love, *is due from Knopf in 1998.*

"The Importance of Friends to Support Both Art and Commerce"

Marie Howe

Marie Howe's first book, *A Good Thief,* won the National Poetry series after being a finalist six times. She speaks of the great importance of a supportive network of friends—she had eight or nine—Tom Sleigh, Lucie Brock Broido, Stuart Dischell, among them. "We were all poets and part-time teachers in Cambridge," she says, so they used to call to remind each other of deadlines, as well as assist with the mailing of manuscripts when someone was too physically ill to follow through. "I'm a kind of tribal type, anyway," Ms Howe says while making her point about the importance of writing friends to support both art and commerce.

"There were legendary stories we knew of writers always being runners-up in contests and we used to know all of them—you know, Denis Johnson for example, thirteen times—and we would sit at cafe tables and repeat the eight names and numbers like mantras."

Ms. Howe has two things to share with writers approaching first-book publication. "The first thing that helped me was that I gave it to Tom Sleigh to read and he rearranged it from sections to an arc—didn't touch the poems, just the order—so that later I was sitting on the couch flipping through and sobbing because the book was suddenly revealed to me. I felt frightened and ashamed. Three places at once wanted it after that. I really think you go to the most exacting editor. It was like taking the cloth off the sculpture, undraping it, and I couldn't do it myself."

She laughs as she comes to the second helpful suggestion, as it eases the readers of manuscript competitions. She and Lucie Brock Broido decided to take the manuscripts out of the big black binders and go and have them made spiral bound. "It's such a pain to be eating and the pages flap closed in your lap. Spiral, you can open up and chew your sandwich at the same time."

Responding to the problem of a long wait to publication, Ms. Howe says that it really is better than publishing quickly. You keep writing more poems, changing that first book. "It's hard not to become attached, because it's like your union card," she says, but the farther away from it the better.

Her list of first books that "blew me away" are *Sweet Ruin*, by Tony Hoagland; *The Incognito Lounge*, by Denis Johnson, *Imaginary Timber*, by Jim Galvin, and *What A Kingdom It Was*, by Galway Kinnell. Galvin's book was important to her when she was first starting to write and Hoagland and Kinnell are "wholey, utterly original and necessary." She says that while always a fan of Kinnell's books, it was only last year that she got her hands on his first book and it riveted her. "I couldn't stop talking about it for four months. Everyone should read that as a book. It's deeply inspiring."

Marie Howe's most recent book is What the Living Do *(W. W. Norton, 1997). She teaches at Sarah Lawrence College.*

"First Book Is First World"

Liam Rector

"My advice would fundamentally be what the actor, director, and bon vivant, Orson Welles said in the old Gallo wine ads: No Wine Before It's Time. First book is First World. First book is first child," Mr. Rector states. "Wait, the first book is and remains first-borne. It should be more than a mere collection and more than an assemblage of greatest hits. First books should have found and executed their voice, their voices, amidst the inevitable historical boarding house exorcising of influences and homage."

But he warns the writer not to be, as he puts it, an ungrateful mutt. "A first book should have its own arc. Writers rightly have sentimentia about their first book, as one lives one's whole life with it—there staring, there voicing. Writers who denounce their first books as juvenilia came too quickly, and should be shot. Don't let this happen to you, lest you dwell in juvenilia as a Big Baby Sibling, an *idée fixe* forever," he says, emphasizing anew, "First Book is First World."

Mr. Rector's first collection of poetry, *The Sorrow of Architecture*, had a troubling start. He sent it to about fifteen presses and it was accepted early on by a press that went under before it could publish the book. He started again. "When I received a letter to acceptance from Dragon Gate Press, an ambiguous letter which I didn't take to be an acceptance, I found out the book was also being considered as a finalist at Knopf. Knopf balked, and I went with Dragon Gate, a fine literary press by poet Gwen Head, run out of Port Townsend, Washington. *The Sorrow of Architecture* was beautifully designed by Scott Walker. I got my say on the cover photograph and the type size, and I was and remain happy with *The Sorrow of Architecture* as First World."

The poet and director of Bennington Writer's Workshop, Liam Rector offers a partial list of thirty favorite books. *Prufrock*, by T. S. Eliot, *Howl*, by Allen Ginsberg, and *Open House*, by Theodore Roethke head the list. The first books of Donald Justice, Hedy Lamarr, Robinson Jeffers, Robert McDowell, Lucie Brock-Broido, Linda Gregg, Mark Strand, David Huddle, and Ai also appear on this varied list.

Liam Rector's most recent book is American Prodigal *(Story Line Press). He is the founder and Director of the Writing Seminars at Bennington College.*

"Literary Magazines Are the Lifeblood"

Scott Russell Sanders

Although his very first book was about D. H. Lawrence and came from his doctoral dissertation, it is "really an anomaly because it's the only criticism book I've written out of eighteen." His start as a writer came with the publication in 1983 by William Morrow of Wilderness Plots, a collection of short stories that arose out of research he was doing for a novel. The novel was eventually published, but the collection came together first. "They were like outtakes on a film," Dr. Sanders says. I had finished four unpublished books of fiction and after Wilderness Plots was published, the other three followed." The first helped him break loose and consider the possibility of publishing the others.

A few nonfiction pieces had been published before Dr. Sanders entered Paradise Bombs in the AWP Award for Creative Nonfiction. Because the submission is anonymous, his past publications were not of importance. "On the other hand, Wilderness Plots made it easier to get my other fiction published," including the novel it had interrupted. "Winning the AWP Award was very important in the sense that this new kind of writing that I had started in the last couple of years might be worth pursuing," he says. "The world took small notice of it. The essays reinforced one another and created a whole book." The AWP Award helped attract attention from magazine editors for more essays.

In offering advice to writers concerning the publication of their first books, Dr. Sanders recognizes two major paths. The first is contests, "which are fruitful if you win and does not require your having published anything beforehand." The second path is traditional. "I believe literary magazines are the lifeblood and the best writers get their training by publishing in them and by gradually building a body of work. It's a worthy and viable way to publish that first book.

"The mistake is to put all your energy into getting that first book published," he says. "And the writer may be right in believing that it is utterly worthy. But even if you have no luck in getting it published, if you believe deeply enough in yourself to keep on writing that second and third and fourth book, you will grow as a writer." Instead of the book, "believe in your talent."

Scott Russell Sanders, names Henry David Thoreau's *A Week on the Concord and Merrimack Rivers* and Walt Whitman's first poetry book *Leaves of Grass* as his favorite first books.

Scott Russell Sanders is Distinguished Professor of English at Indiana University. His first collection of stories, Wilderness Plots, *was published by William Morrow and his first collection of essays,* The Paradise of Bombs, *won the AWP Award in Creative Nonfiction, and his latest book,* Writing From the Center, *won the 1996 Great Lakes Book Award.*

9

FAVORITE FIRST BOOKS
OF WRITERS: A LISTING

Writers	First Books
Cathryn Alpert	*Girl Interrupted*, Susanna Kaysen; *Reeling and Writhing*, Candida Lawrence; *The Other America*, Michael Harrington
Andrea Barrett	*Housekeeping*, Marilyn Robinson; *Learning by Heart*, Margot Livesey; *The Voyage Out*, Virginia Woolf; *Tales of the Fire*, Kim Edward
Douglas Bauer	*Principles of American Nuclear Chemistry: A Novel*, Thomas McMahon; *A Bigamist's Daughter*, Alice McDermott; *Housekeeping*, Marilyn Robinson
Sven Birkerts	*Buddenbrookf*, Thomas Mann; *V*, Thomas Pynchon; *The Leopard*, Lampedusa
Sophie Cabot Black	*Sleeping With One Eye Open*, Mark Strand; *The Lost Pilot*, James Tate; *Colossus*, Sylvia Plath; *Too Bright to See*, Linda Gregg; *Death of a Naturalist*, Seamus Heaney
Laurel Blossom	*Dance Script With Electric Ballerina*, Alice Fulton; *The Ocean Inside Kenyi Takezo*; Rick Noguchi, *Out of Canaan*; Mary Stuart Hammond,
T. C. Boyle	*V.*, Thomas Pynchon; *The Collector*, John Fowles; *Love Medicine* (fiction), Louise Erdrich
Melanie Braverman	*Beginning with O*, Olga Brumas; *Maps to Any where*, Bernard Cooper; *The Virgin Suicides*, Jeffrey Eugendeis
Nick Carbó	*White Elephants*, Reetika Vazrani; *Likely*, Lisa Coffman; *Ismalia Eclipse*, Khaled Mattawa

Writers	First Books
Ron Carlson	*This Side of Paradise*, F. Scott Fitzgerald
Susan Cheever	Genesis; *War & Peace*, Tolstoy
Steven Cramer	*Lyrical Ballads*, William Wordsworth & Samuel Taylor Coleridge; *Some Trees*, John Ashbery; *Silence in the Snowy Fields*, Robert Bly; *Stop-Time*, Frank Conroy
Eric Darton	*Two Little Trains*, Margaret Wise Brown; *A Boy's Will*, Robert Frost; *In Our Time*, Ernest Hemingway; *Counter-Statement*, Kenneth Burke
Toi Derricotte	*A Street in Bronzeville*, Gwendolyn Brooks; *Howl*, Allen Ginsberg; *Colossus*, Sylvia Plath
Mark Doty	*Autobiography of a Face*, Lucy Grealy; *Refuge*, Terry Tempest Williams
Susan Dowd	*Here We Are In Paradise*, Tony Earley; *In The Garden of the North American Martyrs*, Tobias Wolff; *Same Place, Same Things*, Tim Gautreaux
Stephen Dunn	*Harmonium*, Wallace Stevens; *The Lost Pilot*, James Tate; *Heart's Needle*, W. D. Snodgrass
Thomas Sayers Ellis	*Death of a Naturalist*, Seamus Heaney; *Annotations*, John Keene; *Invisible Man*, Ralph Ellison
Elaine Equi	*The Anxiety of Influence*, Harold Bloom
Carolyn Forche	*Disfortune*, Joe Wenderoth; *The Tulip Sacrament*, Annah Sobelman; *Candy Necklace*, Calvin Bendient; *Cities of Memory*, Ellen Hinsey; *New Intimacy*, Barbara Cully; *The Little Door*, Jeff Clark
Lynn Freed	*Lost in Translation*, Eva Hoffman; *My Old Sweetheart*, Susana Moore
John Haines	*The Sleepwalkers*, Herman Broch

Writers	First Books
Shelby Hearon	*Mysteries of Pittsburgh*, Michael Chabon; *The Movie Goer*, Walker Percy
Amy Hempel	*Edisto*, Padgett Powell; *The Ice at the Bottom of the World*, Mark Richard
Robert Hershon	*Delores: The Alpine Years*, Pansy Maurer-Alvarez; *The Business of Fancy Dancing*, Sherman Aletie; *The Very Stuff*, Stephen Beal; *Air Pocket*, Kimiko Hahns
Edward Hirsch	*White Buildings*, Hart Crane; *Harmonium*, Wallace Stevens
Jane Hirshfield	*Views of Jeopardy*, Jack Gilbert; *North and South*, Elizabeth Bishop; *Leaves of Grass*, Walt Whitman
Tony Hoagland	*Airships*, Barry Hannah; *Keeping Still Mountain*, John Engel; *Incognito Lounge*, Denis Johnson
Marie Howe	*Incognito Lounge*, Denis Johnson; *Sweet Ruin*, Tony Hoagland; *Imaginary Timber*, Jim Galvin; *What A Kingdom It Was*, Galway Kinnell
David Lehman	*Meditations in An Emergency*, Frank O'Hara; *Some Trees*, John Ashbery; *Harmonium*, Wallace Stevens; *Ommateum*, A. R. Ammons; *Lucky Jim*, Kingsley Amis; *Ko, or A Season On Earth*, Kenneth Koch
Philip Levine	*Leaves of Grass*, Walt Whitman; *Harmonium*, Wallace Stevens
Carole Maso	*At The Bottom of The River*, Jamaica Kincaid; *The River*, Jayne Anne Philips
Allison Mattison	*Golden State*, Frank Bidart
Richard McCann	*After Leaving*, Jane Rhyes; *The Body and His Dangers*, Alan Barnet; *Tell Me a Riddle*, Tillie Olsen

Writers	First Books
Jill McCorkle	*The Heart is a Lonely Hunter,* Carson McCullers
Robert McDowell	*A Boy's Will,* Robert Frost; *Californians,* Robinson Jeffers; *The Sorrow of Architecture,* Liam Rector
N. Scott Momaday	*Blue Highways,* William Least Heat Moon
Carol Muske	*Letters from a Stranger,* Thomas James; *A Change of World,* Adrienne Rich; *Cooking for John,* Jon Anderson; *Presentation Piece,* Marilyn Hacker; *Winter Morning with Crow,* Clare Rossini
Robert Pinsky	*Prufrock & Other Observations,* T. S. Eliot; *Poems,* William Carlos Williams; *In The Blood,* Carl Phillips; *Little Star,* Mark Halliday; *The Key to the City,* Anne Winters
C. L. Rawlins	*Jacklight* (poetry), Louise Erdrich; *In The Wilderness: Coming of Age,* Kim Barnes; *Pleasure of Believing,* Anastasia Hobbet
Liam Rector	*Prufrock & Other Observations,* T. S. Eliot; *Howl,* Allen Ginsberg; *Open House,* Theodore Roethke
Scott Russell Sanders	*A Week on the Concord and Merrimack Rivers,* Henry David Thoreau; *Leaves of Grass,* Walt Whitman
Gerald Stern	*Views of Jeopardy,* Jack Gilbert; *Poems,* Alan Dugan; *Vesper Sparrows,* Deborah Digges; *Catch 22,* Joseph Heller; *Too Bright to See,* Linda Gregg
David Trinidad	*Idols,* Dennis Cooper; *Howl,* Allen Ginsberg; *To Bedlam and Part Way Back,* Anne Sexton

PART 6

IN YOUR OWN HANDS:
MAKING YOUR FIRST BOOK A SUCCESS

INTRODUCTION

Ruth Greenstein

There comes a time for most writers when their work seems to be done: their first book is in the final stages of production, and they don't quite know what to do with themselves. Instead of feeling relieved, they anxiously imagine all the things that might be going on—or going wrong—with their book. At the publishing house, the editor steps back as the publicist comes to the fore. Where does the author fit in?

After all the hard work that goes into writing a good book and getting it published, writers who then sit back and leave the rest to their publishers are doing themselves a great disservice. The fact is that most first books don't receive a lot of promotional attention from their publishers. Terry McMillan discovered this early on, and decided to take matters into her own hands. She made her first book a success, and so can you. Here are just a few of the things you can do:

Know your publisher's game plan

Find out as much as you can about your publisher's plans for your book. How many copies are they printing? How many do they hope to sell? Are they producing bound galleys? Do they have a budget for advertisements or a book tour? If not, negotiate. Are they willing to help you make arrangements and to split the expenses with you? Are you willing to cover certain expenses yourself?

Start early

Well before your book is published, you should develop an action plan and timetable for promoting it. (See the Promotional Action Plan Worksheet included in this section.) Set aside some money for your promotional activities. Will you need to hire someone to type mailing lists? Do you want to have postcards printed up, or to hire an outside publicist?

Prepare your pitch

How can you make your book stand out from the crowd? Is there an unusual story behind the writing of it? Is it topically related to a current events story? Is there something relevant in your own life story that may spark peoples' attention?

Summon your forces

What writers do you know or admire who might be willing to comment on your book? Do you have any media contacts who may be willing to help get the word out? Look at your resume—what schools and organizations have you been affiliated with that may help support your debut publishing "event"? What special interest groups might be interested in buying your book? Have you armed your publisher with this information?

Start locally

Talk to your local booksellers and librarians, and to organizations that sponsor literary events or that may be interested in you and your book. Let them know when your book is coming out. Find out if they'd like to host a reading, a talk, or a book party.

Work with your publisher

Publishers are only too happy to have authors who are eager to promote themselves and their work. But when authors go off on their own without first speaking with their publicist, they may find themselves duplicating efforts, working at cross-purposes, and stepping on some very sensitive toes. Be smart: meet with your publicist, and be sure to keep him or her continually apprised of your efforts.

What You've Heard Is True

◆

It Pays to Invest

I cannot emphasize enough the importance of your investing in your work. Carole Maso recently purchased a full-page advertisement for her book *Aureole* in the *American Poetry Review*. Maso has an established reputation as a fiction writer, but with this book, she wanted to get the word out to poetry readers as well. And she wanted to do more for the book than her publisher was doing. Like many writers, Maso believes that her financial contributions toward promoting her work are a good investment—no different than an investment in a house or a car.

–J. S.

Work with your agent

If you have an agent, use her or him! An agent's role is to represent your interests throughout the publishing process, not just when the book deal is being signed. Is your agent aware of and satisfied with the publication plans for your book? Who do they know who can help promote your work? If you have a new project in the works, when do they want to pitch it to the publisher?

Be mindful of timing

In today's book business, the unfortunate marketplace reality is that most booksellers will only keep hardcover books in stock for a few short months. Be mindful of this brief window of opportunity, and work aggressively with your publisher to keep you book alive throughout it. Then look ahead for ways of giving your book new life, such as submitting it for awards, printing a paperback edition, setting up additional public appearances, etc.

Final perspectives

Remember that regardless of how many copies your first book ultimately sells, it will move you ahead considerably in your craft. And when your second book comes out, you will have a new opportunity to sell your first book again.

Promotional Action Plan Worksheet

Jason Shinder

Here is an outline of critical questions to ask your publisher as you assume responsibility for helping to promote your book and to maximize its readership and sales. As soon as a publisher has agreed to publish your book, you can begin collecting some of this information. In most cases, a promotional action plan should be in place six months before your book is scheduled to be published.

Catalogs

- Who is writing the catalog copy? What aspects of the book are they highlighting, and why?

- What is the deadline for catalog copy? Can I review the copy before the deadline?

- How much catalog space will my book receive? Will it include a photo of the cover? A photo of me?

- Will the copy include information about promotional plans, special sales offers, public events?

- When is the catalog being sent out and to whom?

- Can copies be sent to people on my mailing list?

- How many copies can I receive?

Cover Art and Copy

- Who is creating the cover art? Who is designing the cover? What aspects of the book are they highlighting, and why?

- What is the deadline for the final design?

- Will the cover be black-and-white, two-color, or four-color?

- Can I speak with the artist and/or designer?

- Can I review the cover before the deadline?

- Who is writing the cover copy?

- What is the deadline for the copy?

- Can I review the copy before the deadline?

Sales Meetings

- When will the book be introduced to the sales force and/or distributors? (Initial sales meetings are usually scheduled a season before the book is being published.)

- How will it be introduced? What will be the focus?

- Can I help out by speaking at a sales meeting or by securing advance comments on the book?

Special Sales

- What organizations might be interested in purchasing a quantity of books at a discount? (For instance, a book about the movies may be of interest at video stores and movie houses. A memoir about a swimmer may be of interest at health clubs and sporting goods stores.)

- Who will approach these organizations? When? How?

- Will a special sales package be developed?

Publicist

- Is a publicist being assigned to my book? When?

- Has the publicist read my book yet? Has he or she worked on similar books before?

- Can I meet with the publicist and review the promotional action plan? (If you are able to, consider hiring your own publicist. An independent publicist should be hired for a minimum of three months, beginning one month prior to publication. Be sure you and your publicist develop very specific objectives and strategies for achieving those objectives. Be sure you and your publicist work closely with your publisher. In some cases, hiring a publicist may help you leverage additional promotional support for your publisher. You may want to hire a publicist only under the condition that your publisher will then contribute to your promotional efforts.)

Blurbs

- Is the publisher soliciting blurbs for the book? When? From whom? (Most authors need at least two months to write a blurb. Give your publisher a list of people you think might comment on your book, and help contact those people you know.)

- What aspects of the book are they hoping the blurbs will address?

- What kinds of people are they approaching? Nationally celebrated writers? Regionally popular writers? Writers or experts associated with a specific subject or style?

Bound Galleys

- Are bound galleys being produced? When will they be ready?

- Will the galleys show the cover art? Will they include blurbs?

- How many copies are being printed? To whom are they being sent?

- Can copies be sent to people on my mailing list? (Develop a concise mailing list of key authors, book reviewers, and editors, especially those with whom you have some connection.)

- Will follow-up calls be made after the mailing?

- How many copies of the bound galleys can I receive?

Publication

- What is the bound book date? What is the official publication date? When will books arrive in stores? Are these dates firm, or is there a chance they will slip? Why?

- How many copies are being printed? If the publisher is printing hardcovers and paperbacks simultaneously, how many are being printed of each?

Sales

- How many copies has the book advanced (orders for the book placed prior to publication)?

- How many copies does the book need to sell to break even? By when?

- What will the book be priced at? (If the price of the book seems unusually high or low, ask the publisher to explain how they arrived at this price.)

Press Release

- Who is writing the press release?

- When is it being sent out? To whom?

- Can I review the copy before it is sent out?

- Will the release include blurbs? Cover art? An author photo?

- Are any special markets being targeted for the mailing?

- Will follow-up calls be made after the mailing?

- Will there be a special sales press release—one that offers a discount and includes an order form?

- Can I provide a mailing list?

- How many copies of the press release can I receive?

Press Kit

- Is a press kit being produced? When?

- What will the press kit include? (Press release, copy of book, author photo, special appeal letter?)

- Who will the press kits be sent to?

- Can I review the press kit before it is sent out?

Advertisements

- Will my book be advertised? Alone or with other books?

- When and where will the ads appear? How many ads will there be?

- Can I review the ads before they are finalized?

- If the publisher does not have a budget for ads, are they willing to split the costs with me? If I pay for running an ad, will the publisher design it for me? (Some small magazines will run book ads for free in exchange for offering the books at a special discount to its members or subscribers. Many magazines offer special ad rates to writers who are purchasing ad space for their own books.)

Postcards/Posters/Bookmarks

- Will the publisher be printing any promotional items to announce the book? When?

- How many are being printed and to whom will they be mailed?

- Can I review the items before they are printed?

- Will the items include blurbs? Cover art? Dates of upcoming events?

- If the publisher does not have a budget for promotional items, are they willing to split the costs with me?

Book Party

- Will the publisher be sponsoring a party for my book? When?

- Who will be invited? When will the invitations be mailed?

- If the publisher does not have a budget for a book party, are they willing to split the costs with me?

Readings

- Will the publisher be arranging readings for my book? When? Where?

- Will I be reading alone or with other writers? Who?

- How will the publisher promote these readings?

- If I hire an outside events coordinator to arrange readings, will the publisher contribute to his or her fee? Will they promote the readings?

- If I arrange readings on my own, will the publisher cover my travel expenses? Will they promote the readings?

- Has the publisher confirmed that books will be available for sale at every reading?

Publicizing Your Novel

Terry McMillan

Right after I learned that my publisher, Houghton Mifflin, wasn't going to take ads in the *New York Times* (among other places) for my first novel *Mama*; that they weren't going to be able to send me on the twenty-city book tour I'd dreamed about; that my novel wouldn't form a pyramid in the (then) Scribner's window on Fifth Avenue in New York; that my chances of getting on *Good Morning America* and *The Oprah Winfrey Show* were slim to zero; and that the meager amount of money that had been allocated for publicity was too embarrassing to mention, I was disappointed and hurt, but more than anything, I felt I'd been misled by them. After all, hadn't my editor exclaimed his excitement over my book? And hadn't they sent me their booklet, "A Guide for Authors," telling me the various ways in which they would determine the most appropriate strategy for drawing attention to my book?

I found out that the most they were actually going to do was send out the standard media kit—a press release with my photo, a copy of the book, and any advance reviews—to reviewers and TV and radio producers. If they got a lead, they would follow it up with a phone call. More often than not, the people to whom they send the media kits already have a pile a mile high of just such kits, some of which never get opened, let alone read.

I learned quickly that this is standard operating procedure for most first novels, and even some second novels if the first one wasn't well received. Let me warn you now. Get used to hearing, "Don't expect much. This is just your literary debut." And get used to hearing, "Don't expect a review in the *New York Times Book Review* because chances are there won't be one. And if you get one, consider yourself lucky." And especially get used to hearing: "We can't. We wish we could, but we can't."

I had worked hard on my novel and I wanted as many people as possible to know that it existed. I'd heard too many horror stories about first novels never being reviewed, never being available in bookstores. Most terrifying to me of all was the thought of being remaindered, reviewers panning my novel and thus, never selling enough copies of my book to see a royalty check. I didn't want to be one of those writers, and I also didn't want to spend another year as a freelance word processor for a law firm in Manhattan.

I didn't need long to realize that *my* publisher wasn't the only guilty one. Other friends whose first novels had also been accepted said, "My publisher's doing absolutely nothing to promote my book" and "My galleys were late and if I don't hear from the authors I've asked for blurbs in the next two weeks, the back of my book will be blank!" The question that came to my mind over and over was, How can you expect to sell a product if no one's ever heard of it?

If you happen to be one of the lucky ones and have published poetry or stories in all the right places, or established yourself writing nonfiction, or are "well-connected" (i.e. you know everybody who is anybody in the literary world), you might not have to be concerned about the attention your book is likely to get from your publisher. But if you're like me, and hundreds of other first novelists, who have few if any other publications to their credit and don't know anyone who may give them that fantastic blurb (three days before my deadline, of the eighteen authors to whom I'd written, I received one blurb from Grace Paley, whom I'd never met), then you'll do well to do what I did: take matters into your own hands.

In July 1986 I found out just how little was going to be done to promote my book. My publication date was January 15, 1987. I had all kinds of books about all facets of writing, so I searched through them until I found one that dealt with promoting and publicizing books. Entitled *How to Get Happily Published*, it proved to be invaluable. A chapter called "Why and How to Be Your Own Best Sales Force" explained in detail the steps authors can take to drum up excitement, interest, and an audience for their books without feeling the least embarrassed. The book suggests that authors need not be intimidated by their publishers and that the best way to get them excited about your book is to "nag" them.

Let me say this now. If you have access to a computer, it'll make everything that much simpler, cheaper, and easier. Because I was a freelance word processor, I had access to one, but if you don't, there are many inexpensive word-processing services that can facilitate printing letters from multiple mailing lists. Your promotion and publicity campaign will be time-consuming, so if you're not willing to sacrifice a few hours a day and some of your weekends, forget this notion. What will help is if you know an eager teenager, child, or lover who will help seal envelopes and even sign letters for you— or at least someone who'll do it for minimum wage! Most of my time was spent at the library, photocopying mailing lists, typing them into the computer, and merging the names to the letters I had written. (More about the letters follows.) How extensive your campaign becomes will determine how much time and money you'll spend. I sent out over 4,000 letters over a six-month period, and spent over $700. Most independent book publicists charge $3,000, and they basically end up doing the same thing you can do yourself.

The first thing I did was to tell my publicist (you will automatically be assigned a publicist by your publisher) that I was going to do everything I could to help promote my book, and that I would keep her apprised of my actions. She was delighted to hear this, as most publicists are, because it takes some of the burden of guilt off of them. So, during a heat wave in July, while all my friends were out sunbathing at the beach, I spent a week answering the questionnaire that all publishers send authors. *Take time to answer it*, because this may be the only opportunity you'll have to provide the publicity department with information that can help them zero in on your target audience. The more mailing lists and names of people you can give them, the less work you'll have to do in the long run. Included with the questionnaire will most likely be mailing labels on which the publishers asks you to provide names of people who you would like notified once your book is published. Not only did I go through my phone book, but also I picked names of authors, those I'd heard of and respected, from a listing in *A Directory of American Poets and Fiction Writers*. So what if E. L. Doctorow and Ann Beattie had never heard of me? By the time my book came out, they would.

Publishers periodically hold conferences with their sales representatives (the men and women who take your book around to the bookstores and try to get orders for it), at which they give a short synopsis of each of the books on the list for the upcoming season. You hope that the sales reps have read your book, that they like it and are excited about it, but you have no guarantee of this. Lots of times they haven't read it, even though at this meeting, they'll sit and listen to how the publisher wants to market each book. Editors never tell you all the details of this meeting, but if you can get on the good side of the sales reps, your book will benefit. I got all their names and addresses (they live all over the United States because they work by regions), and I sent them all notes (on note cards), telling them that I hoped they liked my book and were excited by it. I also told them how much I appreciated their efforts to secure a home in as many bookstores as possible for *Mama*. Although I never received any written responses, I was told by my editor and the publicity director how much the sales reps all appreciated my note.

I made up lists of my target audience. Because I'm black and a woman, I had to target groups right there. I spent much time in the library getting lists of all the black organizations in the United States. I also got a list of over 500 women's studies programs and a list of all black newspapers, magazines, and radio and TV programs. I knew I wanted all the black colleges and Afro-American studies programs to know about my novel, so I got listings of them too.

Since I had no guarantee that the sales reps would be enthusiastic about my book, I decided to write bookstores myself. Unenthusiastic sales reps can sometimes cause book buyers not to order your book, or encourage them to "wait and see." This usually mean they'll wait to see what the prepublication reviewers, *Publishers Weekly, Kirkus Reviews, Library Journal, and Booklist,* have to say about your book before consulting the *American Book Trade Directory (ABTD)*, which lists 25,500 bookstores, wholesalers, distributors, and bookstore chains (including the names of the buyers), alphabetically by state and city. I'm from Michigan, so I made a special effort to write down as many of the bookstores there as possible. Why? Because it's likely that the bulk of your initial sales will take place in the area you're from. Most of the bookstores are listed as "general," "antiquarian," "women's," "Afro-American," etc., so that's how I came up with many of the stores to which I later wrote. After I spent at least a hundred dimes photocopying these pages, I picked cities I knew had large populations of blacks. *Poets & Writers* also publishes a book entitled *Literary Bookstores: A Cross-Country Guide*, from which I made another list. (Some of them were in *ABTD*, but many of them weren't.) In total, I wrote letters to 1,010 bookstores.

If you belong to any organizations or have friends or relatives that do, try to get mailing lists from them. My sister worked at the Ford Motor Company, and she told her supervisor about my novel, and in their Christmas newsletter was a half-page article about *Mama*. That newsletter reached over 2,500 people. If your book is about dogs, think of any and all organizations that deal with dogs. In your publisher's questionnaire you can provide the names of your local newspapers, TV and radio programs, auxiliary groups, churches, and especially your old high school and/or college. Both Detroit newspapers, as well as that city's slick monthly magazine, carried reviews and articles about me. My hometown newspaper actually had a full-color spread! The local bookstore couldn't keep *Mama* in stock.

The college audience is a big market, so I went to the back of *Webster's Dictionary*, checked off 260 colleges and universities, and plugged them into my computer. At these institutions, as well as at the black colleges, I included "variables" in my computer so I could write to different people at the same school. I wrote to the trade book buyer of the campus bookstore and also to the acquisitions librarian. Each person to whom I wrote was in charge of ordering books.

I know how valuable readings can be, and I wanted as many as I could get before and around my publication date. Most places that have a regular reading series, planned at least six months to a year in advance. I had time. I made a list of all local places that had regularly scheduled readings. I used the New York City Poetry Calendar and *Author & Audience: A Readings and Workshops Guide*, which is published by Poets & Writers, Inc. This book lists universities and other places—by state and city—that have reading series, and it usually tells the honorarium. I ended up with a list of over 200 places, to which, over a two-month period, I sent out the first twenty-five pages of my novel (by this time my book was in galley form). I ended up with over forty readings. Each time I got an invitation, I sent my publicist an updated itinerary so that she would have plenty of time to try to get press coverage before I arrived (she had agreed to do this when I told her I would get as many readings as I could). Some places already had their series planned, but others said they would keep me in mind for a future date.

Exactly what kind of letters did I write? Simple. The first paragraph told the name of my novel and who was publishing it in the United

States and elsewhere. The second paragraph told why I was writing them; in hopes that they would consider ordering my book or adding it to their library, consider me for a reading or a lecture, consider using my book as a text in their class, or whatever. In this same paragraph I told them why I was writing to them directly, because as a new novelist I was afraid my novel might not be widely distributed and I wanted them to know that I was doing all that I could to help generate an audience. (I received lots of letters from bookstores, thanking me for writing. Some even said how refreshing it was to receive a personal letter from the author, and in some cases, I was invited to bookstores for readings and autographings.) The third paragraph was my own synopsis of my book. In the fourth paragraph I thanked them for their time, interest, and consideration.

Because I had been living in Brooklyn, New York, for six years, I picked up copies of all the neighborhood throwaways (newspaper) and wrote them (at least three of which reviewed the book and interviewed me); I wrote the "People" page of the *Daily News* and got my picture in the Brooklyn section. Around my publication date, my three-year-old son and I spent days gallivanting around Brooklyn and Manhattan to bookstores to see if they had *Mama* on their shelves. The shocker was that most of them did, and when I told them I was the author all of them asked me to autograph the books!

To whom didn't I write? I didn't write to public librarians because the list was too massive, and I didn't know where to begin. I assumed libraries had their own method for ordering books. I did not write to a single reviewer, because I was told it was a waste of time. You can't *force* a reviewer to read your book, but you might want to write them if you know them personally.

So after doing all this, exactly what happened? The day before my publication date, I had sold out of my first printing. Six weeks later my book was in its third printing. I was a guest on seven television shows and six radio shows (some nationally syndicated), and was interviewed in approximately fourteen newspapers. *Mama* has been reviewed in more than thirty periodicals. I'm not sure how much, if any, of this good fortune has been due to all my efforts, but my editor and the publicity department seem to think they truly helped. All I know is if I hadn't done it, what would I have to compare it to? It was hard work, but it was worth every penny and every minute I spent. See for yourself.

10

AWARDS FOR PUBLISHED FIRST BOOKS

Editor's note: In some listings, category or deadline information was unavailable and/or under review by the sponsoring organization. Yet all the awards are active. As always, queries should be sent to the mailing addresses provided before applying for any award or fellowship.

ACADEMY OF AMERICAN POETS

Award: Harold Morton Translation Award

*P

Prize: $1,000

Category: Poetry

Open to: U.S. citizens

Deadline: 12/31

Mail to: Academy of American Poets, 584 Broadway, Suite 1208, New York, NY 10012

Award: Lenore Marshall Poetry Prize

*P

Prize: $10,000

Category: Poetry

Open to: No restrictions

Deadline: 6/1

Mail to: Academy of American Poets, 584 Broadway, Suite 1208, New York, NY 10012

Award: Raiziss/de Palchi Translation Award

*P

Prize: $5,000 and $20,000 fellowship

Category: Poetry

Open to: U.S. citizens

Deadline: 11/1

Mail to: Academy of American Poets, 584 Broadway, Suite 1208, New York, NY 10012

AMERICAN ACADEMY OF ARTS & LETTERS

Award: Harold D. Vursell Memorial Award

*F

Prize: $5,000

Category: Fiction

Open to: By nomination only (awards announced in Spring)

Mail to: American Academy of Arts & Letters, 633 West 155th Street, New York, NY 10032

Award: Richard and Hilda Rosenthal Foundation Award

*F

Prize: $5,000

Category: Fiction

Open to: By nomination only (awards announced in Spring)

Mail to: American Academy of Arts & Letters, 633 West 155th Street, New York, NY 10032

Award: Sue Kaufman Prize for First Fiction

*F

Prize: $2,500

Category: Fiction

Open to: By nomination only (awards announced in Spring)

Mail to: American Academy of Arts & Letters, 633 West 155th Street, New York, NY 10032

AMERICAN HISTORICAL ASSOCIATION

Award: Albert B. Corey Prize

*NF

Prize: $500–$1,000

Category: History

Open to: No restrictions

Deadline: 5/15

Mail to: American Historical Association, 400 A Street, SE, Washington, DC, 20003

Award: Albert J. Beveridge Award

*NF

Prize: $500–$1,000

Category: History

Open to: Any book that employs new methodological or conceptual tools or that constitute significant reexaminations of important interpretive problems. Translations, anthologies, and collections of documents are not eligible.

Deadline: 5/15

Mail to: American Historical Association, 400 A Street, SE, Washington, DC, 20003

Award: George Louis Beer Prize

*NF

Prize: $500–$1,000

Category: History

Open to: Only books of a high scholarly historical nature should be submitted. Books submitted must be published between May 1, 1996 and April 30, 1997. Author must be a citizen or permanent resident of the United States or Canada.

Deadline: 5/15

Mail to: American Historical Association, 400 A Street, SE, Washington, DC, 20003

Award: Helen and Howard R. Marraro Prize in Italian History

*NF

Prize: $500–$1,000

Category: History

Open to: Any book or article published between May 1, 1996 and April 30, 1997, which treats Italian history in any epoch, Italian cultural history, or Italian-American relations.

Deadline: 5/15

Mail to: American Historical Association, 400 A Street, SE, Washington, DC, 20003

Award: Herbert Baxter Adams Prize

*NF

Prize: $500–$1,000

Category: History

Open to: Must be the author's first substantial book. Textbooks, pamphlets, anthologies, and edited works do not qualify. Author must be a citizen or permanent resident of the United States or Canada.

Deadline: 5/15

Mail to: American Historical Association, 400 A Street, SE, Washington, DC, 20003

Award: Herbert Feis Award

*NF

Prize: $500–$1,000

Category: History

Open to: Entry must be of high scholarly and literary merit. Eligibility extends to individuals outside academe for a minimum of three years prior to the award year.

Deadline: 5/15

Mail to: American Historical Association, 400 A Street, SE, Washington, DC, 20003

Award: James Henry Breasted Prize

*NF

Prize: $500–$1,000

Category: History

Open to: Only works of high scholarly and literary merit will be considered. Entries must have been published between May 1, 1993 and April 30, 1997.

Deadline: 5/15

Mail to: American Historical Association, 400 A Street, SE, Washington, DC, 20003

Award: Joan Kelly Memorial Prize in Women's History

*NF

Prize: $500–$1,000

Category: History

Open to: Must be books in any chronological period, any geographical location, or in any area of feminist theory that incorporates an historical perspective. Books must be published between May 1,1996 and April 30, 1997.

Deadline: 5/15

Mail to: American Historical Association, 400 A Street, SE, Washington, DC, 20003

Award: John H. Dunning Prize

*NF

Prize: $500–$1,000

Category: History

Open to: Must be of a high scholarly historical nature. It must be the author's first or second book published or completed after May 1, 1995 and before April 30, 1997.

Deadline: 5/15

Mail to: American Historical Association, 400 A Street, SE, Washington, DC, 20003

Award: John K. Fairbank Prize

*NF

Prize: $500–$1,000

Category: History

Open to: Must be of high scholarly and literary merit, and published after May 1, 1996 and before April 30, 1997. Anthologies, edited works, and pamphlets are not eligible.

Deadline: 5/15

Mail to: American Historical Association, 400 A Street, SE , Washington, DC, 20003

Award: Leo Gershoy Award

*NF

Prize: $500–$1,000

Category: History

Open to: Entries must be books published between May 1, 1996 and April 30, 1997, in English on any aspect of the fields of seventeenth- and eighteenth-century western European history.

Deadline: 5/15

Mail to: American Historical Association, 400 A Street, SE, Washington, DC, 20003

Award: Littleton-Griswold Prize

*NF

Prize: $500–$1,000

Category: History

Open to: Must be books published between May 1, 1996 and April 30, 1997.

Deadline: 5/15

Mail to: American Historical Association, 400 A Street, SE, Washington, DC, 20003

Award: Morris D. Forkosch Prize

*NF

Prize: $500–$1,000

Category: History

Open to: Must be of high scholarly and literary merit, and published in the field of between May 1, 1995 and before April 30, 1997.

Deadline: 5/15

Mail to: American Historical Association, 400 A Street, SE, Washington, DC, 20003

Award: Wesley-Logan Prize in African Diaspora History

*NF

Prize: $500–$1,000

Category: History

Open to: Must be books published between May 1, 1996 and April 30, 1997, on some aspect of the history of the dispersion, settlement, and adjustment, and/or return of peoples originally from Africa.

Deadline: 5/15

Mail to: American Historical Association, 400 A Street, SE, Washington, DC, 20003

Association for Library Services, American Library Association

Award: John Newbery Medal

*C

Prize: Medal

Category: Children's Literature

Open to: U.S. citizens

Deadline: 12/31

Mail to: Association for Library Services, American Library Association, 50 East Huron Street, Chicago, IL 60611

Austin Community College

Award: Balcones Poetry Prize

*P

Prize: $1,000

Category: Poetry

Open to: No restrictions

Deadline: 12/1

Mail to: Austin Community College, Northridge Campus, 11928 Stone-hollow Drive, Austin, TX 78758

Austin Writer's League

Award: Violet Crown Book Awards

*F/NF/P

Prize: $1,000 and trophy

Category: Fiction, Nonfiction, and Poetry

Open to: Members of the Austin Writer's League

Deadline: 8/31 (deadline may be extended in 1998)

Mail to: Austin Writer's League, 1501 West 5th Street, Austin, TX 78703

BEREA COLLEGE

Award: W. D. Weatherford Award

*F/NF

Prize: $500

Category: Fiction and Nonfiction

Open to: No restrictions

Deadline: 12/31

Mail to: Berea College, CPO 2336, Berea, KY 40404

THE BERKSHIRE CONFERENCE OF WOMEN HISTORIANS

Award: Publications Award

*NF

Prize: $1,000

Category: History

Open to: American writers

Deadline: 1/15

Mail to: The Berkshire Conference of Women Historians, M.A. and Liberal Studies Program Ramapo College, 404 Ramao Valley Road, Mahwah, NJ 07430

BOSTON GLOBE

Award: L. L. Winship/PEN New England Award

*NF

Prize: $2,000

Category: Nonfiction

Open to: No restrictions

Deadline: 1/1

Mail to: Boston Globe, P.O. Box 2378, Boston, MA 02107-2378

CALIFORNIA LIBRARY ASSOCIATION

Award: John and Patricia Beatty Award

---

*C

Prize: $500

Category: Children's Literature

Open to: No restrictions

Deadline: Subject to change

Mail to: California Library Association, 717 K Street, Suite 300, Sacramento, CA 95814

CHICAGO TRIBUNE

Award: Heartland Award

---

*F/NF

Prize: $5,000

Category: Fiction and Nonfiction

Open to: U.S. citizens

Deadline: 7/31

Mail to: Chicago Tribune, 435 North Michigan Avenue, Chicago, IL 60611

CLAREMONT GRADUATE SCHOOL

Award: Kate Tufts Discovery Award

---

*P

Prize: $500

Category: Poetry

Open to: U.S. citizens

Deadline: 12/15

Mail to: Claremont Graduate School, 160 East 10th Street, Claremont, CA 91711

Award: Kingsley Tufts Poetry Award

*P

Prize: $50,000

Category: Poetry

Open to: U.S. citizens

Deadline: 12/15

Mail to: Claremont Graduate School, 160 East 10th Street, Claremont, CA 91711

THE CLEVELAND FOUNDATION

Award: Anisfield-Wolf Book Awards for Scholarly or Fiction on Race or Human Relations

*NF/F

Prize: (2) $5,000

Category: Nonfiction and Fiction

Open to: No restrictions

Deadline: 1/31

Mail to: The Cleveland Foundation, Harvard University, 1430 Massachusetts Ave., Cambridge, MA 02138

COLUMBIA UNIVERSITY

Award: Bancroft Prizes

*NF

Prize: (2) $4,000

Category: History

Open to: No restrictions

Deadline: 11/1

Mail to: Columbia University, Bancroft Prize Committee, 202A Low Memorial Library, New York, NY 10027

COLUMBIA UNIVERSITY GRADUATE SCHOOL OF JOURNALISM

Award: Pulitzer Prizes

*F/J/D

Prize: (several) $3,000

Category: Fiction, Journalism, and Drama

Open to: inquire within.

Deadline: 11/1 fiction; 2/1 journalism; 3/1 drama

Mail to: Columbia University Graduate School of Journalism, Graduate School of Journalism, 2950 Broadway, New York, NY 10027

THE CONFERENCE ON LATIN AMERICAN HISTORY

Award: Herbert Eugene Bolton Memorial Prize

*NF

Prize: $500

Category: History

Open to: Unavailable or under review

Deadline: Unavailable or under review

Mail to: The Conference on Latin American History, Institute for Latin America, 508 Lowder Bldg., Auburn University, Auburn University, AL 36849-5258

THE CONTINUUM PUBLISHING GROUP

Award: Continuum Book Award

*F/NF

Prize: $10,000

Category: Fiction and Nonfiction

Open to: No restrictions

Deadline: 2/1 and 9/1 (may be discontinued in 1998)

Mail to: The Continuum Publishing Group, 370 Lexington Avenue, New York, NY 10017

FRIENDS OF AMERICAN WRITERS

Award: Young People's Literature Award

---

*C

Prize: (2) $800

Category: Children's Literature

Open to: Inquire within

Deadline: Inquire within

Mail to: Friends of American Writers, 15237 Redwood Lane, Libertyville, IL 60048

FRIENDS OF CHICAGO PUBLIC LIBRARY

Award: Carl Sandburg Literary Awards

---

*F/P

Prize: (4) $1,000

Category: Fiction and Poetry

Open to: Chicago residents

Deadline: 8/1

Mail to: Friends of Chicago Public Library, 400 South State Street, 10S-7, Chicago, IL 60605

GREAT LAKES COLLEGES ASSOCIATION

Award: New Writer Awards

*F/P

Prize: (2) $300 and reading

Category: Fiction and Poetry

Open to: No restrictions

Deadline: 2/28

Mail to: Great Lakes Colleges Association, 2929 Plymouth Road, Suite 207, Ann Arbor, MI 48105-3206

HADASSAH MAGAZINE

Award: Harold U. Ribalow Prize

*F

Prize: $1,000 and publication of either an excerpt or a review

Category: Jewish Fiction

Open to: No restrictions

Deadline: 4/1

Mail to: Hadassah Magazine, 50 West 58th Street, New York, NY 10019

HARIAN CREATIVE BOOKS

Award: Workshop Under the Sky Writing Award

*F

Prize: $500

Category: Fiction

Open to: No restrictions

Deadline: 9/1

Mail to: Harian Creative Books, 47 Hyde Blvd., Ballston Spa, NY 12020

HARVARD REVIEW

Award: August Kleinzahler Award

*P

Prize: $1,500 and reading

Category: Poetry

Open to: No restrictions

Deadline: Unavailable or under review

Mail to: Harvard Review, Poetry Room, Harvard College Library, Cambridge, MA 02138

THE HISTORIC NEW ORLEANS COLLECTION

Award: General L. Kemper Williams Prizes in Louisiana History

*NF

Prize: $500 and plaque

Category: History

Open to: No restrictions

Deadline: 2/1

Mail to: The Historic New Orleans Collection, 533 Royal Street, New Orleans, LA 70130-2179

JEWISH BOOK COUNCIL

Award: National Jewish Book Awards

*F/NF

Prize: $750

Category: Fiction and Nonfiction

Open to: American authors of books on Jewish content

Deadline: 10/31

Mail to: Jewish Book Council, 15 East 26th Street, New York, NY 10010

LATIN AMERICAN WRITER'S INSTITUTE

Award: Latino Literature Prize

*F/P

Prize: (2) $1,000

Category: Fiction and Poetry

Open to: Latino writers living in the United States

Deadline: 2/28

Mail to: Latin American Writer's Institute, Hostos Community College, 500 Grand Concourse, Bronx, NY 10451

LITERARY ARTS—OREGON BOOK AWARDS

Award: H. L. Davis Award for Fiction

*F

Prize: $1,000

Category: Fiction

Open to: Oregon residents

Deadline: 3/31

Mail to: Literary Arts—Oregon Book Awards, 720 SW Washington, Suite 745, Portland, OR 97205

Award: Hazel Hall Award for Poetry

*P

Prize: $1,000

Category: Poetry

Open to: Oregon residents

Deadline: 3/31

Mail to: Literary Arts—Oregon Book Awards, 720 SW Washington, Suite 745, Portland, OR 97205

Award: Mary Jane Carr Award for
Young Reader's Literature

*C

Prize: $1,000

Category: Children's Literature

Open to: Oregon residents

Deadline: 3/31

Mail to: Literary Arts—Oregon Book Awards, 720 SW Washington, Suite 745, Portland, OR 97205

LOS ANGELES TIMES BOOK PRIZES

Award: Art Seidenbaum Award

*F

Prize: $1,000 and citation

Category: Fiction

Open to: By nomination only

Deadline: No deadline (by nomination only)

Mail to: Los Angeles Times Book Prizes, Times Mirror Square, Los Angeles, CA 90053

MEDIEVAL ACADEMY OF AMERICA

Award: John Nicholas Brown Prize

*NF

Prize: $500

Category: History

Open to: Writers who are residents of North America

Deadline: 11/1

Mail to: Medieval Academy of America, 1430 Massachusetts Avenue, Cambridge, MA 02138

The National Book Awards
Award: National Book Awards

---

*F/NF/P/C

Prize: (3) $10,000 and (some) $1,000 runners-up

Category: Fiction, Nonfiction, Poetry, and Children's

Open to: American authors

Deadline: 7/15

Mail to: The National Book Awards, National Book Foundation, 260 Fifth Ave., Room 904, New York, NY 10001

New Jersey Council for the Humanities
Award: New Jersey Council for the Humanities Book Award

---

*NF

Prize: $1,000

Category: Humanities

Open to: Writers from or living in the state of New Jersey

Deadline: 2/1

Mail to: New Jersey Council for the Humanities, 25 West State Street, 6th Floor, Trenton, NJ 08608-1602

Organization of American Historians
Award: Avery O'Craven Award

---

*NF

Prize: $500

Category: History

Open to: No restrictions

Deadline: 10/1

Mail to: Organization of American Historians, 112 North Bryan Street, Bloomington, IN 47408-4199

Award: Elliot Rudwick Prize

*NF

Prize: $2,000

Category: History

Open to: No restrictions

Deadline: 9/1

Mail to: Organization of American Historians, 112 North Bryan Street, Bloomington, IN 47408-4199

Award: Frederic Jackson Turner Award

*NF

Prize: $1,000

Category: History

Open to: No restrictions

Deadline: 9/1

Mail to: Organization of American Historians, 112 North Bryan Street, Bloomington, IN 47408-4199

Award: James A. Rawley Prize

*NF

Prize: $750

Category: History

Open to: No restrictions

Deadline: 10/1

Mail to: Organization of American Historians, 112 North Bryan Street, Bloomington, IN 47408-4199

Award: Merle Curti Award

*NF

Prize: $1,000

Category: History

Open to: No restrictions

Deadline: 10/1

Mail to: Organization of American Historians, 112 North Bryan Street, Bloomington, IN 47408-4199

Award: Ray Allen Billington Prize

*NF

Prize: $1,000

Category: History

Open to: No restrictions

Deadline: 10/1

Mail to: Organization of American Historians, 112 North Bryan Street, Bloomington, IN 47408-4199

PASSAIC COUNTY COMMUNITY COLLEGE

Award: Paterson Fiction Prize

*F

Prize: $500

Category: Fiction

Open to: No restrictions

Deadline: 4/1

Mail to: Passaic County Community College, Poetry Center, One College Blvd., Paterson, NJ 07509-1179

Award: Paterson Poetry Prize

*P

Prize: $1,000

Category: Poetry

Open to: No restrictions

Deadline: 2/1

Mail to: Passaic County Community College, Poetry Center, One College Blvd., Paterson, NJ 07509-1179

Award: Paterson Prize for Books for Young People

*C

Prize: $500

Category: Children's Literature

Open to: No restrictions

Deadline: 3/1

Mail to: Passaic County Community College, Poetry Center, One College Blvd., Paterson, NJ 07509-1179

PEN AMERICAN CENTER
Award: Hemingway Foundation/ PEN Award for Short Fiction

*SF

Prize: $7,500

Category: Short Fiction

Open to: U.S. citizens

Deadline: 12/16

Mail to: PEN American Center, 568 Broadway, New York, NY 10012-3225

Award: PEN Award for Poetry in Translation

*TR

Prize: $1,000

Category: Translation

Open to: No restrictions

Deadline: 12/16

Mail to: PEN American Center, 568 Broadway, New York, NY 10012-3225

Award: PEN/Book-of-the-Month Club Translation Prize

*TR

Prize: $3,000

Category: Translation

Open to: No restrictions

Deadline: 12/16

Mail to: PEN American Center, 568 Broadway, New York, NY 10012-3225

Award: PEN/Martha Albrand Award for Nonfiction

*NF

Prize: $1,000

Category: Nonfiction

Open to: U.S. citizens

Deadline: 12/16

Mail to: PEN American Center, 568 Broadway, New York, NY 10012-3225

Award: PEN/Spielvogel-Diamonstein Award
for the Art of the Essay

*NF

Prize: $5,000

Category: Nonfiction

Open to: No restrictions

Deadline: 12/16

Mail to: PEN American Center, 568 Broadway, New York, NY 10012-3225

PEN/ FAULKNER AWARD,
FOLGER SHAKESPEARE LIBRARY

Award: PEN/Faulkner Award for Fiction

*F

Prize: $15,000 and (4) $5,000 nominee prizes

Category: Fiction

Open to: U.S. citizens

Deadline: 12/31

Mail to: PEN/Faulkner Award, Folger Shakespeare Library, 568 Broadway, New York, NY 10012-3225

PLOUGHSHARES

Award: John C. Zacharis First Book Award

*F

Prize: $1,500

Category: Fiction

Open to: No restrictions

Deadline: By nomination only

Mail to: Ploughshares, Emerson College, 100 Beacon Street, Boston, MA 02116

Award: John C. Zacharis First Book Award

*P

Prize: $1,500

Category: Poetry

Open to: No restrictions

Deadline: By nomination only

Mail to: Ploughshares, Emerson College, 100 Beacon Street, Boston, MA 02116

THE POETRY CENTER

Award: Book Award

*P

Prize: $500 and reading

Category: Poetry

Open to: No restrictions

Deadline: 12/31

Mail to: The Poetry Center, San Francisco State University, 1600 Holloway Avenue, San Francisco, CA 94132

POETRY SOCIETY OF AMERICA

Award: Norma Farber First Book Award

*P

Prize: $500

Category: Poetry

Open to: U.S. citizens

Deadline: 12/22

Mail to: Poetry Society of America, 15 Gramercy Park South, New York, NY 10003

Award: Robert H. Winner Memorial Prize

*P

Prize: $2,500

Category: Poetry

Open to: Poets over 40 years of age

Deadline: 12/22

Mail to: Poetry Society of America, 15 Gramercy Park South, New York, NY 10003

Award: Williams Carlos Williams Prize

*P

Prize: $500–$1,000

Category: Poetry

Open to: U.S. citizens

Deadline: 12/22

Mail to: Poetry Society of America, 15 Gramercy Park South, New York, NY 10003

PUBLISHING TRIANGLE

Award: Ferro-Grumley Awards for Gay and Lesbian Literature

*F/NF

Prize: (2) $1,000

Category: Fiction and Nonfiction

Open to: No restrictions

Deadline: Unavailable or under review

Mail to: Publishing Triangle, P.O. Box 114, Prince Street Station, New York, NY 10012

QUALITY PAPERBACK BOOK CLUB

Award: New Visions Award

*NF

Prize: $5,000

Category: Nonfiction

Open to: American writers

Deadline: Internal nomination only

Mail to: Quality Paperback Book Club, 1271 Avenue of the Americas, New York, NY 10017

Award: New Voices Award

*F

Prize: $5,000

Category: Fiction

Open to: American writers

Deadline: Internal nomination only

Mail to: Quality Paperback Book Club, 1271 Avenue of the Americas, New York, NY 10017

ROBERT F. KENNEDY AWARDS

Award: Robert F. Kennedy Annual Book Award

*F

Prize: $2,500

Category: Fiction

Open to: All books published in 1997

Deadline: 1/2

Mail to: Robert F. Kennedy Awards, 136 Connecticut Ave., NW, Suite 200, Washington, DC, 20036

SOCIETY FOR HISTORIANS OF AMERICAN FOREIGN RELATIONS
Award: Stuart L. Bernath Book Prize

*NF

Prize: $2,000

Category: History

Open to: No restrictions

Deadline: Unavailable or under review

Mail to: Society for Historians of American Foreign Relations, Temple University, Department of History, Philadelphia, PA

SOCIETY OF AMERICAN HISTORIANS
Award: Francis Parkman Prize

*NF

Prize: $2,500

Category: History

Open to: No restrictions

Deadline: 1/15

Mail to: Society of American Historians, Butler Library, Box 2, Columbia University, New York, NY 10027

Award: James Fenimore Cooper Prize for Historical Fiction

*F

Prize: $2,500

Category: Fiction

Open to: No restrictions

Deadline: 1/15

Mail to: Society of American Historians, Butler Library, Box 2, Columbia University, New York, NY 10027

SOCIETY OF MIDLAND AUTHORS
Award: Literary Competition

*P/F/NF/C

Prize: (6) $300 and plaque

Category: Poetry, Fiction, Nonfiction, and Children's

Open to: Inquire within

Deadline: 1/15

Mail to: Society of Midland Authors, P.O. Box 10419, Chicago, IL 60610-0419

SONS OF THE REPUBLIC OF TEXAS
Award: Summerfield G. Roberts Award

*F/NF

Prize: $2,500

Category: Fiction and Nonfiction

Open to: All creative writers writing about the Republic of Texas

Deadline: 1/15

Mail to: Sons of the Republic of Texas, 1717 8th Street, Bay City, TX 77414

SOUTHERN HISTORICAL ASSOCIATION
Award: Charles S. Sydnor Award

*NF

Prize: $1,000

Category: History

Open to: U.S. citizens

Deadline: Unavailable or under review

Mail to: Southern Historical Association, Department of History, University of Georgia, Athens, GA 30602

Southern Review/Louisiana State University

Award: Southern Review/LSU Short Fiction Award

*SF

Prize: $500

Category: Short Fiction

Open to: U.S. citizens

Deadline: 1/31

Mail to: Southern Review/Louisiana State University, 43 Allen Hall, Baton Rouge, LA 70803

Texas Institute of Letters

Award: Carr P. Collins Award

*NF

Prize: $5,000

Category: Nonfiction

Open to: Authors living in and/or writing about Texas

Deadline: 1/1–1/8

Mail to: Texas Institute of Letters, Texas Christian University Press, P.O. Box 30783, Fort Worth, TX 76129

Award: Jesse H. Jones Award

*F

Prize: $6,000

Category: Fiction

Open to: Authors living in and/or writing about Texas

Deadline: 1/1–1/8

Mail to: Texas Institute of Letters, Texas Christian University Press, P.O. Box 30783, Fort Worth, TX 76129

Award: Natalie Ornish Poetry Award

*P

Prize: $1,000

Category: Poetry

Open to: Authors living in and/or writing about Texas

Deadline: 1/1–1/8

Mail to: Texas Institute of Letters, Texas Christian University Press, P.O. Box 30783, Fort Worth, TX 76129

Award: Soeurette Diehl Fraser Award

*TR

Prize: $1,000

Category: Translation

Open to: Authors living in and/or writing about Texas.

Deadline: 1/1–1/8

Mail to: Texas Institute of Letters, Texas Christian University Press, P.O. Box 30783, Fort Worth, TX 76129

Award: Steven Turner Award

*F

Prize: $1,000

Category: Fiction

Open to: Authors living in and/or writing about Texas

Deadline: 1/1–1/8

Mail to: Texas Institute of Letters, Texas Christian University Press, P.O. Box 30783, Fort Worth, TX 76129

UNITARIAN UNIVERSALIST ASSOCIATION

Award: Melcher Book Award Celebrating Religious Liberalism

*NF

Prize: $1,000 and citation

Category: Nonfiction

Open to: No restrictions

Deadline: 1/1

Mail to: Unitarian Universalist Association, 25 Beacon Street, Boston, MA 02108

UNIVERSITY OF ROCHESTER

Award: Janet Heidinger Kafka Prize

*F

Prize: $1,000

Category: Fiction

Open to: A woman who is an U.S. citizen who has written a recently published, book-length work of prose fiction, whether novel, short stories, or experimental writing. Works primarily for children and publications from vanity presses cannot be considered.

Deadline: 3/14

Mail to: University of Rochester, Susan B. Anthony Center, Lattimore Hall, Room 538, Rochester, NY 14627-0434

WESTERN HISTORY ASSOCIATION
Award: Athearn Book Award

*NF

Prize: $500 author/$500 publisher

Category: History

Open to: No restrictions

Deadline: 6/1

Mail to: Western History Association, University of New Mexico, Department of History, Albuquerque, NM 87131

Award: Caughey Western History Association Award

*NF

Prize: $2,500

Category: History

Open to: No restrictions

Deadline: 6/1

Mail to: Western History Association, University of New Mexico, Department of History, Albuquerque, NM 87131

Award: W. Turrentine Jackson Prize

*NF

Prize: $1,000

Category: History

Open to: No restrictions

Deadline: 6/30

Mail to: Western History Association, University of New Mexico, Department of History, Albuquerque, NM 87131

WESTERN STATE ARTS FEDERATION

Award: Western States Book Awards

*P/F/NF

Prize: $5,000 author/$5,000 publisher

Category: Poetry, Fiction, and Nonfiction

Open to: Under review by sponsoring organization

Deadline: Under review by sponsoring organization

Mail to: Western State Arts Federation, 236 Montezuma Avenue, Santa Fe, NM 87501

WRITER'S DIGEST

Award: National Self-Publishing Awards

*F/NF/P/C

Prize: $1,000 and promotion

Category: Varies—contact publisher (new annual guidelines available in August)

Open to: No restrictions

Deadline: 12/15

Mail to: Writer's Digest, 1507 Dana Avenue, Cincinnati, OH 45207

AWARDS FOR PUBLISHED FIRST BOOKS

BY PRIZE

Award Name	Prize
Kingsley Tufts Poetry Award	$50,000
Raiziss/de Palchi Translation Award	$5,000 and $20,000 fellowship
PEN/Faulkner Award for Fiction nominee prizes	$15,000 and (4) $5,000
Continuum Book Award	$10,000
Lenore Marshall Poetry Prize	$10,000
National Book Awards	(3) $10,000 and some $1,000 runners-up
Hemingway Foundation/ PEN Award for Short Fiction	$7,500
Jesse H. Jones Award	$6,000
Anisfield-Wolf Book Awards for Scholarly or Fiction on Race or Human Relations	(2) $5,000
Carr P. Collins Award	$5,000
Harold D. Vursell Memorial Award	$5,000
Heartland Award	$5,000
New Visions Award	$5,000
New Voices Award	$5,000
PEN/Spielvogel-Diamonstein Award for the Art of the Essay	$5,000
Richard and Hilda Rosenthal Foundation Award	$5,000
Western States Book Awards	$5,000 author/ $5,000 publisher

Award Name	Prize
Bancroft Prizes	(2) $4,000
PEN Book-of-the-Month Club Translation Prize	$3,000
Pulitzer Prizes	(several) $3,000
Caughey Western History Association Award	$2,500
Francis Parkman Prize	$2,500
James Fenimore Cooper Prize for Historical Fiction	$2,500
Robert F. Kennedy Annual Book Award	$2,500
Robert H. Winner Memorial Prize	$2,500
Sue Kaufman Prize for First Fiction	$2,500
Summerfield G. Roberts Award	$2,500
Elliot Rudwick Prize	$2,000
L. L. Winship/PEN New England Award	$2,000
Stuart L. Bernath Book Prize	$2,000
August Kleinzahler Award	$1,500 and reading
John C. Zacharis First Book Award—Fiction	$1,500
John C. Zacharis First Book Award—Poetry	$1,500
Carl Sandburg Literary Awards	(4) $1,000
Ferro-Grumley Awards for Gay and Lesbian Literature	(2) $1,000
Latino Literature Prize	(2) $1,000
Art Seidenbaum Award	$1,000 and citation

Award Name	Prize
Balcones Poetry Prize	$1,000
Charles S. Sydnor Award	$1,000
Frederic Jackson Turner Award	$1,000
H. L. Davis Award for Fiction	$1,000
Harold Morton Translation Award	$1,000
Harold U. Ribalow Prize	$1,000 and publication of either an excerpt or a review.
Hazel Hall Award for Poetry	$1,000
Janet Heidinger Kafka Prize	$1,000
Mary Jane Carr Award for Young Reader's Literature	$1,000
Melcher Book Award	$1,000 and citation
Merle Curti Award	$1,000
Natalie Ornish Poetry Award	$1,000
National Self-Publishing Awards	$1,000 and promotion
New Jersey Council for the Humanities Book Award	$1,000
Paterson Poetry Prize	$1,000
PEN Award for Poetry in Translation	$1,000
PEN/Martha Albrand Award for Nonfiction	$1,000
Publications Award	$1,000
Ray Allen Billington Prize	$1,000
Soeurette Diehl Fraser Award	$1,000
Steven Turner Award	$1,000
Violet Crown Book Awards	$1,000 and trophy

Award Name	Prize
W. Turrentine Jackson Prize	$1,000
Young People's Literature Award	(2) $800
James A. Rawley Prize	$750
National Jewish Book Awards	$750
Albert B. Corey Prize	$500–$1,000
Albert J. Beveridge Award	$500–$1,000
George Louis Beer Prize	$500–$1,000
Helen and Howard R. Marraro Prize in Italian History	$500–$1,000
Herbert Baxter Adams Prize	$500–$1,000
Herbert Feis Award	$500–$1,000
James Henry Breasted Prize	$500–$1,000
Joan Kelly Memorial Prize in Women's History	$500–$1,000
John H. Dunning Prize	$500–$1,000
John K. Fairbank Prize	$500–$1,000
Leo Gershoy Award	$500–$1,000
Littleton-Griswold Prize	$500–$1,000
Morris D. Forkosch Prize	$500–$1,000
Wesley-Logan Prize in African Diaspora History	$500–$1,000
Williams Carlos Williams Prize	$500–$1,000
Athearn Book Award	$500 author/$500 publisher
Avery O'Craven Award	$500
Book Award	$500 and reading
General L. Kemper Williams Prizes in Louisiana History	$500 and plaque

Award Name	Prize
Herbert Eugene Bolton Memorial Prize	$500
John and Patricia Beatty Award	$500
John Nicholas Brown Prize	$500
Kate Tufts Discovery Award	$500
Norma Farber First Book Award	$500
Paterson Fiction Prize	$500
Paterson Prize for Books for Young People	$500
Southern Review/LSU Short Fiction Award	$500
W. D. Weatherford Award	$500
Workshop Under the Sky Writing Award	$500
Literary Competition	(6) $300 and plaque
New Writer Awards	(2) $300 and reading
John Newbery Medal	Medal

Awards for Published First Books

by Genre

Short Fiction

Translation

11

𝐹IRST 𝐵OOK 𝒜MERICAN CLASSICS

⌘

Claude McKay

Songs of Jamaica
London: Jamaica Agency, 1912
Schomburg Center for Research in Black Culture

𝐼n 1912, Claude McKay (1889–1948) left his home in Jamaica for the United States and the famous Tuskagee Institute, to find himself and a larger audience for his poetry: "I had read my dialect poems before many of these poetry societies before and the members used to say 'Well, he's very nice and pretty, you know, but he's not a real poet as Browning and Byron and Tennyson are poets.' I used to think I would show them something. Someday; would write poetry in straight English and amaze and confound them." *Songs of Jamaica* was, it turned out, McKay's farewell to his native land. Although he loved Jamaica passionately, he was to return to it only in his poetry. McKay stayed only a year at Tuskagee before he left for Kansas State College; he then left his studies altogether for radical New York in 1914, near the beginning of the New Negro movement. He spent 1920 in London, and in 1922 he was feted in the Soviet Union. He later traveled for twelve years through France, Germany, Spain, and North Africa, returning to Harlem in 1934. He died in 1948, after converting to Catholicism and working for the poor of Harlem in the Catholic Friendship House.

In *Songs of Jamaica* and its companion, *Constab Ballads*, McKay creates authentic portraits of Jamaican life, particularly through his use of dialect; McKay's books are free, as James Weldon Johnson said, "of both the Minstrel and the Plantation traditions, free from exaggerated sweetness and wholesomeness." Although he rarely used dialect after he left Jamaica, the lessons he learned in craft and expression were never forgotten. His later books included poetry, novels, short stories, nonfiction, and autobiography.

From the beginning, McKay confronted prejudice and bigotry head on with courage and poise. His most famous poem, "If We Must Die," written in response to lynchings and massacres of black Americans that occurred in the Red Summer of 1911, was read before Parliament by Winston Churchill for inspiration in the worst days of World War II.

Hilda Doolittle (H.D.)

Sea Garden
London: Constable, 1916

*I*n the fourth issue (January 1913) of Harriet Monroe's new *Poetry, a magazine of verse* appeared three poems entitled as a group "Verses, Translations and Reflections from the Anthology" and attributed to a poet identified only as "H.D. Imagiste." Two of these poems, augmented by twenty-six others, were published in 1916 as *Sea Garden*, the first publication of the newly anointed American poet Hilda Doolittle of Bethlehem, Pennsylvania, who had followed her fiancé, the irrepressible, green-eyed, red-haired Ezra Pound, to London in 1911. The poet herself, nicknamed Dryad by Pound, credited the young poetry impresario with the publication of her new poems, describing the fateful moment in the British Museum tea room when he "scrawled 'H.D. Imagiste' at the bottom of the page," before sending them off to Chicago and Harriet Monroe. In literary legend, this moment is often considered the birth of the movement of imagism, which flourished briefly in London among the American expatriate writers who gathered there before World War I, and provided the break from Victorianism and the past needed for the beginning of literary modernism.

H.D.'s early poems are *the* quintessential imagist poems: spare, powerful, and sharp presentations of feeling embodied in natural images of surpassing clarity. H.D. herself applied the lessons of

imagism to her great modernist *Trilogy*, published in Oxford during
World War II as three booklets, *The Walls Do Not Fall* (1944), *Tribute to
the Angels* (1945), and *The Flowering of the Rod* (1946). These works, and
her psychoanalytic sessions and correspondence with Freud, provided
a breakthrough for H.D., whose later work in both poetry and prose
differed from her earlier "imagist" poems in length, in complexity, and
in their more open personal nature, as well as in their expanding, epic
vision of the world. About the early poems in this book, which include
those for which she is best known—"Orchard," "Heat," "The Helms-
man," "Sea Rose," and "Pear Tree"—H.D. wrote: "It is nostalgia for a
lost land. I call it Hellas. I might psychologically just as well have listed
the Casco Bay off the coast of Maine."

Edna St. Vincent Millay

Renascence and Other Poems
New York: Mitchell Kennerly, 1917
Estate of Carter Burden

One of the most famous poems of the early twentieth century,
"Renascence" changed the life of its young author, who was to become
in the public's eye, for a time, the absolute epitome of the poet. Edna St.
Vincent Millay (1892–1950) had been pushed by her mother to enter a
national poetry contest sponsored by the *Lyric Year* magazine. "Renascence," a long meditative poem concerned with the author's near death
experience as a child, won acclaim if not first prize. The occasion caused
a small literary scandal, as the editor of the volume in which her poem
appeared had enthusiastically informed Millay that her poem was
certain to take first prize of $500, only to have the selection committee
opt to give the prizes to three more conventional, established poets. In
the hearts of readers and critics, however, the true winner was Millay.
The poet, identified only as "E. Vincent Millay," turned out to be an
ethereal, low-voiced twenty-year-old woman with flowing red hair.
When she recited "Renascence" in public a few months later, an
astounded stranger offered her a college scholarship. She entered Vassar
College and became its most famous graduate. Her first book, *Renascence*

and Other Poems, was published by Mitchell Kennerly in 1917, in black-ribbed cloth. A special limited edition, printed on Vellum and bound in white, was issued in only seventeen copies. Only three of these special copies were sold; the other fourteen were given as gifts by Kennerly, who kept them in his desk drawer for years.

Thomas Wolfe

The Crisis in Industry
Chapel Hill: Published by the University of
North Carolina, 1919

$\mathcal{T}$homas Wolfe's (1900–1938) first year at the University of North Carolina was miserable: he wanted to attend Princeton or the University of Virginia, but his father would only pay for UNC, whose law school he wanted Wolfe to attend. But he threw himself into campus life beginning in his sophomore year, writing at least two one-act plays and contributing to the *Carolina Magazine* and *Tar Heel,* which he also edited. In his junior year, his essay on the resolution of labor disagreements won the Worth Prize from the Department of Philosophy; his adviser justified the award as acceptable "if philosophy could throw any light on the problems of labor." Published by the university in an edition of two hundred copies, the essay became his first book publication.

Ernest Hemingway

Three Stories and Ten Poems
Paris: Contact Editions, 1923
Rare Books Division

$\mathcal{E}$rnest Hemingway (1899–1961) came to Paris with his new wife, Hadley Richardson, in December 1921, and quickly made friends with Gertrude Stein, who later reviewed his first book, *Three Stories and Ten Poems*, in the *Paris Tribune* of November 27, 1923: "So far so good, further than that, and as far as that . . . I should say that Hemingway should stick to poetry and intelligence and eschew the hotter emotions. . . ."

Hemingway's signature style was probably developed from Stein, though he vehemently denied it. The two were to quarrel, attacking each other in the *Autobiography of Alice B. Toklas* and *A Moveable Feast*.

In July 1923, three hundred copies of *Three Stories and Ten Poems* were printed in Dijon by Maurice Darantiere, who had the previous year printed James Joyce's *Ulysses*. The publisher was the American émigré Robert McAlmon, who was married to the novelist Bryher (Winifred Ellerman), and traveling with her and the poet and novelist H.D. Spending some of Ellerman's money but exercising his own exquisite taste, he set up Contact Editions, headquartering at Sylvia Beach's Shakespeare & Company Books, 12 rue de L'Odeon, in Paris.

First published in this volume, "Up in Michigan" was the only manuscript to survive a theft from Hemingway's wife in the Gare de Lyon of a valise containing everything he had written up to that point: the manuscript of "Up in Michigan" had fortunately been left in a drawer. "Out of Season" was written later, and six of the poems and "My Old Man" were already at their respective serial publishers (*Poetry* magazine and *Best Short Stories*). Along with four previously unpublished poems, they made up Hemingway's first book.

❧◉❧

William Faulkner

The Marble Faun
Boston: The Four Seas Company, 1924

*W*illiam Faulkner (1897–1962) often referred to himself as a "failed poet." At the beginning of his career, he pursued his failure with a single-minded dedication that alarmed some of his relatives, who shook their heads as he padded about Oxford, Mississippi, in bare feet and drifted from job to job. From his teens until well into his twenties, Faulkner wrote hundreds of poems, laboriously reworking many of them; forged poetic sequences inspired by Conrad Aiken's "verse symphonies"; devoured Eliot and parodied him ("Shall I walk, then, through a corridor of profundities"); and produced hand-made books in which his often feverish poems throbbed between hand-painted watercolor boards. Faulkner's first appearance in print was in the August 6, 1919, issue of *The New Republic*, which paid $15 for "L'apres-midi d'un faune" (title from Mallarme). The magazine rejected another handful of his poems, so Faulkner, as a joke, typed up Coleridge's "Kubla Khan" and submitted it. This time Faulkner received some feedback from the editor: "We like your poem, Mr. Coleridge, but we don't think it gets anywhere much." Thirteen of Faulkner's poems and some criticism appeared in *The Mississippian*, the student paper at the University of Mississippi, where he had enrolled in 1919 after very brief service in the Royal Air Force–Canada in World War I.

The Marble Faun, whose nineteen interlocking poems create a pastoral fantasy out of the voices of the nymphs and shepherds, was published in 1924. The Four Seas Company was a "subsidy" or vanity book publisher, which also published Stephen Vincent Benet's first book, *Five Men and Pompey*, as well as books by Williams Carlos Williams, Gertrude Stein, Conrad Aiken, H. L. Mencken, and H.D. Although the records are not clear, from a variety of sources it appears that only 500 copies of this volume were printed and that fifty to sixty of them were given as gifts to people in and around Oxford. Some copies, at least twenty, were destroyed in the fire that gutted the house and collection of Faulkner's mentor Phil Stone, who had paid for either half or all of the publication (it's not clear whether Faulkner contributed).

Countee Cullen

Color
New York: Harper Brothers, 1925

*I*n 1925, Harvard University graduate student Countee Cullen (1903–1946) published his first book *Color*, and he published it with a major American publisher. That same year, his poem "To One Who Say Me Nay" took second prize in the annual literary contest run by *Opportunity: The Journal of Negro Life*. One of the few black students at New York's academically stringent DeWitt Clinton High School, from which James Baldwin later graduated, Cullen had been a frequent contributor of poems to *Magpie,* the school literary magazine. While at New York University, he published his work in national literary magazines such as *Poetry* and *Harper's.* His second book, *Copper Sun,* was published just two years after his first, and other prizes were showered on him, including a Guggenheim grant to study in Europe. In 1928 he married the daughter of W. E .B. Du Bois in a huge, well-publicized ceremony (Langston Hughes was an usher). Nevertheless, in May 1926, racist practices still stopped him from reading from his poetry in Baltimore's Emerson Hotel, to which he had been invited by the Baltimore Civic Club.

Cullen published three more books of poetry, an autobiographical novel, two children's books, and an important anthology of black poetry, *Caroling Dusk* (1927). An intense Francophile, he spent long periods in Paris and taught French at a New York City junior high school. The New York Public Library's 135th Street branch was named in his honor after his sudden death of uremic poisoning in 1946.

Hart Crane

White Buildings
New York: Boni & Liveright, 1926

*W*hen Crane submitted the manuscript of *White Buildings* to the publisher Thomas Seltzer in May 1925, he sent the following cost estimate from the Polytype Press at 38 West 8th Street (where designer/printer Samuel Jacobs had done e. e. cummings's *Tulips and Chimneys,* which Crane admired). The estimate was for an edition of five hundred copies, the book to be "admirable in every detail." Jacobs had agreed to donate the composition costs:

500 copies—White Buildings—64pp.

Stock (Warren's Oldstyle)	$17.00
Makeup (by Pelley Press)	16.00
Lockup and Press work	40.00
Casing and Shipping	2.00
Binding (@25 cents per copy)	125.00
Total	$200.00

The book was finally published not by Seltzer, but by Boni and Liveright, where Crane's friend Waldo Frank, to whom the book was dedicated, had placed it. The foreword to the volume was written (and signed) by Allen Tate, who had offered to have it printed under Eugene O'Neill's name, since the publishers had agreed to accept the book only if O'Neill would write a preface (they published it anyway). For the younger poet, who did not finish high school and was largely self-educated, it must have been like first love, the "realization of one's dreams in flesh, form, laughter and intelligence."

Wallace Stevens

Harmonium
New York: Alfred A. Knopf, 1931

Harmonium was published in 1923, a year after Joyce's *Ulysses* and Eliot's *The Waste Land*. It was mostly ignored and remaindered; there were three different bindings—checkered, striped, and plain blue—and of the plain blue, for example, 715 of the 1,500 copies were remaindered. For another five or six years, Stevens wrote little poetry, devoting himself instead to his newly born daughter and to consolidating his career in insurance law (he became an expert on surety bonds). Despite the remaindering of the first edition, Knopf reprinted *Harmonium* in 1931, in response to pressure from other poets and literary people. Stevens added fourteen poems and removed three. Even today, "The Comedian as the Letter C," the long poem from *Harmonium*, can be read as a summary of Stevens's poetic life up to the publication of *Harmonium*, and a prophesy for the future: "In the presto of the morning, Crispin trod/ Each day, still curious, but in a round/ Less prickly and much more condign than that/ He once thought necessary." He went on to write many more fine poems and many long ones, such as "The Man with the Blue Guitar," and to compose several philosophical essays on poetry.

Stevens went every year to Florida, escaping from his hibernation in the cold north of Hartford. He loved France and the French language, but visited Europe only in his imagination and poetry. As a young man, Stevens had been fond of hikes, of long walks, murmuring poetry for companionship; he once walked from New York City to Paterson, New Jersey, and back in an afternoon. Until his retirement from Hartford Accident and Indemnity at age seventy, he continued to walk to work every day across Elizabeth Park in Hartford, composing his magnificent poems.

❧❀☙

Eudora Welty

The Key with a note on the Author and her work by Katherine Anne Porter
from Miss Welty's forthcoming *A Curtain of Green*
Garden City, NY: Doubleday, Doran, 1941

*K*atherine Anne Porter (acting as an agent for English novelist Ford Maddox Ford) had in 1938 written to Welty of her admiration of her stories. Ford tried to find an English publisher for a collection, but died shortly after Porter had transferred the Welty stories to him. Meanwhile, Welty's agent, Diarmuid Russell, prodded by Porter, had placed most of her stories in magazines such as *Harper's Bazaar*. Doubleday then agreed to publish the book, with Porter's introduction. *A Curtain of Green* was, however, preceded by this much rarer, glossy pamphlet, used as an advertising or promotional piece for booksellers and reviewers. This pamphlet prints "The Key," a story from *A Curtain of Green*, and is Welty's first "publication." About her new friend's future, Porter was to say, "My money is on her nose for the next race."

❧❀☙

Jack Kerouac

The Town and the City
New York: Harcourt, Brace & Company, 1950

*J*ean-Louis Lebris de Kerouac (1922–1969) began to outline in his mind the novel that was to become *The Town and the City* in December 1945 when he was hospitalized for phlebitis, caused by Benzedrine abuse. At his mother's apartment near the Cross Bay Boulevard in

Ozone Park, Queens, he began the actual writing of the novel after his father's death in 1946. His composition was interrupted by a life-changing meeting with Neal Cassady and a cross-country trip full of adventures, some of which would appear in his most famous novel, *On the Road* (1957). *The Town and the City* is a thinly veiled autobiography in which Kerouac romanticizes his youth in Lowell, Massachusetts, combining it with the family situation of his friends in the Greek-American Sampas family. Mostly completed in December 1948, the novel was rejected by Scribner's, Little, Brown, and Putnam's before it was eventually published by Harcourt, Brace in 1950. Kerouac and his first book had been recommended to the young editor Robert Giroux by the eminent Columbia scholar Mark Van Doren. Kerouac had prompted Van Doren with the Zen parable: "Do what you will when you think of it, at once."

PART 7

ETERNAL LIGHT:
RESOURCES, SERVICES, AND SUPPORT

INTRODUCTION

Ruth Greenstein

I am always surprised at how many writers make the mistake of approaching a publishing company without having first done their homework. Too often the publisher is asked to play the role of librarian, teacher, and adviser, referring such writers to resources that should already be familiar to them. No matter what part of the country you live in, there are organizations, publications, and computer-based resources that are indispensable to the serious professional. Writing is a lonely business; there's no reason to make it lonelier still by working in a vacuum. Here is a brief overview of the resources listed in this section:

Organizations

State and regional arts organizations, funded by your tax dollars, are a conduit of information to the local arts community. They are excellent sources for up-to-date information on awards, grants, workshops, and programs of interest to writers. Why not give your local arts council a call and see what they have to offer? Professional organizations, generally funded by dues-paying members, are good places to network with other writers working in your area of interest. Their offerings may include job banks, educational events, even group medical plans.

What You've Heard Is True

◆

There's No Place Like Home
Often, everything you need to get your first book published can be found right in your own neighborhood. If it's not, be creative. For instance, if there are no writer's workshops offered in your community, you can start a home workshop. Gather several local writers together and split the cost of hiring a professional writer or editor to lead a series of discussions at one of your homes. If the professional cannot come to one of your homes, perhaps he or she can work with you through a regular mail or e-mail correspondence program. In rural areas and other communities that do not offer writer's workshops, home workshops are an increasingly popular option.

—J. S.

Publications

There are a vast array of books, directories, and periodicals that writers can turn to for information on how to write a good book, how to find a literary agent, and how to get published. Your local librarian should be able to point you toward those publications that will be most helpful to you. Have a look at a few trade magazines to learn more about how the publishing business works, to keep abreast of industry changes, and to find out what kinds of books are being published—and by whom.

Web sites

For all writers, but especially those who do not have ready access to traditional resources, the Internet is a godsend. Web sites offer many of the above resources in electronic form, and much more. In addition to being a superb research tool, the Web is also a great place to publicize your work. Check it out!

12

ORGANIZATIONS

STATE AND REGIONAL ART ORGANIZATIONS

State Art Councils & Commissions	Phone	Fax
Alabama State Council on the Arts	(334) 242-4076	(334) 240-3269
Alaska State Council on the Arts	(907) 269-6610	(907) 269-6601
American Samoa Council on Culture, Arts and Humanities	011-684-633-4347	011-684-633-2059
Arizona Commission on the Arts	(602) 255-5882	(602) 256-0282
Arkansas Arts Council	(501) 324-9770	(501) 324-9154
California Arts Council	(916) 322-6555	(916) 322-6575
Colorado Council on the Arts	(303) 894-2617	(303) 894-2615
Connecticut Commission on the Arts	(860) 566-4770	(860) 566-6462
Delaware Division of the Arts	(302) 577-8278	(302) 577-6561
District of Columbia (D.C.) Commission on the Arts and Humanities	(202) 724-5613	(202) 727-4135
Florida Division of Cultural Affairs	(850) 487-2980	(850) 922-5259
Georgia Council for the Arts	(404) 651-7920	(404) 651-7922

State Art Councils & Commissions	Phone	Fax
Guam Council on the Arts & Humanities Agency	011-671-475-CAHA (2242/3)	011-671-472-ARTI (2781)
State Foundation on Culture and the Arts (Hawaii)	(808) 586-0306	(808) 586-0308
Idaho Commission on the Arts	(208) 334-2119	(208) 334-2488
Illinois Arts Council	(312) 814-6750	(312) 814-1471
Indiana Arts Commission	(317) 232-1268	(317) 232-5595
Iowa Arts Council	(515) 281-4451	(515) 242-6498
Kansas Arts Commission	(913) 296-3335	(913) 296-4989
Kentucky Arts Council	(502) 564-3757	(502) 564-2839
Louisiana Division of the Arts	(504) 342-8180	(504) 342-8173
Maine Arts Commission	(207) 287-2724	(207) 287-2335
Maryland State Arts Council	(410) 333-8232	(410) 333-1062
Massachusetts Cultural Council	(617) 727-3668	(617) 727-0044
Michigan Council for Arts & Cultural Affairs	(313) 256-3731	(313) 256-3781
Minnesota State Arts Board	(612) 215-1600	(612) 215-1602
Mississippi Arts Commission	(601) 359-6030	(601) 359-6008
Missouri Arts Council	(314) 340-6845	(314) 340-7215
Montana Arts Council	(406) 444-6430	(406) 444-6548
Nebraska Arts Council	(402) 595-2122	(402) 595-2334
Nevada Arts Council	(702) 687-6680	(702) 687-6688

State Art Councils & Commissions	Phone	Fax
New Hampshire State Council on the Arts	(603) 271-2789	(603) 271-3584
New Jersey State Council on the Arts	(609) 292-6130	(609) 989-1440
New Mexico Arts Division	(505) 827-6490	(505) 827-6043
New York State Council on the Arts	(212) 387-7000	(212) 387-7164
North Carolina Arts Council	(919) 733-2821	(919) 733-4834
North Dakota Council on the Arts	(701) 328-3954	(701) 328-3963
Commonwealth Council for Arts and Culture (Northern Mariana Islands)	011-670-322-9982	011-670-322-9028
Ohio Arts Council	(614) 466-2613	(614) 466-4494
Oklahoma Arts Council	(405) 521-2931	(405) 521-6418
Oregon Arts Council	(503) 986-0087	(503) 986-0260
Pennsylvania Council on the Arts	(717) 787-6883	(717) 783-2538
Rhode Island State Council on the Arts	(401) 222-3880	(401) 521-1351
South Carolina Arts Commission	(803) 734-8696	(803) 734-8526
South Dakota Arts Council	(605) 773-3131	(605) 773-6962
Tennessee Arts Commission	(615) 741-1701	(615) 741-8559
Texas Commission on the Arts	(512) 463-5535	(512) 475-2699
Utah Arts Council	(801) 236-7555	(801) 236-7556

State Art Councils & Commissions	Phone	Fax
Vermont Arts Council	(802) 828-3291	(802) 828-3363
Virgin Islands Council on the Arts	(809) 774-5984	(809) 774-6206
Virginia Commission for the Arts	(804) 225-3132	(804) 225-4327
Washington State Arts Commission	(360) 753-3860	(360) 586-5351
West Virginia Division of Culture and History, Arts and Humanities Section	(304) 558-0240	(304) 558-2779
Wisconsin Arts Board	(608) 266-0190	(608) 267-0380
Wyoming Arts Council	(307) 777-7742	(307) 777-5499

Regional Arts Organizations	Phone	Fax
Arts Midwest	(612) 341-0755	(612) 341-0902
Consortium for Pacific Arts and Cultures	(808) 946-7381	(808) 955-2722
Mid-America Arts Alliance	(816) 421-1388	(816) 421-3918
Mid-Atlantic Arts Foundation	(410) 539-6656	(410) 837-5517
New England Foundation for the Arts	(617) 951-0010	(617) 951-0016
Southern Arts Federation	(404) 874-7244	(404) 873-2148

KEY SERVICE ORGANIZATIONS

American Book Producers Association
160 Fifth Ave.
New York, NY 10010
(212) 645-2368

Associated Writing Programs
Old Dominion University
Norfolk, VA 23529-0079

Authors Unlimited
31 East 32nd St.
Suite 300
New York, NY 10016

CLMP (Council of Literary Magazines and Presses)
154 Christopher St.
Suite 3C
New York, NY 10014-2389
(212) 741-9110; fax: (212) 741-9112

Dial-a-Writer Referral Service
American Society of Journalists and Authors
1501 Broadway, Suite 302
New York, NY 10036
(212) 997-0947; fax: (212) 768-7414

Editorial Experts, Inc.
66 Canal Center Plaza
Suite 200
Alexandria, VA 22314-1538
(703) 683-0683; fax: (703) 683-4915

A publications consulting company that provides writers, editors, proofreaders and word and data processors for its clients, Editorial Experts also has an informative newsletter, *The Editorial Eye*.

Editorial Freelancers Association
71 W. 23rd St.
Suite 1504
New York, NY 10010
(212) 929-5400; fax: (212) 929-5439

Members have access to information about job opportunities through a telephone bulletin board. The EFA also offers a newsletter, a directory, and insurance at group rates, plus educational and supportive meetings.

The Foundation Center (NY)
79 Fifth Ave.
New York, NY 10003-3050
(212) 620-4230

With national offices in New York and Washington, field offices in San Francisco and Cleveland, and cooperating collections in libraries throughout the United States and abroad, the Foundation Center is a splendid source of information about thousands of foundations that offer grants to individuals and groups.

The Foundation Center (DC)
1001 Connecticut Ave. NW
Suite 938
Washington, DC 20036
(202) 331-1400

The Foundation Center (CA)
312 Sutter St.
Suite 312
San Francisco, CA 94108
(415) 397-0902

The Foundation Center (OH)
1422 Euclid Ave.
Suite 1356
Cleveland, OH 44115-2001
(216) 861-1934

International Association of Business Communicators
One Hallidie Plaza
Suite 600
San Francisco, CA 94102
(800) 776-4222; fax: (415) 362-8762

Poets & Writers, Inc.
72 Spring St.
New York, NY 10012

Through their publications and referral services, Poets & Writers can boost the income as well as the spirits of people who write fiction, poetry, and nonfiction.

State Council for the Arts
See listing in this section (page 285) and inquire for more information.

U.S. Government
Federal agencies engaged in all sorts of activities (Education, Commerce, Agriculture, Defense, etc.) have libraries and issue press releases about where funds are going and what they've been earmarked for. There's grist for sales and promotion plans when and if money is allocated to a particular region for study of the particular subject you've written about, so ask to be put on the mailing lists of agencies whose bailiwicks are relevant to your writing/publishing efforts. And find out if they have special-interest libraries that might buy your book.

Volunteer Lawyers for the Arts
1285 Avenue of the Americas, 3rd Fl.
New York, NY 10019

Founded in New York to provide legal services for artists who can't afford lawyers' fees, Volunteer Lawyers for the Arts has affiliates across the country— in California (San Francisco, Los Angeles and La Jolla), Colorado (Denver), Connecticut (Hartford), the District of Columbia, Florida (Clearwater, Fort Lauderdale, Miami, and Tallahassee), Georgia (Atlanta), Illinois (Chicago), Iowa (Cedar Rapids and Dubuque), Kentucky (Lexington and Louisville), Louisiana (New Orleans), Maine (Augusta), Maryland (Baltimore), Massachusetts (Amherst and Boston), Minnesota (Minneapolis), Missouri (St. Louis), Montana (Missoula), New Jersey (Trenton), New York (Albany, Buffalo, Huntington, and Poughkeepsie, as well as New York City), North Carolina (Raleigh), Ohio (Cleveland and Toledo), Oklahoma (Oklahoma City), Pennsylvania (Philadelphia), Rhode Island (Narragansett), South Carolina (Greenville), Tennessee (Nashville), Texas (Austin and Houston), Utah (Salt Lake City), and Washington (Seattle). And there's an office in Toronto too. Write or call the affiliate nearest you to find out about services and costs, or send $10 to the NYC office for the group's directory.

Women in Communications
2101 Wilson Blvd.
Suite 417
Arlington, VA 22201

Job hotlines and programs that hone professional skills are just two of the benefits Women in Communications offers members. Contact the national headquarters for information on nearby chapters.

WHERE TO FIND GROUP HEALTH INSURANCE FOR WRITERS

American Craft Association
21 South Eltings Corner Rd.
Highland, NY 12528
(800) 724-0859

American Society of Journalists and Authors
1501 Broadway, Suite 302
New York, NY 10036
(212) 997-0947

The Authors Guild, Inc.
330 West 42nd Street, 29th Floor
New York, NY 10036
(212) 563-5904

Editorial Freelancers Association
71 West 23rd Street
New York, NY 10010
(212) 929-5400

International Women's Writing Guild
P.O. Box 810
Gracie Station
New York, NY 10028
(212) 737-7536

Mystery Writers of America, Inc.
17 East 47th Street, 6th Floor
New York, NY 10017
(212) 888-8171

National Writers Union
837 Broadway, Suite 203
New York, NY 10003
(212) 254-0279

PEN American Center
568 Broadway
New York, NY 10012

Society of Children's Book Writers and Illustrators
22736 Vanowen Street, Suite 106
(818) 888-8760

Support Services Alliance
102 Prospect Avenue
Schoharie, NY 12157
(800) 322-3920

United States Federation of Small Businesses
26 North Broadway
Schenectady, NY 12305
(800) 637-3331

OTHER PROFESSIONAL ORGANIZATIONS

American Medical Writers Association
9650 Rockville Pike
Bethesda, MD 20814-3998
(301) 493-0003

American Society of Journalists & Authors, Inc.
1501 Broadway
Suite 302
New York, NY 10036
(212) 997-0947

American Translators Association
1800 Diagonal Rd.
Suite 220
Alexandria, VA 22314-0214
(703) 683-6100

Associated Writing Programs
Tallwood House MS1E3
George Mason University
Fairfax, VA 22030
(703) 993-4301

Association of Authors Representatives
10 Astor Pl.
3rd Floor
New York, NY 10003
(212) 353-3709

Association of Desk-Top Publishers
3401-A800 Adams Avenue
San Diego, CA 92116-2429
(619) 563-9714

The Authors Guild
330 W. 42nd St.
29th Floor
New York, NY 10036
(212) 563-5904

The Authors League of America, Inc.
330 W. 42nd St.
29th Floor
New York, NY 10036
(212) 564-8350

Copywriters Council of America, Freelance
Linick Bldg. 102
7 Putter Lane
Middle Island, NY 11953-0102

The Dramatists Guild
1501 Broadway
Suite 701
New York, NY 10036
(212) 398-9366

Editorial Freelancers Association
71 W. 23rd St.
Suite 1504
New York, NY 10010
(212) 929-5400

Education Writers Association
1331 H. St. NW
Suite 307
Washington, DC 20005
(202) 637-9700

Freelance Editorial Association
P.O. Box 380835
Cambridge, MA 02238-0835
(781) 643-8626

International Association of Business Communicators
1 Hallidie Plaza
Suite 600
San Francisco, CA 94102
(415) 433-3400

International Association of
Crime Writers Inc., North
American Branch
JAF Box 1500
New York, NY 10116
(212) 243-8966

International Television
Association
6311 N. O'Connor Rd.
Suite 230
Irving, TX 75039
(972) 869-1112

International Women's
Writing Guild
P.O. Box 810
Gracie Station
New York, NY 10028-0082
(212) 737-7536

Mystery Writers of America
17 E. 47th St.
6th Floor
New York, NY 10017
(212) 888-8171

National Association of
Science Writers
Box 294
Greenlawn, NY 11740
(516) 757-5664

National Writers Association
1450 S. Havana St.
Suite 424
Aurora, CO 80012
(303) 751-7844

National Writers Union
113 University Place
6th Floor
New York, NY 10003
(212) 254-0279

New Dramatists
424 W. 44th St.
New York, NY 10036
(212) 757-6960

PEN American Center
568 Broadway
New York, NY 10012
(212) 334-1660

Poetry Society of America
15 Gramercy Park South
New York, NY 10003
(212) 254-9628

Public Relations Society
of America
33 Irving Place
New York, NY 10003-2376
(212) 995-2230

Romance Writers of America
13700 Veterans Memorial Dr.
Suite 315
Houston, TX 77014

Science-Fiction and Fantasy
Writers of America
Suite 1B
5 Winding Brook Dr.
Guilderland, NY 12084

Seattle Writers Association
P.O. Box 33265
Seattle, WA 98133
(206) 860-5207

Society of American Business
Editors & Writers
c/o Janine Latus-Musick
University of Missouri
School of Journalism,
76 Gannett Hall
Columbia, MO 65211

Society of American Travel Writers
4101 Lake Boone Trail
Suite 201
Raleigh, NC 27607
(919) 787-5181

Society of Children's Book Writers and Illustrators
345 North Maple Drive #296
Beverly Hills, CA 90210
(310) 859-9887

Society of Professional Journalists
16 S. Jackson
Greencastle, IN 46135
(765) 653-3333

Writers Guide of America (East)
555 W. 57th St.
New York, NY 10019
(212) 767-7800

Writers Guild of Alberta
11759 Groat Rd.
Edmonton, AB T5M 3K6 Canada

Writers Guild of America (West)
8955 Beverly Blvd.
West Hollywood, CA 90048
(310) 550-1000

13

PUBLICATIONS

TRADE MAGAZINES

Advertising Age
Crain Communications Inc.
740 N. Rush St.
Chicago, IL 60611
(312) 649-5200

Weekly magazine covering advertising in magazines, trade journals and business.

American Journalism Review
8701 Adelphi Rd.
Adelphi, MD 20783
(301) 431-4771

10 issues per year magazine for journalists and communications professionals.

Daily Variety
Daily Variety Ltd./Cahners Publishing Co.
5700 Wilshire Blvd.
Los Angeles, CA 90036
(213) 857-6600

Trade publication on the entertainment industry, with helpful information for screenwriters.

Editor & Publisher
The Editor & Publisher Co.
11 W. 19th St.
10th Floor
New York, NY 10011
(212) 675-4380

Weekly magazine covering the newspaper publishing industry.

Folio
Cowles Business Media
11 Riverbend Dr. South
P.O. Box 4949
Stamford, CT 06907-0949
(203) 358-9900; fax (203) 358-5811

Monthly magazine covering the publishing industry.

Gifts & Decorative Accessories
Geyer-McAllister Publications, Inc.
51 Madison Ave.
New York, NY 10010-1675
(212) 689-4411

Monthly magazine covering greeting cards among other subjects, with an annual buyer's directory in September.

Horn Book Magazine
11 Beacon St.
Suite 1000
Boston, MA 02108
(617) 227-1555; fax (617) 523-0299

Bimonthly magazine covering children's literature.

Party & Paper Retailer
4 Ward Corp.
70 New Canaan Ave.
Norwalk, CT 06850
(203) 845-8020

Monthly magazine covering the greeting card and gift industry.

Poets & Writers Inc.
72 Spring St.
New York, NY 10012
(212) 226-3586

Bimonthly magazine, primarily for literary writers and poets.

Publishers Weekly
Bowker Magazine Group
Cahners Publishing Co.
245 W. 17th St.
New York, NY 10011
(212) 645-0067

Weekly magazine covering the book publishing industry.

Science Fiction Chronicle
P.O. Box 022730
Brooklyn, NY 11202-0056
(718) 643-9011; fax (718) 522-3308

Monthly magazine for science fiction, fantasy, and horror writers.

Travelwriter Marketletter
The Waldorf-Astoria
Suite 1880
New York, NY 10022

Monthly newsletter for travel writers with market listings as well as trip information.

The Writer
120 Boylston St.
Boston, MA 02116
(617) 423-3157

Monthly writers' magazine.

Writer's Digest
1507 Dana Ave.
Cincinnati, OH 45207
(513) 531-2222

Monthly writers' magazine.

Writing for Money
Blue Dolphin Communications, Inc.
83 Boston Post Rd.
Sudbury, MA 01776

Bimonthly freelance market reports.

KEY BOOKS AND DIRECTORIES

AV Market Place
R. R. Bowker
A Reed Reference Publishing Co.
121 Chanlon Rd.
New Providence, NJ 07974
(908) 464-6800

The Complete Book of Scriptwriting
J. Michael Straczynski
Writer's Digest Books
1507 Dana Ave.
Cincinnati, OH 45207
(513) 531-2222

The Complete Guide to Self Publishing
Marilyn and Tom Ross
Writer's Digest Books
1507 Dana Ave.
Cincinnati, OH 45207
(513) 531-2222

Copyright Handbook
R.R. Bowker
A Reed Reference Publishing Co.
121 Chanlon Rd.
New Providence, NJ 07974
(908) 464-6800

Dramatists Sourcebook
Kathy Sova, Ed.
Theatre Communications
Group, Inc.
355 Lexington Ave.
New York, NY 10017
(212) 697-5230

Editors on Editing: What Writers Need to Know About What Editors Do
Gerald Gross, Ed.
Grove Atlantic Press
841 Broadway
New York, NY 10003

Forty essays by America's most distinguished trade book editors on the art and craft of editing.

Grants and Awards Available to American Writers
19th Ed
PEN American Center
568 Broadway
Suite 401
New York, NY 10012-3225
(212) 334-1660

Guide to Literary Agents
Kristen Holm, Ed.
Writer's Digest Books
1507 Dana Ave.
Cincinnati, OH 45207
(513) 531-2222

The Guide to Writers Conferences
ShawGuides, Inc.
Educational Publishers
Box 1295
New York, NY 10023
(212) 799-6464

How to Write Irresistible Query Letters
Lisa Collier Cool
Writer's Digest Books
1507 Dana Ave.
Cincinnati, OH 45207
(513) 531-2222

**The Insider's Guide to Book Editors,
Publishers & Literary Agents**
Jeff Herman
Prima Publishing
3875 Atherton Rd.
Rocklin, CA 95765
(916) 632-4400

**International Directory of Little
Magazines & Small Presses**
Len Fulton
Dustbooks
P.O. Box 100
Paradise, CA 95967
(916) 877-6110

**Literary Market Place and
International Literary Market Place**
R.R. Bowker
A Reed Reference Publishing Co.
121 Chanlon Rd.
New Providence, NJ 07974
(908) 464-6800

Magazine Writing That Sells
Don McKinney
Writer's Digest Books
1507 Dana Ave.
Cincinnati, OH 45207
(513) 531-2222

My Big Sourcebook
66 Canal Center Plaza
Suite 200
Alexandria, VA 22314-5507
(703) 683-0683

**National Writers Union Guide to
Freelance Rates & Standard
Practice**
Alexander Kopelman
Writer's Digest Books
1507 Dana Ave.
Cincinnati, OH 45207
(513) 531-2222

Professional Writer's Guide
Donald Bower and James Lee Young,
Eds.
National Writers Press
1450 S. Havana St.
Suite 424
Aurora, CA 80012
(303) 751-7844

**Standard Directory of Advertising
Agencies**
National Register Publishing
A Reed Reference Publishing Co.
121 Chanlon Rd.
New Providence, NJ 07974
(908) 464-6800

Successful Scriptwriting
Jurgen Wolff and Kerry Cox
Writer's Digest Books
1507 Dana Ave.
Cincinnati, OH 45207
(513) 531-2222

The Writer's Legal Companion
Brad Bunnin and Peter Beren
Addison-Wesley Longman
Publishing Co.
1 Jacob Way
Reading, MA 01867
(617) 944-3700

**Writing Tools: Essential Software
for Anyone Who Writes with a PC**
Hy Bender
Random House Electronic
Publishing
201 E. 50th St.
New York, NY 10022
(212) 751-2600

TARGETED BOOKS AND DIRECTORIES

Author & Audience: A Readings and Workshops Guide
Updated periodically
Poets & Writers
72 Spring St.
New York, NY 10012

The listings here will help you pinpoint places to give your own readings and/or workshops.

Awards, Honors, and Prizes
Gita Siegman, Ed., Updated periodically
Gale Research, Inc.
P.O. Box 33477
Detroit, MI 48232-5477

This is a two-volume general reference work about all kinds of awards in the United States and abroad. Its subject index will lead you to those for which you're eligible.

Communication Unlimited Catalog
P.O. Box 6405
Santa Maria, CA 93456

Featuring the works of Gordon Burgett, Communication Unlimited sells tapes and reports as well as books on topics that include writing greeting cards, setting up seminars, and marketing mailing lists.

Copyediting: A Practical Guide
Karen Judd, 1990, second ed.
Crisp Publications, Inc.
95 First St.
Los Altos, CA 94022

Speaking from experience at Random House and elsewhere, Karen Judd shows how to get manuscripts ready for publication. A delightful, effective primer for anyone who'd like to make money publishing other people's prose.

Desktop Publishing Success: How to Start and Run a Desktop Publishing Business
Felix Kramer and Maggie Lovaas, 1991
Business One Irwin/ DPT Success
P.O. Box 844, Cathedral Station
New York, NY 10025

Remarkably thorough, readable and friendly, this is a book you'll want to buy if you're thinking of cashing in on desktop expertise.

The Financial Side of Book Publishing: A Home/Office Study Course on Financial and Business Analysis for the Non-Accountant in Book Publishing
Robert J.R. Follett, 1988, Revised ed.
Alpine Guild
P.O. Box 183
Oak Park, IL 60303

An experienced publisher who learned financial terms, techniques and skills the hard way, Follett now makes it easy for beginners to get the hang of them.

The Foundation Center Catalog
The Foundation Center
79 Fifth Ave., Dept.CE
New York, NY 10003-3050

Getting Yours: The Complete Guide to Government Money
Matthew Lesko, 1987, 3rd ed.
Viking Penguin
40 West 23rd St.
New York, NY 10010

Good leads to state and federal funds. Be sure to check the lengthy index for the subject(s) your work covers.

Ghostwriting: How to Get Into the Business
Eva Shaw, 1991
Paragon House
90 Fifth Ave.
New York, NY 10011

Drawing on her own fund of experience, Shaw explains the whole process of ghostwriting—not just how to get into the business, as the subtitle says, but how to structure and price your services and how to work with the source of your material.

Grants and Awards Available to American Writers
Updated periodically
PEN American Center
568 Broadway
New York, NY 10012

An indispensable—and inexpensive—reference for writers in search of funds. Well-worth perusing whether you write fiction, nonfiction, poetry, children's books, plays, or all of the above.

Guide to Literary Agents
Writers Digest Books
1507 Dana Ave.
Cincinnati, OH 45207
(800) 289-0963
$21.99 for the 1996 edition

A great resource guide with a list of 475 agents, of which 300 charge no fee. This annual guide has chapters on the business aspects of working with an agent and understanding book contracts, and an insider's view of particular agencies. It also offers a viewpoint for fee-charging agents and a section of addresses for them, which is best avoided. Listings include number of clients and what percentage are new or unpublished, recent sales, tips for contacting agents, terms for representation, and the kind of work they handle.

How to Get Money for Research
Mary Rubin and the Business and Professional Women's Foundation, 1983
The Feminist Press
311 East 94th St.
New York, NY 10128

The advice in Rubin's short primer is directed to women and those doing research about women but it can be applied to a variety of projects.

How You Can Make $25,000 a Year Writing (No Matter Where You Live)
Nancy Edmonds Hanson, 1987, revised ed.
Writer's Digest Books
1507 Dana Ave.
Cincinnati, OH 45207

This peppy, can-do manual focuses on the kinds of writing you do primarily for money. Hanson makes the very good point that writers outside New York have at least as much chance of making it as writers in the city.

International Directory of Little Magazines and Small Presses
Len Fulton, Ed.
Dustbooks
P.O. Box 100
Paradise, CA 95967
len@dustbooks.com
http://www.dustbooks.com
$31.95 paper 32nd edition, 1996–97

Great for small presses and literary magazine market, as well as small magazines that are not strictly literary. Over 6,000 markets for writers in the current edition. Has subject and regional indexes. Listings include address of publisher, editors' names, what they accept, sometimes a quote about the kind of work accepted, often names of writers they've published, circulation or number of titles, payment, and reporting time.

Literary Agents of North America
Author Aid Associates
$33.00 for 5th edition, 1995

This book is updated every two years, and is forthcoming on the Web and has about 1,000 listings. The best part of the book is the People Index, where you can look up either names of agents whose agencies you do not know or names of writers to find out who their agents are. There is also a Policy Index so that you can look under "Multiple submissions (reads)" or "Diskette submissions." The listings for agents include the following details: commission percentage, year established, agency policies, manuscript categories, subject interests, number of current clients and agents, and professional listings.

Literary Market Place (LMP)
Updated annually
R. R. Bowker
121 Chanlon Rd.
New Providence, NJ 07974

This is the directory of the American book publishing industry. The 1997 edition was designed by splitting off the yellow pages section. The yellow pages are where you look up names and addresses. The white pages have the detailed information, a reverse of a telephone book. The Literary Agent section of *LMP* has fewer details than other books mentioned here. This is where to find who handles fiction, who handles fiction crime, who handles contracts, what genres they represent, and what their response time and their commission is.

Marketing for the Home-Based Business
Jeffrey P. Davidson, 1990
Bob Adams, Inc.
260 Center St.
Holbrook, MA 02343

Solid, specific pointers with lots of real-life examples and handy lists, including one called "When to Call" that tells you the times when certain people—accountants, bankers, pharmacists, priests, etc.—are most accessible.

Mark My Words: Instruction and Practice in Proofreading
Peggy Smith, 1987
Editorial Experts, Inc.
66 Canal Center Plaza, Suite 200
Alexandria, VA 22314-1538

Those of you who like catching typos and errors can upgrade proofreading skills through the exercises in here, and sell them when they're good and strong. Smith is also the author of *Simplified Proofreading: How to Catch Errors Using Fewer Marks.*

Million Dollar Directory
Dun's Marketing Services, Updated periodically
A Division of Dun & Bradstreet
Three Century Dr.
Parsippany, NJ 07054

Businesses often need writers—to prepare annual reports, speeches, feature stories, newsletters and manuals. Try using the geographic and industry classification indexes in this multi-volume work to zero in on companies that might hire you. Entries cover more than 160,000 U.S. businesses with net worths over $500,000.

Poet's Market; Novel & Short Story Writer's Market; Writer's Market
Writer's Digest Books
1507 Dana Ave.
Cincinnati, OH 45207
(800) 289-0963
$22.99; $22.99; $27.99, respectively

Annual reference guides unparalleled in their content: chapters on the submission process and business end of things, features with individual writers and editors. The listings are of literary journals and large circulation magazines, small and university presses, and mid-size and large publishers. The listings include addresses, editors, payment, reporting times, list of writers they've published, themes or subject interests, reading periods. The *Poet's Market* often includes a sample poem or lines from a longer poem to help you figure out its style. The *Writer's Market* has listings for poetry and fiction, as well as nonfiction.

Publication Grants for Writers and Publishers
Oryx Press, 1991
4041 North Central @Indian School Rd.
Phoenix, AZ 85012-3397

A handbook rather than a directory, this explains how to write and submit proposals to the federal government, to selected foundations, and to several less conventional funding sources.

Research Centers Directory
Karen Hill, Ed., Updated periodically
Gale Research, Inc.
P.O. Box 33477
Detroit, MI 48232-5477

By affiliating with institutions, individuals can become eligible for some grants offered to nonprofit groups. To find the centers most likely to take you under their wing, look up your project's subject in the directory's index and then study the description of each group listed under that heading.

Securing Your Organization's Future: A Complete Guide to Fundraising Strategies
Michael Seltzer, 1987
The Foundation Center
79 Fifth Ave.
New York, NY 10003

Because it's so comprehensive, so imaginative and so well written, Michael Seltzer's handbook can help individuals (including writers) as well as groups (for which it's designed) to amass the funds they need.

Small-Time Operator: How to Start Your Own Home Business, Keep Your Books, Pay Your Taxes, & Stay Out of Trouble!
Bernard Kamoroff, Updated periodically
Bell Springs Publishing
P.O. Box 640
Laytonville, CA 95454

Kamoroff has years of experience as a financial adviser and tax accountant for small businesses and years of ex-

perience running small businesses of his own. This very popular guide covers everything from getting started (figuring out how much money you need and then getting your hands on it) to bookkeeping to the legal and financial technicalities of partnership, payrolls, and, yes, taxes. Bell Springs has other books about small businesses too; ask for the brochure.

Speaking for Money
Gordon Burgett and Mike Frank, 1985
Communication Unlimited
P.O. Box 6405
Santa Maria, CA 93456

Burgett covers seminars and Frank covers speeches in this detailed, common-sensical manual.

Substance & Style: Instruction & Practice in Copyediting
Mary Stoughton, 1989
Editorial Experts, Inc.
66 Canal Center Plaza, Suite 200
Alexandria, VA 22314-1538

Primarily a book of exercises, it also includes interesting short essays on topics such as "Is It Wrong to Tamper with a Quotation?" and "Fair Use and Copyright."

Sure-Fire Business Success Catalog
Jeffrey Lant,
Jeffrey Lant Associates
50 Follen St., Suite 507
Cambridge, MA 02138

The author of *The Unabashed Self-Promoter's Guide* unabashedly uses his books as tools for promoting himself. Fortunately, he also supplies canny tips and he's able to poke fun at his own audacity. His publications may embolden you to spot and pull all the strings you can for your book, magazine, or whatever. The catalog is free.

Thomas Register of American Manufacturers
Updated periodically
Thomas Publishing Co.
One Penn Plaza
New York, NY 10001-0107

A great source of leads to companies that might buy your work in bulk. *The Thomas Register,* a twenty-six-volume set, is available in libraries.

The Writer's Legal Guide
Tad Crawford, 1978
Allworth Press
10 East 23 St., Suite 400
New York, NY 10010

Crawford, lawyer-writer, offers some good guidance on money matters and presents a sample ledger you can use to get into the habit of recording your expenses so you're prepared at tax time.

Working from Home: Everything You Need to Know about Living and Working Under the Same Roof
Paul Edwards and Sarah Edwards, 1990, revised ed.
Jeremy P. Tarcher, Inc.
5858 Wilshire Blvd., Suite 200
Los Angeles, CA 90036

A useful commonsense guide on setting up and managing any home-based business.

14

WEB SITES OF INTEREST

AcqWeb: http://www.library.vanderbilt.edu/law/acqs/acqs.html

Although geared toward librarians and researchers, AcqWeb provides reference information useful to writers, such as library catalogs, bibliographic services, *Books in Print*, and other web reference resources.

Book Zone: http://www.bookzone.com

A catalog source for books, audio books, and more, with links to other publishing opportunities, diversions and distractions, such as news, classifieds, contests, magazines, and trade groups.

Books A to Z: http://www.booksatoz.com

Information on publications services and leads to other useful web sites, including areas for book research, production services, self-publishing, bookstores, organizations, and publishers.

**Books and Writing Online:
http://www.clark.net/pub/iz/Books/books.html**

A collection of sources directing you to other sites on the net, this is a good place to jump to other areas on the Web with information pertaining to writing, literature and publishing.

BookWeb: http://www.ambook.org

This ABA site offers book news, markets, discussion groups, events, resources, and other book-related information.

Bookwire: http://www.bookwire.com

A gateway to finding information about publishers, booksellers, libraries, authors, reviews, and awards. Also offers information about frequently asked publishing questions and answers, a calendar of events, a mailing list, and other helpful resources.

Children's Writing Resource Center: http://www.mindspring.com/~cbi

Presented by *Children's Book Insider*, the newsletter offers information on numerous aspects of publishing and children's literature, such as an InfoCenter, a Research Center, results of various surveys, and secrets on getting published.

Internet Entertainment Network: http://www.HollywoodNetwork.com

Home to Showbiz Online.com, this site covers everything in Hollywood whether its dealmaking, music, screenwriting, or profiles of agents and Hollywood executives.

Internet Road Map to Books:
http://www.bookport.com/b_roadmap.html

Leads to publishers' web sites, resources for writers, book reviews, online editing, and other helpful areas.

Ultimate Book List and Writer's Page: http://www.missouri.edu/~writery

Provides links and information on resources, references, authors, online writing, publishing, handouts, other web sites of interest, prizewinners, and more.

The Write Page: http://www.writepage.com

Online newsletter for readers and writers of genre fiction, featuring information on authors, books about writing, new releases, organizations, conferences, web sites, research, public service efforts writers can partake in, and writer's rights.

Writer's Resources:
http://www.interlog.com/~ohi/www/writesource.html

An elaborate site that provides information about workshops, how-to information, copyright, quotations, writing tips, resources, contests, market information, publishers, booksellers, associations, mailing lists, newsletters, conferences, and more.

INDEX

J

K

L

M

Unpublished first-book manuscripts
   awards exclusively for, 71–76
   awards favorable to, 77–103
   publishers favorable to, 147–74
Unsolicited manuscript, about, 135–36
User's guide, 17
U.S. Government, 291
Utah Arts Council, 92–94, 95–96
Utah Arts Council Publication Prize, 92
Utah's Original Competition for a Short
      Story, 93
Utah's Original Writing Competition for
   Fiction Novel, 95
   Short Story, 93
   Short Story Collections, 95
   Young Adult Book, 94
Utah State University, 68, 96

V

Vilet Crown Book Awards, 234
Vintage, 7
Violet Crown Book Awards, 234
Volunteer Lawyers for the Arts, 291

W

Walt Whitman Award, 35–36
Waring, Belle, 31
W. D. Weatherford Award, 235
Web sites, 284, 307–8
Weil, Wendy, 194
Welty, Eudora, 279
Wesley-Logan Prize in African Diaspora
      History, 233
Western History Association, 258
Western State Arts Federation, 259
Western States Book Awards, 259
West Town Press, 127
West Virginia Commission on the
      Arts, 97
West Virginia Literature Fellowship in
      Fiction, 97

Wharton, Edith, 109
White Eagle Coffee Store Press, 127, 128
White Pine Poetry Prize, 68–69
White Pine Press, 68–69, 169
Whitman, Walt, 106–7
Wick Poetry Chapbook Series, 128
Willa Cather Fiction Prize, 47
Williams, William Carlos, 182–83
Williams Carlos Williams Prize, 251
Winning a contest, experiences of, 27–33
Winter Poetry Competition, 127
Wolfe, Thomas, 274
Women authors, contests restricted for,
      86, 257
Women in Communications, 291
Workshop Under the Sky Writing
      Award, 240
Wright, Nancy Means, 27–33
Writer, The, 298
Writers at Work, 69
Writer's Digest, 259, 298
Writer's workshops, 283
Writing for Money, 298
W. Turrentine Jackson Prize, 258
W. W. Norton, 168, 178

Y

Yale Series of Younger Poets, 70
Yale University Press, 70
Yamashita, Karen Tei, 19–20
YMCA National Writer's Voice, xiv
Young adult books. *See also* Children's
      literature
   unpublished first-book manuscripts
      awards exclusively for, 41, 42
      awards favorable to, 92, 94
Young People's Literature Award, 239

Z

Zacharis. *See* John C. Zacharis First
      Book Award

ABOUT THE EDITOR

Jason Shinder's books include the collections of poems, *Every Room We Ever Slept In*, and the forthcoming, *Among Women*. He is also the editor of the first series of literary anthologies dedicated exclusively to parent and child relations and the first collection of 20th century American movie poems. He is also the general series editor of the new annual series, *Best American Movie Writing*. Forthcoming books include *Tales From the Couch: Writers On the Talking Cure*. Mr. Shinder is the founder and director of the YMCA National Writer's Voice, a network of more than 30 literary art centers at YMCAs nationwide. He teaches at Bennington College and the New School for Social Research in their MFA programs.